Tim Harkness

is a leading psychologist and world-class sports scientist, with
interests ranging from sports data to the rules of public discourse.
He developed the **10 Rules for Talking** over a lifetime of
conversations, having grown up in South Africa during
apartheid and working as a psychologist in private
practice. Tim is married with three sons.

'Combining his knowledge in psychology and sports science,
Tim always knows exactly what you feel and what you need
to hear when you need it most.'
ALI FARAG, 2019 SQUASH WORLD NO.1 AND WORLD CHAMPION

'Tim is an elite performance psychologist with global experience
of working in business and sport. I resonate deeply with many
of the strategies and techniques that I've learned from him
and have often leveraged his ideas and stories in my own
work with my team. I strongly recommend this book
for what it says about partnerships and teams in the
personal, professional and political realms.'
RAJIV BAJAJ, MD OF BAJAJ AUTO

'Effective communication is an art which we all need to master.
Tim is a great teacher because he speaks simply and persuasively.
This book can help us all to do better professionally
and personally!'

'I am privileged to have been able to count on Tim as a close mentor for seven successful years as Chelsea FC Technical Director and have unfettered access to his exceptional knowledge on, and passion for, communication, leadership and practical solution-oriented behaviours to everyday conflicts.'
MICHAEL EMENALO, *FORMER CHELSEA FC TECHNICAL DIRECTOR*

'There can be a world of difference between what a person says and another hears. Tim's knowledge and experience shows us how we can bridge that gap.'
RICK DI MASCIO, *CEO OF INALYTICS*

10 Rules for Talking

How To Have Difficult Conversations in an Angry World

Tim Harkness

BLINK
bringing you closer

First published in the UK by Blink Publishing
An imprint of Bonnier Books UK
80–81 Wimpole Street, London, WIG 9RE
Owned by Bonnier Books
Sveavägen 56, Stockholm, Sweden

facebook.com/blinkpublishing
twitter.com/blinkpublishing

Trade Paperback – 978-1-788-702-66-9
Paperback – 978-1-788-704-09-0
Ebook – 978-1-788-702-67-6
Audio – 978-1-788-702-68-3

A CIP catalogue of this book is available from the British Library.

Typeset by IDSUK (DataConnection) Ltd.
Printed and bound in Great Britain by Clays Ltd, Elcograf S.p.A.

1 3 5 7 9 10 8 6 4 2

Every reasonable effort has been made to trace copyright holders of material reproduced in this book, but if any have been inadvertently overlooked the publishers would be glad to hear from them.

Blink Publishing is an imprint of Bonnier Books UK
www.bonnierbooks.co.uk

This book is dedicated to my wife and my parents.
To Claudia, who has been my partner in everything,
including psychological work and discussion,
since I borrowed her neuropsychology exam study notes in 1995,
to my mother, Jenny, for her continued daily love and guidance,
and to my father, Ken, who was a precise and accurate thinker,
and who valued and practised honesty and kindness.

CONTENTS

INTRODUCTION: VIOLENCE, RHETORIC AND TALKING

A few months after my wife Claudia and I moved into our first house in Durban, South Africa, in 1998, I was surprised by an intruder in our back garden. I was sitting on the veranda when he appeared from up the side path. He was a small man with unkempt hair and was wearing old clothes and a glossy red backpack of a size and design which suggested it had previously belonged to a nursery school child.

In South Africa, as a white homeowner, it wasn't completely unusual to meet unknown black people in your garden. Because of the racially based gap in wealth and opportunity, many white people employed poor black people to work as domestic workers or gardeners. Even small homes of white people would have a separate building at the back where the black servants would live. The white people would befriend white neighbours and entertain visitors in the front rooms, and the black people would befriend black neighbours and would socialise in the back buildings and garden.

So although my reading of the situation was that the man had stolen the backpack and was now scouting my garden for items with which to fill it, when he responded to my challenge by saying that he was there to visit the gardener, it was a plausible response. But when I asked him the name of the gardener he was looking for and he couldn't answer, I deemed this justification to escalate the situation and we engaged in a brief scuffle. I won it using a technique known to junior school scufflers everywhere: the arm twisted behind the back, which is especially useful when fighting someone smaller than yourself. I marched him to the back veranda and locked him in the outside toilet.

Once he was inside, there was a brief pause during which we both assessed the situation. I decided that I was going to call the police. The man started to rattle the door and beg to be let free. The toilet door had a small bolt with which it could be locked from the outside. I realised it was so flimsy that the man could easily break free. So I threatened him by saying, 'Hey! If you touch that door, I'm going to *hurt* you!' and the rattling stopped.

I am a psychologist and I worked from home. I had a client, so I had to break away from this situation to do a counselling session. I left Claudia in charge whilst I finished the session and the police arrived.

The policeman marched him down the side path and told him to get into the back of the police van. The understanding between us all was that there would be no charges pressed, but that the man would be loaded into the police van, driven away somewhere and dropped off with some kind of informal reprimand, the nature of which I had not considered. The man had not resisted much, but on seeing the inside of the van suddenly quailed with fear and shrank from the entrance. The policeman said, 'Hey!' loudly and the man startled and jumped into the van. As he climbed in, his backpack fell open and revealed his solitary worldly possession, a single slice of unbuttered brown bread, an image which has stayed with me since.

Because this is an instructional book and not a work of art, I will not leave you with the full responsibility of interpreting this story. It is an account from the benign end of the scale of one of the many crime, inequality and poverty-related conflicts that I experienced as a young man in South Africa.

Others included the man who threatened my mother with an axe, who I had to persuade not to come to our house again, and the man who I fought with after I found him randomly harassing a schoolgirl in the street.

These conflicts left their mark on me. One day, Claudia and I were talking to a friendly man in the street, and as the conversation flowed, the man casually moved to put his hands into his pockets. I instantly interpreted this as a threat and physically threatened him. He calmed me down by showing me his empty hands and assuring me of his good intentions. I had become so vigilant that I saw every threat. It kept me safe. But sometimes I saw threats that were not intended, and my response risked creating something from nothing.

It is a problem to not see what is there, but it is also a problem to see what is not there.

I planned to tell these stories about violence in a book about talking because recognising that I had once been tuned to see certain things in people helped me to gradually realise that, even years later and in quite different situations, I was also tuned to hearing certain things from people. Sometimes I was hearing what was not said and at other times I was not hearing what was said. Some of these errors were because of my past exposure to conflict, which had left me with biases or expectations about people, relationships or myself. And some were just basic mistakes.

But when Claudia read this list of conflicts, because she knew all the fights had been with black men, she exclaimed, 'It sounds really racist!' and then reflected before clarifying, 'I'm not saying you're a racist, but it does sound racist.' And I thought, 'I didn't see that coming.'

And in a sense, when Claudia says the stories sound racist, it's because they are. The reason I recall so vividly the image of the man's slice of bread in his stolen backpack is because, even at the time, I recognised some of the pathos. But what I probably didn't recognise was that our confrontation was not just a conflict between two individuals. The black man was a member of a society that had suffered over three centuries of disempowerment and social disruption. Apartheid didn't just create inequalities in wealth. There was a deeper social injury. For example, in addition to using the taxes and wealth derived from the labour of black people to pay for the privileged education of white children like myself, it also systematically attacked black families, societies and culture by forcing black men to live and work long distances from their wives and children. So when the man with the empty backpack and I squared up to each other in my back garden, there was history between us even though we had never met before. The two of us were part of an institution that was larger than our interaction, and that disadvantaged him and privileged me.

So while my original idea for this introduction was to tell an anecdote that would serve as an origin story of how complex my own past experience of conflict is, and how this led me to a gradual awareness of my own limitations in this area, which initiated a journey of discovery, Claudia pointed out that even my attempt to illustrate this complexity was overly simplistic. What she saw immediately was that I could not tell those stories without

evoking a response in the reader which I could not fully anticipate or control. Claudia highlighted that my challenge in talking
is not just to hear accurately, but also to do my best to ensure that
I am accurately heard. The person that I am talking to has the same
challenge – to accurately hear and be heard. When one of us makes
an error in saying something, or in hearing what has been said, it
takes some skill from the other person to correct the misunder-
standing, disagreement or offence, and return the conversation to
its intended track. When misunderstandings are themselves mis-
understood, arguments can escalate quickly. So maybe the problem
that Claudia pointed out is not a bad one to run into so early in this
book, because being careful about expressing myself accurately,
and being aware of the danger of being misheard is a problem that
will certainly crop up again.

The story of the man with the backpack is an example of the
most basic form of persuasion, which arises from imbalances in
power and the threat of violence. But the persuasion is only as stable as the power imbalance. At the time it seems a compelling and,
if you are on the privileged side of the power imbalance, highly
satisfying short-term solution. But it is only the most temporary
and superficial of fixes, and the fact that South Africa remains a
troubled country is testament to this.

When I moved to London in my thirties, I was looking forward
not so much to no more fights as there being no possibility of a
fight. It took me years before I could walk past any man in the
street without sizing him up. I became able to smile at people as
we peacefully navigated a shared space. So I was particularly dismayed one English spring morning to find myself dismounted
from my bicycle on a bridle-path, being threatened by a man waving a stout walking stick above his head.

I had bought a bike in England instead of a car. I rode backwards and forwards to work every day and became part of the community that shared the path at those times of day – other bike commuters (we would secretly race each other, pretending not to be trying), school children, horse riders and dog walkers.

But there was a heavily set older man who didn't like me. He would march along the path and refuse to give way. Once he dallied at a gate, holding me up, and another time he spat as I rode past. I was aware of his hostility. So when we approached each other one morning, and he took a line that to me appeared designed to force me to ride through a puddle, I instead pushed through the narrow space between him and the water. As I brushed past he swore at me loudly. I decided that this conflict had gone on for long enough, so I got off my bike and said to him firmly, 'You can't talk to me like that.' He instantly became enraged and swore repeatedly and threatened me with fists and walking stick.

But now I was living in a country which did have a police and legal system with the resources to attend to conflicts of this kind, so I said to him, 'I'm just going to phone the police.' I turned away and continued my ride to work and phoned the police from my office to tell them my side of the story. It was only when the officer repeatedly asked me, 'But what did he actually say to you?' and I couldn't answer the question, that I recalled that the man hadn't said anything at all. He had been swearing clearly, and waving his stick, but he had produced no other words, only a weird sing-song wail. And I suddenly realised – stroke! Why hadn't I seen it before?

Strokes cause localised damage in the brain, and if one occurs in the speech centre in the left temporal region, the victim suffers catastrophic language loss without necessarily incurring broader cognitive impairment (they are just as intelligent but can't speak). Swearing is a separate function from language (it originates in the brain area responsible for exclamations and alarm cries), so stroke victims can lose the ability to speak but retain the ability to swear fluently. Additionally, many stroke victims lose spatial awareness and become less confident with moving objects.

My fast-moving bicycle frightened him because he couldn't judge whether I was going to crash into him or not, and he lacked the language to explain this to me and to ask me to ride past him more slowly. I said to the police officer, 'It's OK, I'll sort it out.' The next time I saw the man I dismounted my bike at a safe distance, walked up to him slowly and said, 'I'm sorry.' We shook hands and in that moment became friends, and in the subsequent years spent many hours walking together during my commutes, he with his walking stick, and me pushing my bike.

I remember this confrontation as an argument between two men, one rendered speechless by injury, the other by emotion, to the point that neither realised that they had no words to share. And it is in that light that I offer you this book on communication.

WHY WE NEED TO LEARN HOW TO TALK

This book is a story of the struggler, or the late developer. While in my day job as a psychologist I am (hopefully) reasonably good at a specific kind of conversation (time-limited one-to-ones in a quiet space with a cooperative person discussing an issue in which I am not emotionally invested), it took me some time to realise that I wasn't good at other kinds of conversations – those that involved disagreement, emotion, high stakes, with no recourse to an adjudicator or power structures that would arbitrate when consensus failed. But I am not the only one who struggles with these kinds of conversations.

DIFFICULT CONVERSATIONS

The purpose of communication is to exchange knowledge and ideas. Sometimes this exchange is easy – if I have no information about a topic, I will readily accept yours. But when we both have ideas and knowledge, when they do not overlap perfectly or conflict, we need to pool them and then select the best. We have to allow our ideas and knowledge to compete. But often when we converse, rather than selecting the best facts and ideas from a common pool, with the objective of achieving the best solution, we get stuck in a competition of just trying to jam our own ideas into the conversation. Then we find it difficult to dispassionately compare and select ideas.

We are not very good at recognising the limits of our own knowledge. It is not easy for us to accept that our ideas could be improved, corrected or replaced. We are possessive and competitive, so become biased by our preference for our own ideas. Talking *should* be a competition, but it should be a competition between ideas, not protagonists. The problem with many personal and public conversations is that it is a competition without purpose or rules, a competition of power.

A lot of difficult conversations are predictions requiring consensus. If a family is discussing whether to get a pet, they are trying to predict, and agree, how it will affect the family dynamics. If a business is making a strategic decision about what to buy or sell, or a politician is proposing a policy, these are also predictions about the future that are ideally shared. Consensus can be difficult to reach because you and I could have been exposed to different information, have different prior opinions, and have competing agendas. But consensus matters. If we prioritise my agenda 100 per cent and your agenda 0 per cent, is this really better for either or both of us than developing a new shared agenda?

When I won the argument with the intruder in my back garden, I was exploiting our failure to agree either on the processes by which the disagreement would be resolved, or its objective. My choice was that power and violence would be used to assert property rights, his preference was that excess (I had too much stuff to pay attention to, everything he owned was in one bag) and compassion would be used to address basic needs.

When we don't recognise the limits of our knowledge on the subject of talking itself, we are stuck in a state of unconscious incompetence when it comes to communicating.

HOW DO WE GET BETTER?

There is a psychological theory called the four stages of competence. It says that we progress from a state of:

Unconscious incompetence: we are unaware of our own inability and potential

To

Conscious incompetence: we realise our inability, but also what we might achieve

To

Conscious competence: we begin to exercise new skills, but only at a basic level and by thinking about them really hard

To

Unconscious competence: we execute the new skill competently and naturally

Among our psychological quirks as humans is our tendency to believe that we are better than average at easy things and worse than average at difficult things. And most communication is actually quite easy, because a lot of the time we are discussing low stakes issues that we agree on. It's only rarely that we find ourselves in genuinely difficult conversations where there is disagreement, high stakes and high emotion.[1] I always thought of myself as a good communicator, but in some ways this was because I was judging myself on my ability to have easy conversations and, like the 80 per cent of drivers who think they are better than average, I may have misjudged my level of skill.

In my late thirties, I had a friend at work, Ralph, and we had great fun disagreeing and arguing with each other. I remember slowly realising that the reason we were able to sustain such vigorous debate was due to Ralph's skills rather than mine. He was able to have vigorous debate with many people and I wasn't. I became curious about what it was that he was doing. Ralph's skills fell into two categories. The first set of skills enabled him to keep the conversation safe; he was a friendly and charismatic person, who was able to project a sense that any disagreement was less important than our relationship and would not impact on his generally positive opinion of me. When I argued with Ralph, I always felt that he respected and liked me, and also that he respected my needs and wishes. This is what made the conversation safe – he was challenging my conclusions, not my integrity or my needs. I felt challenged but not threatened by Ralph. But at the same time he was an intelligent and rigorous thinker, so he would not avoid issues or accept weak arguments or unsatisfactory compromises. This was his second set of skills – his ability to demand logical, informed discussions that would deliver rigorous conclusions.

These became the two principles that inform the 10 Rules – talking has to be both safe and effective.

---

[1] The Harvard Negotiation Project define difficult conversations as those with differing opinions, high stakes, and elevated emotion.

TALKING OR DEBATING?

The reason why talking has to be safe and effective is that talking is not debate. The key difference between the two is that debate is externally adjudicated and talking is not. A debate is actually much less skilled an arena than a talk. In a debate, you don't have to maintain a relationship with the person you are talking to. You don't even talk to them directly; you don't have to change their mind and you don't have to achieve consensus. You don't even have to produce a complete, logical or correct argument. All you have to do is sound slightly more plausible than the other point of view and the structure of the debate determines that a third party (judge, voter, viewer or reader) will rule 100 per cent in your favour. You can use whatever scorched earth or underhanded tactics you want to achieve this; you can leave your opponent fuming, humiliated or tongue tied. It doesn't matter, as long as the adjudicator is won over.

Debates deliver definitive rather than proportionate conclusions, and because they make no accommodation for maintaining the connection between adversaries, they tend to be one-off events, rather than a repeated and progressive development of knowledge, opinion, or a relationship. Knowledge is best developed collaboratively and incrementally, so, in addition to limiting our ability to achieve agreement, debates may actually stifle our ability to understand important personal and public matters. If you want to improve your knowledge through learning, maintain a collaborative relationship with your adversary and achieve consensus, you will have to talk, not debate.

Debate is not the only limiting but popular form of social discourse. Monologues happen when one party has more access to a communication channel than another and uses it to talk more than they listen. The simplest kind of monologue is when one person in a duo or group dominates the conversation through spending more time talking, having a louder voice, a position of social dominance or more fraught emotional energy.

Western culture has a tradition of valuing monologues from political orators and writers, but monologues are not talking. They are designed to overwhelm opposing opinion and look to replace, rather than add to what you already know or believe. The opinion piece written for a newspaper is of course a monologue, but so is the output of political news channels, the fossil fuel industry or advertising campaigns. They are all monologues which are meant to overwhelm opposing opinion and are uninterested in learning from their audience.

Another category of communication is the retort. Retorts are aggressive replies which often only address part of the argument and prioritise making a winning point over continuing the conversation. Like debates and monologues, retorts are not designed to foster collaboration or to change minds. They allow the 'retorter' to vent emotion and to express their determination to entrench their own position. I am sure you will struggle to think of examples of times you have been on the receiving end of a retort and changed your position as a consequence. Retorts are having their day right now. The normal retort limiters – our lack of quick wittedness in the moment and the inhibitory effect of seeing hurt or disapproval on the face or in the body language of the person to whom we are retorting – are completely removed in social media. When you are talking, you have to share the conversation bandwidth with at least one other person. On social media, this bandwidth is shared with a large number of people, giving you a small share. People adapt to this by resorting to the retort which, for the above reasons, is currently more popular than it is useful.

A subcategory of retort is the sound bite. Sound bites are prepared in advance of a conversation rather than developed in response to a question and they often derive their power from the planning and intelligence of several people. Public figures can get away with using sound bites out of the context of a conversation because the context is not reported and does not reveal that the speaker is not even applying the main skill of the retort. A retort is at least a response to the flow of the conversation. To retort you first have to listen. A sound bite does not even require that the speaker responds to the person that they are talking to.

While these rhetorical elements are an improvement on violence, they are still unsatisfactory when used in private and public discourse because, like violence, they fail to establish a safe, collaborative, iterative, learning conversation and thus fail to achieve consensus. A critical ingredient of convincing somebody is leaving them feeling that their change of mind was achieved through fair means.

In debates, if one party appears to have preferential access to systems or adjudicators (more expensive lawyers, more court time, influence over judges, etc.), the debate is seen as unfair. If a monologist is considered to be using a privileged position to dominate communication channels or bandwidth, and a retorter has access to a larger social media audience, the process is considered unfair and consensus fails.

REALISING OUR INCOMPETENCE

Our lack of skill in achieving consensus could be the master weakness which underlies so many desperately important but intractable personal and public conversations. Don't be fooled into thinking that because you often agree with people you are good at achieving agreement. Being *in* consensus is not the same as *achieving* consensus.

I remember picking up the first book about communication that I read. I opened it thinking that within I would find the answer to a problem that had long vexed me: how to convince all the idiots that disagreed with me that I was right. It was disappointing to gradually realise that, in fact, not everybody who disagreed with me was wrong.

In his book *Thinking Fast and Slow*, Nobel Laureate Daniel Kahneman calls the human mind 'a machine for jumping to conclusions'. I began to realise how good I was at convincing myself that I was right. Once I had formed an opinion, I excelled at seeing only those facts which confirmed my opinion. I dealt with the problem of people who held different opinions in the simplest way, by making an *ad hominem* attack – believing that their contrary opinion was due to some flaw in their knowledge, reasoning or character – rather than by seeking to use their knowledge and opinion to upgrade the quality of (not replace) my own.

A series of incidents helped shift me from a state of unconscious incompetence to a state of conscious incompetence when it came to my own talking. Here is one: I have always taken pride in my driving. My father was a fast, skilled rally driver, and I consider myself to also be an above average driver. One day, I was driving the family on a slightly wet road and a squirrel darted out in front of the car. I calculated that, at its current trajectory, the only way to save the squirrel's life was to swerve slightly towards it and drive the car right over it so that it would pass unharmed between the wheels of the car.

Unfortunately, the squirrel saw me coming and stopped, and I ran it over and killed it. Claudia said, 'You shouldn't have swerved,' and I found myself aware of my inability to reply effectively because I was so offended at being criticised. Claudia later told me that my face told a story, but this is a book about talking, not emoting.

After a year or two of pondering questions posed by books on conversation, I began to run low-key communication workshops as a way of teaching the principles that I had developed. My main themes at this point were two ideas: first, that conversations should be emotionally safe, which is achieved when people feel that they and their needs are being respected; and second, that we should be aware of the limitations in our own knowledge as this would make us more open to the ideas and opinions of others.

I found that people were quite receptive to these ideas and were able to implement them within personal conversations quite quickly. But the feedback I got was that although people were finding themselves in fewer arguments, they were achieving this by being excessively accommodating. They were becoming so aware of the validity of the other person's opinion that they were sacrificing their own. This wasn't really progress. Because just as you are rarely completely right in an argument, so are you rarely completely wrong.

At the same time, from about 2012 onwards, I became aware of a shift in public discourse. My attitude towards politics was shaped by my history as a South African. Living through the dismantling of apartheid had left me profoundly optimistic about the direction of politics. I clearly remember feeling, even in the depths of apartheid, that things would get better. When democracy arrived in 1994, it seemed to be confirmation that negotiations and talking worked.

I moved to the UK in 2009, and my attitude was that politics there was skilled, benevolent and settled – too stable to be very interesting. While in South Africa we had apparently resolved a civil war and 350 years of oppression, in Britain the most exciting thing seemed to be whether Gordon Brown would succeed Tony Blair.

Though I soon realised that Britain isn't perfect. A friend of mine, born in London but of African ancestry, told me that when he was a young boy watching football in London in the 1980s, he would sit in the stands of his football club and pull his hoodie tight over his head and the sleeves of his jacket over his hands so that the fans around him who were racially abusing black players on the pitch would not see that he was black also. At the same time, in South Africa I was able to go with black friends to rugby matches attended by large white crowds without any fear or chance of racially based harassment.

Also, in Britain, there seems to be little awareness of the less glorious parts of the country's past, which includes the slave trade, opium wars, concentration camps and colonisation. In South Africa, we commemorate the Sharpeville massacre, in which police fired on unarmed civilians, killing 69 people. In Britain, there doesn't seem to be public awareness of, for example, the Jallianwala Bagh massacre, when in 1919 British troops in India trapped a large crowd of unarmed civilians in a town square and fired on them until their ammunition ran out, killing many hundreds of men, women and children. In South Africa, we know that we have a troubled history. One of the ways that you live with a troubled history is by not hiding from it.

So my initial optimism and complacency about the high quality and low stakes of public debate in Britain were slowly replaced by concern. The MPs' expenses scandal demonstrated that, even in the United Kingdom, many people will be as corrupt as they can get away with. The newspaper phone-hacking scandal exposed a lack of integrity and purpose in parts of the media. And the Brexit referendum was accompanied by the use of lies, denigration of logical process and the consolidation of the cult of personality. Subsequent to the Brexit referendum and Brexit elections, we have seen opposing political positions become increasingly entrenched. These developments are not unique in Western democracies. It may be that instead of historically or culturally being good at achieving consensus, we have just been fortunate to find ourselves already mostly in agreement.

The benefit of moving from unconscious incompetence to conscious incompetence is that you can start learning skills to create competence. As a society, a plausible initial point of agreement may be that we are not as good at talking as we once thought. A valuable topic of conversation may be talking itself. After all, it's hard to have a conversation when we haven't agreed the terms of that conversation. We use communication media that favour the retort and the monologue, and political and legal structures that favour the debate. We celebrate personalities who value metaphor, deduction, division and sentiment over talking.

But recognising ourselves as individually or collectively incompetent at talking is hard. It's unpalatable to acknowledge an inability of which you were previously unaware. Sometimes it's easier to carry on being wrong than to acknowledge that you were wrong in the first place. And it's discouraging to consider that even if we accept that we need to get better at talking, there is no guarantee that we will ever be able to master the skills or the rules.

Taking myself as an example, certainly among my colleagues and acquaintances, you would find people critical of my own talking ability. Surely, they will say, for someone of his training, he should have handled that situation better? And my family would be able to provide you examples, some very recent, of me displaying incompetence in conversations. But no endeavour is best started with perfection as a goal.

Many of our conflicts are recurring – think of the individual arguments you have at work or with family. Chances are they contain themes that you have visited repeatedly, and chances are the arguments remain unresolved because of a surge of emotion, or a point of view or a behaviour that was also used the last time this conversation didn't work out. This is true of public debates as well – the themes of the debates and the reasons for their failure tend to be the same again and again.

In these recurring situations, conscious incompetence, or just knowing what you are doing wrong, is highly valuable. If you can just stop doing those things, you have already increased your chances of success. And in recurring situations, you have the opportunity to prepare. Conscious competence may be awkward, and take effort, but just having a prepared line or response can increase your chances of success. For example, simply inserting the phrase 'it is complex' early into a contentious conversation, or spending some time keeping quiet and listening, can make it more likely that a conversation will go well.

Achieving mastery, or consistent unconscious competence in the skills and rules of talking would be difficult and unlikely, but as with many skills, there is meaningful value in achieving small gains.

WHY WE NEED RULES

A trivial yet impressive social example of achieving broad consensus is sport. The most basic way of settling competitions about who is the fittest, strongest and most skilled is by fighting. But rule-free fighting is unsatisfactory because it is damaging and not definitive. If you sneak up behind me and hit me on the back of the head with a rock you have won the fight, but have you really established yourself as having superior fitness, strength and skill? If you bite off my ear but I gouge out your eye, who has really won? This is an important question, because both of us need to decide whether to accept a claimed result or re-engage in the competition, and others may want to decide which one of us to ally with in future conflicts.

The accomplishment of sport in managing to create mostly harm-free and mostly definitive tests of fitness, strength and skill is a remarkable global social achievement. Everybody agrees that France are the 2018 football world champions. This agreement rests on a massive body of work and knowledge. In every country, there are official organisations for training players to play the sport and training people to referee it. Fans who watch the game can evaluate skill and whether players are playing within the rules and the spirit of the game. Every country has sophisticated systems for recognising the best players and for progressing them through the ranks to play at the highest level of competition. When there are global competitions to determine the fittest, strongest and most skilled people, these take place according to rules that are sophisticated, documented and mutually agreed.

When Mike Tyson bit off a chunk of Evander Holyfield's ear during a boxing match, this deviation from the agreed rules of boxing was instantly and universally recognised as an illegitimate technique. Everybody understands that it is better to be an agreed winner and that this is only possible if you stay within the agreed rules.

There is no similar mechanism for deciding private and public disagreements. Despite the fact that resolving the question of who is the most fit, strong or skilled is a trivial matter compared to some of our public and private conflicts, there is no investment in educating people and societies in the skills of allowing ideas to compete and no mechanism for agreeing the rules under which this competition would take place.

I don't know whether we can solve what seems to be a pressing and intractable modern problem of reaching public consensus on important issues where opinions and agendas vary. I am slightly more optimistic about achieving gains in the private sphere. But I am confident about the following three assertions. Firstly, that many private and public debates are competitions of ideas and agendas which have most chance of being resolved in an arena governed by prior agreed rules. Secondly, there are many examples, including sport, traffic and tax, that prove that individuals and societies are capable of learning and following sophisticated new social skills and rules, and that these rules make things better, if not perfect. And thirdly, that even small or occasional escapes from unconscious incompetence are worthwhile.

THE 10 RULES FOR TALKING

These 10 rules are 10 *of the* Rules for Talking, not the *only* 10 Rules for Talking. I hope that these rules are useful enough to be debated, amended, improved or replaced over time. But to move from unconscious incompetence to a point where we can have better private and public conversations, these are my suggestions. The rules are designed to meet the two requirements of a conversation – that it is safe, in that participants feel engaged, respected and that their emotions are not clouding their thinking; and that it is effective, in that it mutually establishes a pool of well-observed facts and applies an agreed logic and shared experience correctly to draw a consensual opinion.

Each of the chapters that follow on Rules 1 to 10 will have a 'rules in real life' summary. Each summary will list the key concepts of a rule and give an example of how to use it. Please do not expect a 'gotcha!' or 'aha!' moment every time. Conversations are complex, and these rules are nudges to keep the talking going in a slightly better direction rather than stopping it in its tracks. Discussions work better when they are gradual and collaborative rather than dramatic monologues.

Rules 3, 5 and 6 are mostly about safety; Rules 1, 7 and 8 are mostly about effectiveness and Rules 2, 4, 9 and 10 are about both. But all rules affect both requirements, because difficult conversations have to be safe to be effective, and they have to be effective to be safe.

THE 10 RULES

1. Agree what you are talking for
2. Accept that agreement takes skill and effort
3. Remember most people are good, competent and worthy of respect
4. Talk fast and slow
5. Keep the conversation safe
6. Use resilience
7. Use rigor
8. Use complexity
9. Listen
10. Reach out

RULE 1: AGREE WHAT YOU ARE TALKING FOR

This first rule is important because there are many potential objectives in a conversation. We talk to express emotion, to develop our ideas, to learn, to collaborate, but also, sometimes, to try to influence somebody else. It is surprisingly easy to go into a conversation without knowing why you are in it. The person you are talking to has a similarly wide range of possible objectives and these objectives can shift rapidly during the conversation. Three common priorities that we pivot to as the conversation becomes difficult are expressing our own emotion, keeping the peace and prioritising our point of view. Each of these threatens the success of the conversation, especially as the other person could be pivoting their priorities also. Agreeing what you are talking for creates a reference point to which you can return when the conversation goes off track and allows you to set realistic and step-by-step goals for the conversation. It also allows competing or misaligned agendas to be identified early on, so this can become a topic in itself.

RULE 2: ACCEPT THAT AGREEMENT TAKES SKILL AND EFFORT

When conversations turn out to be more difficult than we expect, we can have an emotional reaction which can then become a new major difficulty. When we underestimate the complexity of a conversation, our lack of preparedness or motivation for the scale of the task can imperil the outcome. Human beings are good at learning complex skills and undertaking difficult and arduous tasks. Our failure to succeed in difficult private and public conversations is not always to do with the inherent difficulty of these conversations. Sometimes it is because we think these conversations should be easier than they actually are, and so do not prepare ourselves with sufficient skill or patience. Accepting the scale of the task allows us to allocate the necessary time and resource, to do the necessary preparation and to be encouraged by progress rather than demanding perfection.

RULE 3: REMEMBER MOST PEOPLE ARE GOOD, COMPETENT AND WORTHY OF RESPECT

The fundamental attribution error is a psychological principle that says I attribute my own success to skill and intent and my failures to bad luck, while I attribute your success to good luck and your failures to poor skill and malign intent. Not everybody is a good person (and following Rule 1 creates an important platform for engaging with people who aren't), but most are, and remembering this casts disagreement as a more interesting and challenging but also more solvable problem: why does this informed, intelligent and virtuous person disagree with me?

RULE 4: TALK FAST AND SLOW

Tversky and Kahneman are the psychologists who debunked the myth of '*Homo economicus*' – the idea that people act as if they are essentially rational. Their work into the predictable biases and shortcuts that we are vulnerable to helped establish the idea humans have two forms of thinking – fast and slow. Fast thinking is automatic and intuitive but subject to bias and error-causing shortcuts, while slow thinking is effortful and too time consuming to deliver immediate answers, but more accurate and less subject to bias and error. Tversky and Kahneman called fast thinking System 1 and slow thinking System 2. Rule 4 applies some of their key concepts about thinking to talking.

Different conversations require different systems. Creativity, spontaneity and intuition are useful fast-thinking elements of a conversation and stimulate fun, optimism and agreeableness. But when we are not already in agreement, or when we are unaware of our errors because we are too much in agreement, we need to think and talk slow. Building agreement depends on a shared view of the world, which may need to be carefully constructed using slow thinking. If we are to progress from unconscious incompetence to unconscious competence, the role of slow talking is to discover and correct our errors and limitations. Once we have restored the conversation to safe ground, we can progress with unconsciously competent fast talking. But slow talking is always necessary to detect our unconscious incompetence – the frequent and inevitable occasions when we make errors of which we are not immediately aware.

RULE 5: KEEP THE CONVERSATION SAFE

The marriage expert John Gottman calls criticism, defensiveness, contempt and stonewalling the 'four horsemen of the apocalypse' which destroy relationships. Conversations can tip into 'silence or violence', in which we withdraw or attack, and to keep conversations on track we need to maintain two conditions: mutual respect and mutual purpose.[2] Mutual respect is demonstrated by a tone of voice that is free of aggression or contempt, by turn-taking, protagonists having similar word counts and allowing each participant to articulate complete arguments. Mutual respect is maintained when participants affirm that they see each other as good, competent and worthy, rather than ignorant, incompetent or evil. It also helps us attribute differences of opinion to logical interpretations of different observations.

Rule 1 is to establish purpose and Rule 3 is to respect. Rule 5 is to practically apply these principles in the conversation to the point where all participants feel safe enough to talk effectively.

RULE 6: USE RESILIENCE

Resilience is an accurate response to threat or opportunity – not being excessively or insufficiently anxious or motivated.

---

[2] According to the team at VitalSmarts from their book, *Crucial Conversations*.

To be resilient, we need to be able to gauge threat and also the resources that we have available to respond to that threat. Resilience is a personal matter. In some ways it is an individual skill that we can bring to bear on adversity. But it is also a political matter – some of us are more resilient than others because we have access to more resources and more safety nets than others.

Many public debates involve some degree of disagreement about resilience – should this group of people get more help or more money from society, or should they just be more resilient? These debates can degenerate into name-calling. We use terms like trolls, snowflakes and triggers. Discussing resilience publicly matters because understanding what level of adversity and challenge an individual or a group can cope with is part of the conversation about what is fair in society. It is more realistic to strive for a self-correcting conversation than a perfect one. Misunderstandings, disagreements and conflict may be inevitable in some conversations. When we apply resilience, we are able to stay calm and focused enough to resolve these incidental challenges rather than being alarmed enough to escalate them into a new and unhelpful priority for the conversation.

RULE 7: USE RIGOR

The idea of making careful observations, drawing cautious logical conclusions, testing these ideas with further observation of whether the conclusion applies in a wider range of circumstances, and repeating, is responsible for most of what allows us to have a modern civilisation. Human beings are intractably emotional, impulsive and tribal, but we are also very good at individual and social learning.

The scientific method is arguably our greatest collective accomplishment and most important idea. It is slow and painstaking, but when the alternative is protracted and repetitive arguments its implementation can be the fastest way to a resolution. Reality is what exists independently of your opinion. We can be rigorous about our use of rigor; we can check for precision, accuracy, evidence, method, verifiability, meaningfulness and inference. Rigor is our most reliable way of building a picture of reality that is as independent of the observer as possible and thus allows two observers to independently arrive at the same or similar opinions, which is the best way to achieve consensus.

RULE 8: USE COMPLEXITY

When we acknowledge that a matter is complex, we broaden its scope, and by doing this immediately create the possibility of finding that we and the person we are talking with have overlapping opinions. Laying a foundation of what we do agree on is a good platform from which to tackle disagreements. But it can seem easier to talk fast, and we can wish for our explanations of the world to be coherent and without contradiction. One of the ways of maintaining this is to sacrifice complexity.

In his book on intractable conflicts, Peter Coleman says that as disagreements become more complex, the temptation is to see the answer as increasingly simple. But the chance for overlap between two simple perspectives on the same complex issue is low. Integrative complexity is a way of understanding complex issues. It has three ideas: that a complex topic has multiple dimensions, that each of these dimensions is likely to be graded by degree rather than being binary, and that the dimensions are likely to interact and influence each other. Integrative complexity is useful for reaching conclusions, but also for assessing the method used to achieve them. When we assess an argument, as well as assessing its conclusion, we can assess its scope – has it engaged with the complexity of the topic?

RULE 9: LISTEN

Sometimes listening is easy. When we are hearing what we want to hear, it is easy to follow the classic listening techniques, like attention, stillness, mirroring, remembering, not interrupting and questioning. But it is not always easy to listen. When we listen, we have to be prepared to assimilate – to take the message in. When the message is long, charged or disagreeable, it is harder to assimilate. We also have to be prepared to accommodate the message – to fit it into our understanding of the world. When the message contains ideas that force us to rearrange our beliefs, this can be hard work that we are reluctant to do. And when the message contains or evokes difficult emotions, listening becomes harder again.

But when, in spite of these difficulties, we are prepared to be moved, to learn and to use disagreement rather than be discouraged by it, we can listen and so create the possibility for talking.

RULE 10: REACH OUT

When I locked the garden intruder into my outside toilet and told him not to touch the door, I had secured his compliance. When the policeman got him to scramble into the back of the police van, he had secured his compliance. Both methods were extreme as we used violence or its threat to achieve the man's complete compliance with our points of view. But we had also forced the man into a humiliating capitulation, an acceptance that he had no rights and we had no obligations, that was only possible with extreme coercion.

I wish that instead of fighting the man in my back garden, I had invited him to meet me at my front door. Possibly we could have calmed things down and talked about finding something in between his initial plan of helping himself to my limited belongings without my permission and the actual outcome of him being driven away hungry and destitute in the back of a police van.

This book is my apology to him, and my wish that I can do better.

RULE 1: AGREE WHAT YOU ARE TALKING FOR

'WHAT DID YOU DO THAT FOR?'

One night when I was 20 years old, I was sitting on the terrace of a beachfront bar when my friend Dave turned to me and said, 'I'm bored.' I said to him, 'Let's break into SeaWorld and jump into the shark tank.'

Dave didn't do it, but I did, although it wasn't actually a spur of the moment decision.

I liked to visit the aquarium after closing time by myself at night. I would climb over a wall and find a space to sit in front of the main tank so that I could look at the big fish reflecting silver moonlight as they swam past. On one visit, leaning over the barrier wall at the top of the shark tank and watching the dark shapes circling, I had been seized with a sudden impulse to jump in. The shark tank was about 10 metres long by 5 metres wide, and contained about five raggie (grey nurse) sharks, which are quite docile creatures, three Zambezi (bull) sharks, which are a bit more aggressive, two massive swordfish, which had been caught in an estuary north of

Durban when they were small and were as old as me, and a giant grouper, which was the dominant fish in the tank. Jumping into the tank wasn't totally insane. I knew from experience of diving with sharks that only the Zambezi sharks posed a real risk and even they, I was quite sure, would react reflexively to an unexpected splash by swimming away rather than towards the disturbance. I really wanted to do it but couldn't quite bring myself to give way to the impulse. This failure didn't sit well with me.

So, when my friend Dave proposed an adventure, I had one to hand. Dave said he was going to come with me, but he lost his nerve and didn't even make the climb into the locked facility. I made my way to the dark shark tank alone, climbed over the barrier and stood at the edge of the water. This time I was definitely going to do it. It was just a matter of timing it so that the circling sharks were all clustered mostly on the other side of the tank, then jumping in, and leaping right back out like a dolphin.

I did it. It felt just like jumping into an ordinary swimming pool, just faster. It wasn't a big deal. I looked back into the tank before I left and the sharks were circling much more quickly than before I had jumped in, but I think it was fright rather than thwarted hunger.[3] I was soaking wet when Dave caught up with me walking back down the promenade and said, 'Tim, what did you do that for?'

This question seems to get asked more about things that we have already done ('What did you do that for?'), than things that we are doing ('What are you doing that for?'), or are about to do

---

[3] A couple of years later the grouper got old, and one of the Zambezi sharks sensed an opportunity and hit its long-time tank mate with an attack. The other sharks joined in and within seconds the giant fish had ceased to exist. It did make me think slightly differently about my adventure.

('What are you going to do that for?') This is the case in our own individual motivations, but it also applies to our combined motivations when we talk with someone else. We don't often ask what we are talking for. This chapter is about the value of clarifying and agreeing our motivation before we begin to talk. Just the to and fro of talking often requires close attention, which can distract us from the broader questions of what the conversation is about, and what the objective of the conversation is. Sometimes conversations do not go as well as we want because we do not know what we want.

Rule 1 is a reminder that, in many circumstances, it is worth calculating in advance what we should do something for, and this includes conversations.

CAUGHT IN A LIE

When I was in my first year of high school, my teacher caught me in an obvious lie to her in front of the whole class. It was an Afrikaans language class (not my first language) and I had been required to give an oral review of an Afrikaans book that I had read. I had not read any Afrikaans books, so I came up with the rather weak plan of reviewing an English book that I had read to my little sister at bedtime and pretending that it had been in Afrikaans. Unfortunately for me, I hadn't thought things through carefully enough to translate the name of the main character from English into Afrikaans. This made my subterfuge obvious. My teacher began to question me gently on why the main character in an Afrikaans book had such an obviously English name (Grasshopper), but because I was so embarrassed about having been caught lying, and because I didn't know the Afrikaans word for grasshopper (*sprinkaan*), I just doubled down on the lie and insisted that the book had been written in Afrikaans. When it was finally over, and the teacher had given up on me, as I was walking back to my desk one of my friends laughed at me and said, 'Tim, what *English* book did you read?'

While this was a very unsuccessful lie, what I will say for it, and for lying in general, is that we tend to know exactly what we are lying for. I hadn't done the preparatory work and was lying to conceal that fact.

I have told more successful lies as an adult. A friend of mine who worked in a car dealership had once had a really tough day at work and had driven one of the dealership's unsold cars to a quiet spot to have some thinking time. He had intended this to be a brief, if unscheduled, afternoon break, but the dealership reported the car as stolen. Because he was a young black man being pursued by the (now post-apartheid) police, he was in a genuinely life-threatening situation. In a panic, he dropped the car off at my house and hid in my back room. The police had no warrant to search my house, so I gave them the keys to the car and told them I had no idea where my friend was. Again, I had a very clear idea of what I was lying for.

I do not always have a clear reason for what I say. Sometimes, even though I am not a person given to regret, I ask myself what I said something for. Occasionally, even when I am not arguing with Claudia, I can say something and see from her subsequent hesitation, or suppression of a slightly pained expression, that I have said something not quite right. It is usually a repeat mistake, one of the set pieces that our relationship contains, so I will have said it before and should have known that it would not work, and afterwards will ask myself what I said that for. Sometimes when I am doing a counselling session with a client, I will catch myself saying too much, and sometimes, when talking with a colleague, we will find ourselves repeating, without adding to, a dispute or an agreement that we have had before. Conversations, like any action, are motivated by a complex set of forces, only some of which we are consciously aware. But conversations do work better when both parties are mainly aware and mainly agreed on what they are talking for.

Agreeing what a conversation is for has two parts: deciding what the purpose of the conversation is – what the desired outcome would be; and deciding what the conversation is actually about.

The psychologists Tversky and Kahneman say that when we try to explain our behaviour, we think of ourselves as rational actors taking decisions in our own best interests. We apply this to when we talk also – we think as if every conversation is a logical examination of a logical priority. But what we actually do is act and talk like humans. Sometimes we discuss things that are not imminently important, like the weather, even if we are not going outside, or cars, even if we are not buying a new one. These conversations still have objectives, just not the explicit one – we want to enjoy each other's company and show our care for each other.

One of the most significant hidden objectives of a conversation is to express allegiance to a group. When we are subject to peer or political pressure, we may say things that have the objective of confirming our membership of a group. My father used to play a game when watching sport.

He would say, 'Good decision!' when the referee ruled in favour of his team, and 'Bad decision!' when the referee ruled against them. He was always amused that the people who supported the same team as him took his statements as evidence that he was an expert on the rules, rather than just an ally. This game reveals something quite important in private and public discourse, that sometimes the objective of fitting in or belonging is powerful enough to shape our words and our beliefs, and yet not always obvious enough for ourselves or others to realise when we are doing it.

WHY ARE WE TALKING?

The purpose of a conversation must be both clear and agreed. Lying is an example of a conversation that has a clear purpose that is not agreed. Insults and threats would also fit into this category. But lying that leads to the success of a conversation is rare; conversations with objectives that are clear but not agreed do not normally go well.

Other conversations can have a clear purpose but incomplete agreement. I remember being in an English literature lesson before an exam. Along with most of the other students, I was happy to let the lesson slip by without any specific objective. But one student pinned the lecturer down with a forensic series of questions about what topics were likely to come up in the exam. While she was totally clear on what she was talking for, there was a sense of awkwardness in the room as a consequence of a lack of total agreement between her and the lecturer on what the lecture was for, and specifically how much information it was appropriate to give about the content of the exam. The student was using a combination of emotional pressure and skilled questioning to get him to give away more information than he was really comfortable with. The student (and the rest of us eagerly listening in) benefited from the information, but the lecturer may have felt that the integrity of his exam, and therefore course, had been slightly compromised.

Other conversations have a purpose which may be unclear or implicit, but which is completely agreed. I remember (as a young man new to social conventions) discussing the weather with my aunt, and eventually realising that while the weather didn't really matter to either of us, spending time in conversation together did. We had agreed on an implicit purpose for the conversation.

A Norwegian friend described a similar experience when he moved to the UK. He said it took him some time to work out that when people asked him how he was, that this served as a greeting rather than as a genuine enquiry into his wellbeing. When he realised this implicit purpose, he agreed to it also and conversations flowed more smoothly.

This 'clear and agreed' versus 'unclear and agreed' categorisation of purpose can be used to understand the difference between two significant therapeutic approaches. In cognitive behavioural therapy, the purpose is clear and explicit; it is to consciously improve ways of understanding and responding to threats and opportunity. If I had been talking to a CBT therapist about the example of running over the squirrel that I mentioned in the previous chapter, we would have investigated how my assumption of a right that I did not really have (the right not to be criticised when driving) had led me to an incorrect belief that this right had been violated (you cannot violate a right that does not exist), which had the consequence of an angry response. At any point of the conversation, both the therapist and I would have been able to explain what we were talking for.

In psychoanalytic therapy, the objective is not always as clear. The psychoanalyst Wilfred Bion described the psychoanalytic relationship as 'container-contained'. What he meant by this is that sometimes we simply have the job of absorbing another person's distress and emotion. Sometimes, particularly if the client is experiencing high levels of distress when recounting abuse, trauma or loss, neither the therapist nor the client knows what narrative or emotional turn the conversation will take. In these conversations, while the purpose of the conversation is unclear, there are high levels of agreement. Both parties have agreed to pay attention to the emotional state of the client, and it is this agreement which gives the conversation a chance.

The container-contained relationship applies outside the therapeutic space also. Parenting has significant elements of containing. I once observed a young mother with a baby that was suffering its first cold. The baby was confused and distressed; it was experiencing the unpleasant symptoms for the first time. But the mother remained calm and attentive to the baby – its distress was absorbed by the mother and not reflected back to it. Sometimes this act of containing is hard work; the mother may have been fatigued and worried herself, but she made the effort to put her own feelings to one side so as to not communicate them to her baby.

Psychologist John Gottman says that in fraught conversations between men and women, men are more likely to become 'flooded' – filled with a level of emotion that they cannot contain and that is uncomfortable for them. Men may try to solve this discomfort by withdrawing from the conversation, or by imposing a clear direction or purpose to it. When somebody tries to make a conversation practical, or to quickly find solutions, the person who is talking emotionally can experience this as a failure or a refusal to contain those emotions. Each party might have a different reason for having the conversation. These conversations are an illustration that while a few specific kinds of conversations can work without a clear purpose, and even fewer kinds can work without an agreed purpose, with difficult conversations it is often best to achieve both clarity and agreement of purpose.

Once, after being tailgated by another motorist for longer than I thought necessary, I got out of my car and spoke to him. When I got back into my own car, Claudia asked me what I had done that for. Her unimpressed response to my account made me realise that I had not entered the conversation with any specific objective. I should not have been surprised that the conversation had achieved nothing. Even if I had managed to clarify the purpose to myself, it is unlikely that the other motorist would have agreed – he remained unsympathetic to my emotion and unconvinced by my threats.

I managed a similar subsequent situation more successfully. I was riding my bicycle on a country road and a car came up behind me. The driver felt that I wasn't getting out of his way fast enough. He revved his engine with a sudden roar. It startled me to the point where I almost ended up in a ditch. I caught up with him a few kilometres later and had calmed down enough to decide to try to resolve this through conversation. My objective was to complain that he had frightened me, but also to explain to him why he should change his future behaviour.

I explained to him that when he revved his engine, from my perspective as a cyclist it was quite frightening and could have caused me to lose control of my bicycle and injure myself. I said I was sure that in the future he didn't want anyone to be hurt as a result of his actions, and he agreed and accepted that he should not do it again. I fulfilled both conditions of Rule 1 by having a clear objective and securing his agreement that cyclist safety was a valid topic to discuss and worthy of being prioritised over motorist impatience.

In most of the above examples, the conversation succeeded or failed depending on whether the protagonists found themselves in accordance with or contravention of Rule 1. The purpose of Rule 1 is to allow the protagonists to take control of the conversation rather than being victims of circumstance.

Applying Rule 1 means stopping the conversation that you are having, and starting a conversation about the conversation. The phrasing of Rule 1: Agree what you are talking for, may sound slightly clumsy in contrast to the more obvious 'Agree why you are talking'. But there is a subtle and important difference in meaning between the two. When Claudia and I get lost on a long walk in the countryside and start to argue, the reasons *why* we are arguing include that we are hungry and grumpy. What we are talking *for* is just to agree on a route home. What we are talking *for* is a subset of *why* we are talking, and concentrating on this question allows us to bypass some of the complex and unnecessary forensics that would be required to answer the broader question. This makes the conversation more practical and focused. The point of having a conversation about a conversation is to agree on a purpose for the original conversation. Just asking, 'What are we talking for?' is one way to start this meta-conversation. Others are to ask, 'How would we know that this conversation had succeeded?' and 'If this conversation went well, what would happen or change at the end of it?'

Some friends of ours were considering getting a dog. As a way of informing the family debate, they had agreed to look after their neighbours' dog while the neighbours were on holiday. Because they were doing this as a fact-finding project, they had specifically agreed that the owners of the dog would not pay them a dog-sitting fee. As it turned out, over the course of the week, the mother did all of the work and the three children and husband did nothing. Then the neighbours came back and paid the three children generously for looking after the dog. This led to a considerable family disagreement. The mother's position was that the children should not receive money for doing nothing and that the money should either be returned (to honour the original agreement) or given to her. The children felt that once their fingers had closed around the money in their palms it became theirs, and they shouldn't have to surrender it.

This is a multi-layered problem and the family found themselves mainly expressing emotion (which is hard to do with a clear purpose) while failing to agree whose emotion was legitimate or whose to prioritise. Rule 1 would have instructed them to first achieve clarity of purpose and secondly to agree the purpose.

What seems like a normal family argument can be hard to resolve because there are multiple purposes and multiple levels of disagreement. This could have just been a discussion about how to split the money. It could also have been a discussion about values – is it fair to work for nothing? Is it fair to hand over money that has been given to you? Or it could have been a discussion about parenting – did they want to guide their children to be compromising or to be opportunistic? And it could have been a discussion about family authority – who decides this dispute and how? Finally, it could have been a conversation about the conversation – what would be the signs that the conversation had succeeded?

This is complex and hard work. A legitimate question is whether the disagreement is worth it. John Gottman says that many successfully married couples maintain the harmony of their relationships by avoiding exactly these kinds of disagreements; when a couple judges that they don't have the time, energy or skills to resolve an argument, they just sweep the whole thing under the carpet and carry on with other things. Not everything in life has to be resolved and there is the option to focus on areas where you do agree rather than those you do not.

But if you do choose or need to engage, it is a fallacy to believe that you can take a shortcut past Rule 1. If you are unwilling to invest skill and effort in agreeing the purpose of the discussion, the alternative is to not have the disagreement at all, not to bypass the rule. If you are talking at cross purposes, you are unlikely to succeed because you are not bringing your arguments to bear against each other.

Because it is easier to achieve a general agreement than a specific agreement, a useful application of Rule 1 is to direct the focus of the conversation towards the general. Agreeing that food is nice is easier than agreeing that sweet desserts are nice, which is easier than agreeing that ice cream is nice, which is easier than agreeing that rum and raisin ice cream is nice. Our inclination is to get stuck on the specific, but talking more generally allows us to establish rules or principles which can then be applied to the specific situation. If you can't agree on whether today is a nice day (specific), debate what constitutes a nice day (general) and apply those criteria to today. Even if you don't manage to make a general agreement, you will have a more useful (and general) insight into your disagreement than if you had stayed with the specific argument.

If the family could not reach agreement on the specifics of the dog-sitting money, they should have postponed or abandoned that specific objective and sought more general agreement on what is a fair way to distribute work and money, or a general agreement on how to adjudicate on disagreements within the family.

Talking about what to talk about is a meta-conversation that achieves compliance with Rule 1: you are agreeing what you are talking for.

'HAS THIS CONVERSATION BEEN SUCCESSFUL?'

While some disagreements are intractable, they may have components that can be resolved. And some disagreements that appear intractable may have solutions which appear once their components and layers have been clarified and agreed.

The debate about abortion is settled in many countries, either for its legality or against. But in some countries, like the US or Northern Ireland, it remains an intractable problem. It resembles many difficult public debates which do not have an agreed structure. Like most difficult conversations, it works better when there is clarity and agreement over what you are talking for.

One part of the debate is about living with disagreement, as it is a likely outcome with difficult conversations. What do we do when we lose an argument, hold a minority opinion, get overruled in court or outvoted? It is worth agreeing on the right way to respond to these outcomes before engaging in the processes that deliver them. In some debates, the difficulty comes from securing agreement from people who consider themselves to be above or beneath the law. If this is the case, the debate needs to shift to whether even the powerful or the dispossessed should respect the law, and whether this principle applies in this specific circumstance to this specific person. This is a debate about the process of justice.

Another part of the debate is a moral one. Are some things just wrong, and so should never be done under any circumstances? Or do we sometimes need to do things that harm one party for 'the greater good'?

And another part of the debate is about epistemology – how do we know things? How do we legitimately gain knowledge and develop opinions about these topics? Which of faith, consensus or rigor is most appropriate to this question?

Complex social and political conversations about topics like vaccinations and abortion rights have components that include those mentioned above, process justice, morality, and epistemology. While in themselves complex conversations, it is still simpler to discuss them one at a time. The purpose of Rule 1 is to secure agreement on what exact part of the issue you are talking about.

Our reasons for individual action are complex and the combined reasons why two or more participants should engage in a conversation are even more so. Rule 1 – agree what you are talking for – means knowing what the objective of the conversation is, as well as exactly what you are talking about.

GET SMARTER

When you agree what you are talking for, you are setting a goal for the conversation. Goals work better when they are clear and precise. A classic goal-setting system is the SMART method. This is the idea that goals should be specific, measurable, agreed, relevant and timed. In seeking to make the purpose of conversations clear and agreed, it can help to make them SMART also.

Specific

If, for example, you had the goal of becoming healthier, it could be effective to turn this into a SMART goal by saying that you wanted to gain aerobic fitness by having a fast daily walk and gain muscle strength by gardening. These are two specific health goals.

The family dog-sitting argument could have been made more specific by deciding which of the sub-debates to hold, and in which order to hold them. Likewise, a faith-based debate also needs to be made specific – is it a full pro-choice versus pro-life debate? The Big Bang versus Creationism? Or, is it a more general debate about how to disagree, or how to develop beliefs?

Measurable

Both protagonists should be able to answer and agree on the question, 'How would we know this conversation had succeeded?' When conflict expert Peter Coleman gets people to discuss complex issues, he sets them the objective of mutually producing a paragraph which summarises the topic of discussion and which both parties are prepared to sign. In this situation, success would be measured by when both parties sign the paragraph. Other measurable outcomes could be the acceptance by one or both parties that together you have achieved one or more of the following: elimination of significant disagreement; learning something new; shifting an opinion; feeling listened to; or ending the conversation with a smile, handshake or hug.

Agreed

Just as it is ineffective for a GP to set a patient health goals without the patient agreeing to those health goals, it is ineffective to set an objective for a conversation without both parties agreeing to the objective. The challenge of many difficult conversations is that when emotions begin to run strong, time seems as if it is in short supply. People don't feel like they have time to agree on what they are talking for, so it seems as if they need to each pursue their individual objectives immediately. Also, difficult conversations create a sense of opposition. It seems strange to begin a disagreement by agreeing, but it is often the best time to do it. Arguments tend to finish how they begin.[4] If they start angry, they end angry. If we can start a disagreement by agreeing, there may be more chance of finishing with agreement also. Talking about general principles rather than specific situations, and tackling a component part rather than all of the issue, can help finding an agreement to start with.

Relevant

Sometimes protagonists in a conversation have goals that are not relevant to the ultimate objective. For example, venting emotion probably isn't relevant but feeling listened to often is. 'Agreeing to disagree' is sometimes relevant for unimportant debates; agreeing *how* to disagree is often relevant for more consequential discussions. Some topics may be relevant to one level of the debate, but irrelevant to others. The authority of the courts is a relevant subject of the process justice component of the abortion debate,

---

[4] John Gottman, *The Seven Principles for Making Marriage Work*.

but it is not relevant to the morality component. Whether cold raisins are palatable is irrelevant to the general debate about ice cream, but relevant to the specific debate about rum and raisin ice cream. *Ad hominem* attacks which question the character of the debater, may be relevant to some debates, like whether to accept a lift home with somebody after a party, but irrelevant to others, like whether or not climate change is real.

Timed

Placing unrealistic time goals upon a conversation may lead the protagonists to talk generally rather than specifically, and to take shortcuts rather than to use rigor. Normally, goal setters are encouraged to make short, demanding timed goals, but given our tendency to overestimate our conversational ability and under-estimate the complexity of many difficult conversations, the T of SMART conversational goals should be a reminder to take time rather than to rush it.

When my friend Dave asked my 20-year-old self, 'What did you do that for?' I did not have an answer. One thing I do know about that plunge into the shark tank is that I will not do it again. I was making a statement – which at the time seemed to be about valu-ing curiosity and boldness rather than just ill-judged risk – but I did it, and I got away with it. I wish I could say as much for my talking. Sometimes I hear myself saying things that are insensitive, inappropriate or just incorrect, and at other times I surely make these errors without realising. Sometimes I get into an argument that I have had before and say the same things, and other times I avoid a conversation because I am not quite sure what to talk about. The question, 'What did I say that for?' is retrospective and often accompanied by a measure of regret. But applying this analysis to the future allows us to ask questions like, 'What precisely should I say?' and 'What should I say it for?'

When I read over transcripts of conversations that I have participated in, one of the things that often strikes me is the lack of rigor in the conversation, even though all of the people having the conversation think that they are talking sensibly. What we often think at the time is a logical discussion is sometimes just an argument about values, and sometimes arguments about values are just declarations of allegiance. There is nothing wrong with declaring allegiances, or arguing about values, or having a logical discussion, but these conversations work best when we know what they are – and so does the person we are having them with. If we can begin conversations by clarifying and agreeing why we are having them, it shifts our focus from a past we may regret to a future we can feel hopeful about.

Key principles:

Know what you are having a conversation for

Purpose should be clear *and* agreed

Conversations can be general principles or specific situations. When a specific conversation is not working, it can be helpful to make it more general

Conversations have components. When it is hard to reach an over-arching agreement, it can be helpful to look for agreement on components

Start with points of agreement and progress to the more contentious

Remember SMART – specific, measurable, agreed, relevant, timed

The following conversation is a transcript of a family discussion mentioned previously in this chapter. The family are talking about what to do with the money that the neighbours gave them for looking after their dog. At the end of each chapter, I have selected a personal, professional or political conversation and annotated the transcript to show where the rule covered in that chapter has or could usefully have been applied.

Mother: I am feeling quite angry about this. It is not right that I did the work and you have been paid the money.

Child 1: But if someone has given money to me, now it is my money. Why should I give my money to you?

Child 2: And anyway, you said to the neighbours that you didn't want them to pay us for looking after their dog. So even if you did all the work, you didn't want to be paid for it. So you should be happy.

Child 1: Why is it your problem if the neighbours gave us money? What has it got to do with you?

Father: (laughing) The children are making a good point.

Mother: But it isn't fair. You should either give the money to me, or you can give it back to the neighbours.

Child 1: You can't take our own money away from us.

Father: [applies Rule 1] *What are we actually debating here?*

Child 1: Whether we should get a dog.

Mother: What's fair.

Child 2: Who controls my money.

Mother: *That sounds like three different conversations. Which one should we have first?*

RULE 2: ACCEPT THAT AGREEMENT TAKES SKILL AND EFFORT

WISHFUL THINKING

In one rally in the tennis match between Roger Federer and Kei Nishikori in Wimbledon 2019, Federer ballooned a shot slightly. As the ball drifted towards the baseline it was hard to tell whether it was going to drop in or out. Just before it landed, Federer leapt into the air to look down on the ball. The next point, Nishikori hit a ball fractionally too low and, just before it became certain that the ball would hit the net, Nishikori ducked to look at the ball from underneath. These types of actions are so familiar to sports fans that they draw no comment, possibly because they are busy performing the same action. This is not a random twitch – we twitch right when we want the ball to go left, left for right, up for down, and down for up. Sometimes we also talk to the ball. At any moment of a sports match there are probably thousands of people in the stadium and at home, twitching and talking in synchrony. This impulse is so universal that in some circumstances it is considered rude not to do it.

The reason we are doing this is that, at some level, we misunderstand the laws of cause and effect. We think that in some way our movements or words will affect the flight of the ball. Obviously, at another level, none of us believes this. I even do it when I am watching a replay of a match that has already happened. I do know that I am not capable of time travel or telekinesis. But I still twitch.

I maintain this naive partial belief that I am able to influence the world through intent, desire or will alone, rather than through action because a lot of the time my will is the determining factor in whether things happen. If I want water, I turn the tap and I get water. If I want to open the door, I turn the handle and the door opens. I am more aware of the desire than I am of the mechanics through which that desire is fulfilled. In my daily life, I normally get what I want, so I am less frequently aware of willing something that does not happen because of a lack of ability on my part.

This belief in the power of will is widespread. It takes two forms: desire and confidence, both of which all of us believe in and use at some level. I was watching a match in the 2003 Rugby World Cup when the New Zealander Keven Mealamu scored to establish a significant lead against South Africa. South African commentator Kobus Wiese roared into his microphone, 'And now it's down to who wants it the most!' Kobus Wiese was a World Cup winner himself in 1995, so had knowledge of winning matches, and at that moment was crediting the most important factor in the outcome of this match as being desire.

In the 2014 Football World Cup, USA fans popularised a chant which went, 'I . . . I . . . I believe . . . I believe . . . I believe that we will win!' It's a compelling chant, partly because we do believe, at some level, that believing makes things more likely to happen.

And like desire, belief does often *correlate* with outcome in our everyday lives, even if it doesn't cause it. I believe that the tap will produce water, and it does. I believe that the door will open, and it does.

While we may claim to know that the link between desire, belief and causality is not simple or direct, a lot of the time we act as if it is. When we offer people our best wishes, or tell them that we are thinking of them, we are behaving as if we believe that these desires and beliefs will make a difference to outcomes.

I do remember one stark confrontation between this belief and reality. I was seven years old, and my cousin Paul, who was the same age, had come to stay with me. We had the idea that it would be fun to have an underground network of tunnels running beneath the house and garden and extending through the neighbourhood. We imagined how brilliant it would be to be able to visit friends by popping up from a tunnel into their gardens. We spent the whole morning excitedly planning, in complete agreement the whole time, and I can still feel the vivid disappointment of the moment when the planning was over and it was time to begin construction that we realised we didn't have a clue of how to do it. I can't remember whether we actually had spades in our hands when the realisation struck, but the bewilderment on Paul's face must have been mirrored by my own as we discovered, temporarily, that desire and belief were not enough to make a plan happen.

A THEORY OF MOTIVATION

I became interested in motivation in 1991 when I was a third-year undergraduate biology student. I wanted to move to Cape Town and study great white sharks, but I didn't do enough work to get the marks required to be selected for the programme, so I did psychology instead.

A common predator in Durban is the house gecko, a lizard with adhesive pads on its toes that enable it to run up walls and along ceilings. Our house would have one or two in every room, and in the evenings they would often station themselves in a corner of the ceiling and wait for insects to be drawn in by the electric light. I could sit in the lounge and watch the hunt play out. I became interested in what caused the geckos to chase some insects and not others. It seemed obvious that geckos were generally more likely to chase insects that were large, close and slow moving than those that were small, distant and fast. I represented this as a formula:

Motivation = Reward/Task x Confidence or $M = R/T x C$

Geckos will be more motivated if the reward is larger and less motivated if the task is larger. So their decision of whether or not to chase a moth depends on the relationship between the size of the moth and the distance that the gecko would have to run to catch it; the gecko is as likely to run for a distant fat moth as it is for a close small one. But confidence overrules both of these factors. No matter how large or close the insect, a gecko will not chase it if it is so fast or so well armoured that the gecko is not confident of catching and killing it.

I found it useful to think about motivation in this way because it allowed me to confront my naive and intuitive beliefs about motivation: that it was better to be motivated than not, and that increased motivation increased my chances of success. For geckos, what matters is accuracy, not abundance of motivation. A gecko that is highly motivated to chase small, distant or fast-moving moths will expend more energy hunting than it gains from its prey and will die of starvation. On the other hand, a gecko that is not sufficiently motivated to chase fat, close and slow-moving moths will also die of starvation.

The great white sharks in Cape Town that I wanted to study hunt seals for an average of six seconds or less. Ideally, for the shark it will spot a seal swimming on the surface when it is cruising on the ocean floor. It will then launch a vertical strike on the seal, hitting it with one massive bite and an impact which often launches both seal and shark into the air. After this, ideally, the seal will quickly bleed to death and the shark has a meal which can sustain it for several days. If the shark misses with the initial strike, the seal will use its agility rather than speed to actually turn towards the shark, try to stay in formation just behind the shark's eye and out of reach of its teeth for another few maximum-effort seconds of twisting and turning until the shark makes the $M = R/TxC$ calculation that this seal is not worth the effort and gives up.

Once the shark has lost motivation, there is sometimes another shark waiting to take over the chase. The size of the reward has not changed, but because the seal is now fatigued and the second shark is fresh, the second shark's task may be reduced, and its confidence increased and so it is accurately motivated to continue. The seal will not give up even if it is chased by multiple persistent sharks, because even in the face of an enormous task and diminished confidence, the reward for the seal (survival) justifies effort in a way that the reward for the shark (a meal) does not.

The idea of a shark that is only motivated to do six seconds of work for a meal is at odds with our idea that motivation is morally and practically preferable. Early modern African humans were persistence hunters, who tracked and chased antelope across the savannah for hours, with very high success rates. But persistent human predators, and the ambushing shark and gecko, would only live to hunt another day if they obeyed the laws of M=R/TxC.

When we talk, we need to choose between styles of communication. In the confrontation with the man in my back garden that I mentioned previously, I lost the motivation to pursue a civil conversation and instead became motivated to use violence. My M=R/TxC calculation was as follows:

The reward was to secure my property and the safety of my family.
The task was to physically subdue a smaller, weaker man without harm to myself.
And I was confident that I could succeed.

So the formula explains why I was strongly motivated to use physical confrontation. On the other hand, my motivational equation to converse would have been the reward of securing safety and respecting the needs and dignity of the homeless man. The task of talking through our differences seemed large. I had low confidence that it would succeed. This explains my low motivation to be civil with him.

THE REWARD OF TALKING

Was I correct in this judgement? In retrospect, I undervalued how rewarding it would have been to have treated a vulnerable person with respect. While, 20 years later, I have skills which might have reduced the size of the conversation task and increased my confidence in success, even at that time, holding task and confidence constant, had I been aware of the full reward, I may have been motivated to work harder at a civil interaction.

Another time I abandoned civility was in a conversation with a neighbour. We had been discussing parking spaces on our street for a few minutes on the phone when I suddenly felt I was not getting my point across and so bellowed, 'Listen to me!' I was more motivated to shout than to talk because I was suddenly seized by a conviction that the task of a brief shouting match was smaller than the task of a prolonged discussion. This made me more motivated to shout than to talk. I was wrong in this calculation also; my explosion caused all sorts of relationship damage which required a lot of effort to repair.

But perhaps an even more fundamental error was my misplaced confidence in the effectiveness of shouting. I had made the mistake of acting upon my at-some-level belief that I could affect the direction of a conversation through desire and conviction alone, rather than with skill or persistence. I failed because of something that the hunting gecko and shark knew but I did not – what matters is accuracy rather than abundance of motivation.

Rule 2 is 'accept that agreement takes skill and effort'. Most of our opinions are formed intuitively, rapidly . . . and correctly. This is System 1 decision-making: fast, efficient and accurate – most of the time. But when your System 1 opinion is different from my System 1 opinion, we have no recourse other than to go to System 2 to resolve it.

FAST OR SLOW?

System 2 is slow, methodical, conscious calculation. In System 2, opinions are formed by deliberately applying reason to facts. This means that the disagreeing parties can make the process of their opinion formation explicit, and so have the opportunity to learn from each other and criticise each other as part of the agreement process.

The first step is to establish consensus on what facts are correct, relevant or missing. Because facts are simpler pieces of information than opinions, they are generally easier to agree on. If it is not possible to establish consensus at this step, according to Rule 1, it would be necessary to retreat, and have a preceding conversation about how to collect and measure facts, and how to judge what sources of facts to trust.

The second step is to agree on what logic to apply to the facts. How far may we extrapolate? What confidence level do we require before we have an actionable opinion? What alternative explanations or opinions should we consider?

The third step is to test the opinion. What further piece of information or what alternate explanation would make me change my mind, or not? Under what circumstances would this opinion not be valid?

Applying System 2 to opinion formation is the essence of the scientific method. In his book, *Sapiens*, Yuval Noah Harari calls the discovery of the scientific method 'the discovery of ignorance'. System 1 does not recognise ignorance. When in my day job I speak to elite athletes about their decision-making processes, they very rarely report uncertainty. They always have a solution or decision to hand. It may or may not be the best one, but they always have a sense of what to do. Because time pressure is intrinsic to many sports, inaction is usually punished, so even suboptimal action is favoured. Elite athletes are usually rewarded for confidence and decisiveness. The same is not always true in everyday life, where there are often opportunities for reflection. So when we favour System 1 to form an opinion, we may not be using the best strategy.

When we use System 1 to form opinions, these opinions do not come accompanied with a confidence rating, and a pedigree of their formation. For this reason, it is hard to identify which of our opinions may be weak, or the sources of those weaknesses. When we find our System 1 opinion in conflict with another System 1 opinion, because we can be blind to the weaknesses in either opinion, the easiest route or smallest task can appear to be to pursue a simple solution with vehemence, rather than a complex solution with patience and persistence. But this is a fallacy.

System 2 allows us to discover our ignorance and, while being slower and more difficult than System 1 opinion formation, creates more opportunities to discover where our opinions may diverge from those of others and thus create opportunities for agreement. Rule 2 is 'accept that agreement takes skill and effort' – and that sometimes this skill and effort is worth it. The reward of progress, or of a successful resolution, justifies the task of deliberation.

PUBLIC CONVERSATION

One of the public debates in Britain is about rough sleeping. This debate is split into components. One debate is whether rough sleeping is sufficiently prioritised. Another is what the best solution is. A third closely connected debate is who is responsible for the plight of a rough sleeper.

Homelessness charity Crisis says that not enough is being done to tackle the problem of rough sleeping. The Government says that it is committed to eliminating rough sleeping by 2027 and that it allocated a budget of £100 million to tackle this problem over 2018 and 2019. It is estimated that in 2019 there were around 5,000 people sleeping rough in Britain on any given night and in 2018 over 600 people died while sleeping rough.

One complexity is that while it is easy to agree that rough sleeping is a significant problem, this is not the same as agreeing that rough sleeping is inadequately prioritised relative to other public services. Finding agreement on prioritisation would involve a painstaking investigation into what commitments are currently being made to the full spectrum of public health services, what individual and social impact these investments have, and whether a better distribution could be achieved.

The second debate is the best way to tackle homelessness. There are poles of opinion. On the one side is an approach called Housing First, which believes that homeless people and rough sleepers should be given their own accommodation without strings attached. This means that they do not have to engage in employment guidance, addiction treatment or other self-improvement programmes before receiving accommodation. The other side takes an approach that uses accommodation as an incentive that is made available when people participate in self-improvement programmes. This approach is a safeguard against the 'benefits scrounger', the proliferation of whom is considered by some people to be a risk to the resources of public services.

Scandinavian countries, Scotland and Salt Lake City are examples of countries and a city which use Housing First policies. These places have rough sleeping rates that are falling. By contrast, England and Wales, which both have conditional accommodation approaches, face rising rates of rough sleeping. Because there are many different examples of societies' approaches to rough sleeping and homelessness, and the problems and outcomes of these approaches are documented, the question of what is the best approach is a complex and difficult, but potentially (with skill and effort) answerable question.

The third, and related debate is, who is responsible for rough sleeping? According to the Vagrancy Act, rough sleeping and begging is a crime. Crimes are considered to be the responsibility of the criminal and so, legally, rough sleepers are considered to be responsible for their own predicament. But some rough sleepers have a history of being physically, mentally or sexually abused, come from financially disadvantaged backgrounds, or have suffered poor health and other misfortune. Can they really be held responsible for their circumstances?

In some situations, such as apartheid in South Africa, or colonisation in many parts of the world, privileged people benefit generally and historically from the disadvantage of others and thus can be considered partially responsible for the ill fortune of poor people, despite their possible claims to individual innocence. But do British citizens who did not participate in or benefit from the personal trauma and history of an individual rough sleeper have a responsibility towards that person? Should rough sleeping initiatives be driven by a sense of compassion or a sense of responsibility?

Appreciating the complexity and difficulty of a debate is an important part of accepting the skill and effort required to achieve agreement. It can also help us to be satisfied by, and prepared to work for, partial agreement, rather than being perfectionists who are content with nothing less than total consensus.

INTRACTABLE DISPUTES

Peter Coleman, in his book *The Five Percent*, outlines a method for dealing with complex, intractable conflicts. He describes the problem as having three components: complexity, psychology and spoilers.

The complexity problem is that we think in lines rather than loops, fixed instead of fluid, and short instead of long term. To return to the argument that I had with my neighbour about parking, in my mind there was a direct line between my neighbour's difficult personality and his difficult parking behaviour. I had not seen that, as our competition for parking spots intensified, my perception of his behaviour as difficult or selfish caused me to behave in a way that he perceived as difficult or selfish. This motivated him to respond more extremely, which motivated me to respond more extremely. We were stuck in a loop.

The fixed instead of fluid problem was that I was erroneously attributing this situation to his personality characteristics. My neighbour and I were behaving in ways that were difficult. But what is important is that this behaviour was the consequence of fluid circumstances and influences rather than stable personality traits. We were stressed about our cars being stolen, rather than being nasty people. As for the short instead of long term, the argument erupted about a single incident and my objective was to secure a parking spot for *that* evening. I was so focused on securing an immediate resolution that I was prepared to damage a long-term relationship in order to do so.

The psychology problem is that we marginalise emotion, personalise conflict and simplify. My neighbour and I were both feeling anxious about walking some distance from our parked cars to our front gates and about leaving our cars unattended on the street. But our argument did not reflect this anxiety. We ignored each other's emotions and focused on accusations and counter accusations of trivial rule violations. It was only when we eventually were able to directly acknowledge both of our anger *and* our anxiety that we realised that emotions were central rather than marginal to this conflict.

We had also personalised the situation. We were both making the fundamental attribution error of believing that the situation was caused by the other's ill will. Once we had the opportunity to process the emotion, we could see that this was not a situation that either of us had intended to create or maintain. We had both arrived at this conclusion in part because conflict debilitates reason.

Like an athlete choking under pressure, our ability to think clearly and in complex ways is limited by conflict and emotion. Had we had the time and space, either of us could have worked out how broader issues were influencing our own behaviour. Our ability to comprehend the complexity of the problem was replaced by the fundamental attribution error and our range of options became limited to one: attack.

The spoilers problem is that some people see either the solution or the status quo as unfair or exclusive. Our prevailing social mode is promotion; we seek to help and support others in the expectation that we will benefit from similar sentiments. Had

I been in a promotion state, I would have been prepared to park slightly further away so that I could leave a close space open for my neighbour. But under pressure we move to protection mode. This is where, rather than looking out for others, or maintaining a benevolent social atmosphere, I prioritise my interests. In protection mode I would take the closest parking space for myself or get home slightly early to ensure I had first choice. And if things get worse, we move into punish mode, where we are prepared to incur costs to ourselves to incur greater costs on others for perceived transgressions.

The principle of punishment is an important one for society. Order is maintained partly by its threat. However, punishment applied incorrectly can easily create cycles of revenge in which each party feels that they are legitimately punishing the harmful behaviour of the other.

Coleman proposes a method for dealing with intractable conflicts: complicate to simplify, build up and tear down, and change to stabilise.

The first step to resolving intractable conflicts is complicate to simplify. When complicating, you have to try to see the system rather than component parts. The first question to ask is what dynamic you are trying to understand. For example, can we understand the systems that caused the escalation in rough sleeping? These might include individual stories, education, employment levels, mental health services, the economy, the council housing system, immigration, trends in drug use and availability, the weather and the effectiveness of homelessness and rough sleeping initiatives. Only when you have understood as many of the inputs to the system as possible is it time to simplify.

Simplifying is understanding the key dynamics. The rough sleeping problem is a broader social problem, but it is also a unique, complex problem for each individual rough sleeper. What escalation or pattern or troubles led each person onto the street? What stable system is keeping this individual on the street? For each individual person, which issues out of many, including poverty, mistrust, drug use, abuse or ill health, most urgently need to be reduced or solved to get a roof over their head?

After complicate to simplify, there is build up and tear down. Build up means develop hidden possibilities. A homelessness initiative in Scotland allows caseworkers to draw cash and give it to rough sleepers for simple things like a night in a hotel or a haircut. This means that the caseworkers can build up relationships with people who might otherwise be suspicious of authority. Giving someone a stable place to live would mean that they can build up new friendships and re-establish old friendships, work and family ties. Tear down means breaking cycles. Social isolation, loneliness and poor mental health form a cycle that needs to be torn down for rough sleepers.

The third step is change to stabilise. Sometimes in bad situations, people are more ripe for change than we realise. A rough sleeper who is staying alive by begging on the street may have a long and stable history of financial trouble, mental health problems, or abusive relationships, but they may be ready for a change that will allow a stable and different life. Rough sleeping may have been rising steadily for a decade, but a combination of growing public awareness of, and compassion for mental health struggles, awareness of the scale of the problem and evidence that some approaches work better than others at getting and keeping people into secure accommodation may drive a change to a more stable and successful approach to this national conversation.

THE TALKING EQUATION

Because as humans we have minds which are machines for jumping to conclusions, and because under pressure we have a drive for simplicity, almost any difficult conversation or argument can be improved by inserting the phrase, 'It's complicated'. Part of fulfilling Rule 2 is just recognising the complexity and size of the task of reaching agreement. Then, we need to motivate ourselves to do the work required.

$M=R/T \times C$ (Motivation = Reward/Task x Confidence) is a useful way of thinking about motivation, because it allows a strategic approach to its development and application.

There are many rewards for applying skill and effort to reach agreement. In addition to the reward of partial or complete resolution of a difficult or protracted disagreement, there are the 'IAMP' rewards – rewards of identity, autonomy, mastery and purpose. These are higher level rewards, where we are motivated to behave in a way that is consistent with our identities, act with autonomy, achieve mastery, or do something with purpose, because doing so is intrinsically rewarding.

In that all of us identify in some part as being skilled, driven and agreeable, just following Rule 2 allows us to confirm this part of our identities. It is a powerful reward because it delivers from the beginning of the process – just following Rule 2 is rewarding, it doesn't require complete successful resolution of the problem to deliver.

The autonomy reward can also motivate us to follow Rule 2. One of the signs that you are in a protracted disagreement is the sense of frustration and helplessness that you feel when you are in it. While it is tempting to rush back into the battle, taking a step back and accepting that you need previously unreached levels of skill and effort to resolve the issue can reward you with a sense of autonomy over the process.

The mastery reward is that we like to get better at something. Becoming aware of an increasing skill set, or an increasing willingness to work on something, rewards us because we gain a sense of mastery. And it is rewarding to know the purpose of our efforts. When we apply skill and effort to securing agreement, it is rewarding to know what we are doing it for.

In general, the secret to motivation is to diminish the size of the task. Geckos hunt moths that are close; sharks prefer to eat seals that are bleeding to death. Rule 2 would seem to fly in the face of this – we are expected to be motivated to take on a task that is bigger and more difficult than we had initially anticipated. However, tasks appear smaller and more manageable when they are well defined, and when we can break them into sub-tasks. Complete resolution of a difficult conversation is a big task, but applying just one of the 10 Rules is a valid sub-task, and is worth being motivated for. Also, don't underestimate the size of the alternative; protracted disputes don't require strategic effort or new learning, but they can take up massive amounts of time and energy, and the alternative of applying lots of new skills and effort to making progress, while a significant task, may be relatively inexpensive.

The joker in the pack is confidence. Even if the reward/task balance stacks up, if we are not confident of success, we are not motivated. One way to improve confidence is to consciously define success. What is the smallest meaningful difference that is worth working for? Perfection is great (and shouldn't be ruled out), but what would satisfy you? Another way of improving confidence is to get the right support. Who can help you? Who can teach

RULE 2 | 67

you skills? Who can take other responsibilities away from you so that you have time to work on this task? A third way to improve confidence is to remind yourself of even slightly similar situations where you have succeeded before. Like rewards and task, confidence needs to be strategically constructed to build motivation.

$M=R/TxC$ is strategic motivation. It is helpful in allowing us to prepare to apply more skill and effort to securing an agreement than we have previously. It has another application also. Some disagreements are disagreements of opinion. But some disagreements are disagreements of motivation. I am motivated to do this, and you are motivated to do that. Systematically understanding my R/TxC and your R/TxC can help us understand our different desires and ambitions and explore opportunities for change or synchrony. Which of our identity, autonomy, mastery and purpose rewards are similar or different? How do we perceive tasks so that they seem large or small? What goals do we have and what skills do we possess that make us feel confident or not of certain outcomes?

Often, we don't give up because things are hard, we give up because things are harder than we thought they were going to be. If we start out too optimistic or naive about the size or difficulty of a task, we can be dismayed or disappointed when we enter into it and discover its full scale. Anticipating that a conversation will be difficult can allow us to properly prepare for the task and muster the skills and motivation that we need to succeed.

Rather than the desire and belief that the sports fan thinks affects the flight of his hero's ball, conversations are affected by willingness to put in the work and the ability to do the work. Rule 2, accepting that agreement takes skill and effort, is about mustering the motivation and skill that a conversation actually requires.

Key principles:

    Acknowledge complexity
    Acknowledge emotion
    Commit to talking slowly
    Use M=R/TxC

Some years ago I worked with the sales team in a motor dealership. The vehicle manufacturer had just announced to the dealers that if the dealership got low customer satisfaction ratings, there would be financial consequences for them. The head of the dealership thought he had found a simple solution to this problem by deciding that if any salesperson got less than a 100 per cent customer satisfaction rating when selling a car, they would receive 0 per cent commission. But when he announced this in an early morning sales meeting, it was clear from the ensuing silence that he had underestimated the difficulty of the upcoming conversation.

At this point he had a choice. He could try to force the simple solution, or he could accept that a more difficult conversation was worth having. He chose the second option.

He acknowledged the complexity of the situation with comments like, 'We have to find a way to make sure that we get consistently high customer satisfaction ratings. I know if you get a difficult customer, sometimes the rating they give you is not under your control. What adds to the complexity is that the scores that you get affect my bottom line.'

He acknowledged emotions by saying, 'We come to work in the morning to earn money. It's a shock when something gets in the way of that. I felt quite angry about it at first. I would be surprised if you didn't feel strongly about it also.'

He then made a commitment to work it out. 'Well, we have to find a solution, hopefully one that we all feel is fair, even if not everybody is totally happy with it. That's not the easiest thing to find, but let's try.'

The silence in the room was broken and a constructive conversation ensued.

RULE 3: REMEMBER MOST PEOPLE ARE GOOD, COMPETENT AND WORTHY OF RESPECT

I left school in 1989. It was an all-boys all-boarding school in a remote location in South Africa, so we weren't bound by geographic ties and, once we matriculated, many of us immediately lost contact with everyone other than close friends.

The idea of locking up 500 teenage boys together in a remote rural setting was based on the British public-school model, which was developed partly with the purpose of creating an officer class for the British Army. We came to value hierarchy, self-sufficiency, and physical stoicism without appreciating the design of the system or how it was influencing us. We had a 30-year reunion recently, which gave us the amazing experience of meeting people we had once known almost as intimately as family but then hadn't seen for half a lifetime.

When I left the school, I had strong negative feelings towards three people. One was a prefect, who once cornered me in a room and threatened me with physical violence for a perceived act of disrespect. He was two years older than me, outweighed me by about 30 kilograms, and had me isolated in a room at night with the nearest adult about a kilometre away He menaced me for a year. The second was a teacher – a housemaster who I felt was naive about the prefect and had failed to contain his behaviour. The third was a boy I had nothing to do with except the day he got dropped from the first rugby team and stole some chips from my plate as he walked past my table in the dining hall. When I left, I promised myself I wouldn't return for at least 10 years. I couldn't wait to get away.

Now I consider it, I can think of boys who would have had strong negative feelings towards me. One was Tony, who I had nicknamed The Amoeba. Another was Peter. Peter was a small boy, but he had high status because he used to hang out with the rugby players. One day I found him alone and took the opportunity to be verbally nasty to him. And another was a boy who was shot in the testicles with a hard, unripe plum fired from a wrist-mounted slingshot out of the window of my bedroom. It wasn't me who did it, but he had fair reason to think it was. There would have been others also – boys who struggled with identity, loneliness or anxiety, which would have made life in that environment very difficult, and who I and others treated with passive and occasionally active cruelty.

When I reconnected with some old friends at the 30-year reunion, I wasn't expecting my experiences of strong negative feelings towards people to be so widely shared. One friend joked that, collectively, we had spent a lot of hours in therapy talking about traumas that we had visited upon each other. What I also didn't expect was to find that these feelings, stored for 30 years, would be so easily released. Mostly, all it took was for my memory of a fresh-faced boy to be replaced by the familiar but lined features of a middle-aged man for the feeling to dissipate.

Another old classmate had the grace to apologise. He wrote on a group chat:

'Hi [Name]

It's been a long time and I was waiting for you to join the group as there has been something that has been eating me up for a long time since we left school. What I want to say, and I appreciate that everyone is witness to my shame, is that I'm sorry for all the shit I gave you and a couple of others that are on the group and still to join. I had a huge chip on my shoulder, and it should never have been an excuse to treat you and others the way I did. I hope you find it in your heart to forgive me. I wish I was able to attend this reunion to say this to you in person.

Sorry Brother.

The person to whom the apology was directed replied with this message:

Hey.

I appreciate the sentiments and admit I thought you'd flipped your bean but like [Friend's Name] said to me this week, I made his life miserable, so I might have to also ask forgiveness from some people. Let's put it down to part of growing up. Really hope you can make it to the gaudy.

Cheers buddy.

One friend and I got into a discussion about whether our old enemies really were bad people. Rule 3 is to remember most people are good, competent and worthy of respect. But could we apply this to the people that we had known? And did we also now qualify? Were we good people?

PROMOTION, PROTECTION AND PUNISHMENT

As discussed in the previous chapter, Peter Coleman says that societies operate in promotion, protection or punishment mode. These modes are powerful influences on human behaviour and can operate more strongly than innate characteristics. In promotion mode, people actively seek to support each other. At my school there were many acts of kindness and friendship. We would help each other academically and emotionally and play games together.

But we would slip into self-protection mode quite quickly. Because the school was so hierarchical, there was a strong incentive to challenge perceived slights. There were so many of us crammed into such a small space that territory became very important. When the only personal space you have is your own bed, you defend that vigorously. When I first joined the school, the boy in the bed next to me in the dormitory would throw his used clothes onto my bed. He was a younger but bigger boy, and had been at the school longer, so our relative status was uncertain. At first, I tossed his clothes back onto his own bed. When that didn't work, I asked him to stop. That also didn't work, so then whenever he left anything on my bed, I threw it out of the window.

When an act of protection is seen as illegitimate, it is easy for the other party to construe this as a violation and thus be deserving of legitimate punishment. If a punishment response is seen as disproportionate or illegitimate, it can provoke a retaliatory response.

I was reminded of this propensity for rapid escalation years later when I caught my five-year-old son marching purposefully upstairs early one morning with a metal curtain rod in his hand. I said to him, 'Where are you going?' and he said, 'To get my revenge!'

He had been in an argument with his nine-year-old brother the night before and they had been sent to bed before things had been resolved. In the five-year-old's mind, he had been wronged, he was the moral party, and waking up early and beating his brother with a metal pole was the right thing to do. I do believe that once he had got into the bedroom and gazed upon his sleeping brother's face, mercy would have stayed his hand, but I wasn't sure enough to let things be and find out.

More acts of harm are done in the world through mistaken attempts to do the right thing than deliberate acts of evil. Vengeance fits into this category. It has a legitimate role in social order and, although we may not like to believe this of ourselves, its threat moderates some of our wilder impulses. The problem is not that punishment exists – it is that we are so frequently mistaken when applying it. Escalating cycles of incorrectly applied vengeance in an attempt to maintain social order is responsible for significant and tragic social disruption.

I'M RIGHT AND YOU'RE WRONG

The fundamental attribution error is our tendency to see our own errors and failings as due to circumstance but those of others as due to character defects. Rule 3 is designed to remind us to counteract this.

The fundamental attribution error that I catch myself making most often is when someone steps on my toe. Recently, I was playing a squash match, and in the middle of a vigorous point, my opponent stepped on my foot. It was quite painful. I blamed him immediately. I even complained about it to my family when I got home, possibly more than once. I said that I wasn't accusing him of deliberately stepping on my foot, but I was accusing him of a lack of due caution. I played squash with my son a few days later and stepped on his foot. He found this very funny.

For somebody to be legally guilty, they have to be culpable. This means that they have to have foreseen the negative consequences of their action, desired them, then actioned them. So, when somebody commits burglary, they foresaw the theft, desired it, and actioned it, and are completely culpable. The squash player who stepped on my foot didn't want to hurt me but I held him partly culpable because I thought he should have foreseen the possible consequences of his vigorous movements, and he was the one who made the movements. Exactly the same circumstances applied when I stepped on my son's foot, but because of the fundamental attribution error, I held myself less culpable – I believed my own action had just been unlucky.

SUSPENDING GOODNESS

There are four generally accepted social circumstances under which love and utility can be suspended and harm caused to others in a non-sadistic and moral way. These exemptions are used to justify a range of harm, from mild inequality at the one extreme to war and violence at the other. They are competitiveness, tribalism, vengeance and inertia.

When the fundamental attribution error compromises our vengeance judgements, it is easy for us to slip into a cycle or spiral of punishment, and this dynamic operates all the way from trivial to profound conflicts. We stop believing that the person we find ourselves in opposition to is a good person. We are unaware that the belief we hold on how the conflict has arisen – that I am good but you are not – is a belief our opponent also holds. Explaining conflict between one good and one bad party is often much simpler than explaining how two good people can come to disagree. The purpose of Rule 3 is to remind us to seek the more complex explanation.

While vengeance drives us to the furthest reach of the promotion-protection–punishment continuum, competition is another circumstance in which we feel justified in moving away from promotion mode. Competition is a circumstance where I may legitimately deny you something that you need or are entitled to because there are limited resources and it is fair and moral for me to prioritise my own interests. I know that my friend would have been happier had I not beaten him on the squash court this morning, but I do not consider myself to have been immoral for having denied him this happiness. This may seem an unusual circumstance – but if you live in a privileged society you almost certainly use the competition exemption to justify your privileged status.

Privileged people often believe that there is only so much wellbeing to be had, and that theirs is earned through fair competition against those less fortunate – such as refugees, those suffering from disease or famine, and poverty-stricken people. This is partly how we justify denying these poor people admission to our societies through border control, and unequal distribution of wealth more generally. Remembering that most of the people who we are in competition with are good, competent and worthy of respect is a way of ensuring that we do not slip into a dangerously simple characterisation of the problem. This is the first error of competition – seeing inequality as a legitimate or deserved consequence of the loser's failings or inability, when it could be better explained by circumstance. The second error of competition is to see it as necessary when collaboration is a possibility or a better option. Often in societies it is better to share resources rather than compete for them.

Tribalism is the idea that we are more beholden to those close or related to us and less beholden to those different or distant from us. It is used to justify global inequality – we believe that we are not beholden to some poor people because they live in different countries from us. This logic allows people to accept global levels of hardship and inequality that some would find unacceptable nationally.

If you are one of the winners in the game of global inequality, consider how your privileged existence is maintained by the fact that you are considered less beholden to those people outside your national borders – a distinction between you and them which is as artificial and arbitrary as the one that separated black and white South Africans during apartheid. Tribalism allows us to believe that people who are differentiated from us are also less good, competent or worthy of respect. Rule 3 is a reminder that this is not necessarily true.

Inertia is the idea that status quo has a moral weight that you are not obliged to change. Walking past a poor person with £1,000 in your pocket when they have nothing is not considered to be the same as starting with £990 and taking their only £10, even though the outcome is the same. Inertia relies on the idea that we are responsible for actions, rather than outcomes – if we did not act to create another's suffering, we are not responsible for it or complicit in it.

But in partaking of the world's privileges, we may have been more actively involved than we realise. This could be said for liberal Westerners now, whether the culpability is for the misfortune suffered by people from poor countries, or minorities within their own countries, who are differentially targeted by police and recruited for jobs. If you were able to look at pictures of Alan Kurdi, the drowned three-year-old Syrian boy found face down on a Turkish beach, who became the symbol of the refugee crisis in 2015, do nothing and still consider yourself a good person, you would have been using a combination of the above as exemptions to excuse yourself for your inaction.

It may be that many acts of harm are not caused by moral absence or lapse, but through degrees of error in the application of the exemptions – perspective failings in competitiveness, group-identity failures in tribalism, and errors of intent in vengeance. When testing for bad people, false positives and false negatives both matter. False negatives (believing bad people to be good) can expose us to harm through a failure to use avoidance or deterrence strategies. But false positives also matter because when we treat good people as bad it inclines them to do bad things. Remember Rule 3 and look for a more complex, interesting and accurate interpretation of difference than that your opponent is bad or stupid.

When we make that mistake, we validate both of our use of the tribalism and vengeance exemptions, making conflict escalations more likely, and we decrease the utility of both of our worlds.

CAN I TRUST YOU?

Rule 3 states remember that *most*, but not all, people are good, competent and worthy of respect. When I look back upon my school days, I can see that even the teacher and the boy who stole my chips were good people, but the prefect, a serial bully, possibly was not.

But the most extreme example of a bad person that I ever met was when I was studying postgraduate psychology at university. He was a white 16-year-old boy who went out late one night with some friends looking for black people to assault. Instead they found two white homeless people sleeping in a cemetery and stoned them to death. He found out that one of the men had a son who went to the same school as him, so he taunted the boy by telling him that he had killed his father. This is how he got caught. He was interviewed by my forensic psychology professor while I recorded the interview from behind one-way glass. The boy was calm and collected and cracked jokes as he spoke to my professor. I am confident that he was a bad person.

When we evaluate people, it is important to make judgements that are as accurate as possible. It is useful to start with the base assumption that most people are good. Psychopaths do exist – people who lack empathy or remorse, and whose wilder impulses are therefore not moderated in the way that most of ours are – but they are a small minority and that means that there are a lot of good people out there.

When we evaluate whether to trust somebody or not, it is useful to consider whether the behaviour which we are experiencing as negative is a consequence of our own correctly or incorrectly applied vengeance, competitiveness or tribalism. Sometimes other people act against our own interests because they are competing against us or stuck in a vengeance loop against us. The fundamental attribution error would lead us to judge these people as generally untrustworthy.

Nicholas Christakis says that functioning societies have a 'social suite' of characteristics.[5] These are: individual identity, love for partners and offspring, friendship, social networks, cooperation, in-group bias, mild hierarchy and social learning and teaching. When some of the suite are missing, there is less guidance for positive and less restraint on negative individual behaviour. Some bad individual behaviour is the consequence of a protection/ punishment worldview that comes from being trapped in a society with a historically or currently unhealthy social suite.

The value of using Rule 3 is that it allows us to avoid escalating situations, warns us against the simplification of attributing unwanted behaviour just to ill intent, and allows us to seek circumstances which restore promotion mindsets, where people are motivated by the benevolence of others to become benevolent themselves.

WE CAN ALL BE KIND

Jonathan Haidt's moral foundations theory says that all societies value care over harm, freedom over oppression, fairness over injustice, authority over insubordination, loyalty over betrayal, and divinity over sacrilege. Haidt says that shared moral foundations are an important part of what makes us feel part of a group. While all groups hold the six foundations, they differ in how they prioritise and express them, so groups need to agree on how to prioritise these values. Groups that lean to the left of the political spectrum tend to prioritise freedom and fairness, and groups that lean right tend to prioritise loyalty and authority.

---

[5] In his book *Blueprint*

When it comes to the economic behaviour of markets, freedom and fairness can conflict. Unregulated monopolistic companies can exploit a free and unregulated winner-takes-all economy to acquire a level of power that allows them to behave towards employees and customers in a way that is unfair. They can employ people for low wages and with poor career prospects and can use sophisticated and pervasive marketing to gain strong influence over customers. Groups on the right will prioritise market freedom in this conflict, while groups on the left will prioritise employee and customer fairness, even though both groups will broadly agree that freedom and fairness both matter.

We share and are divided by our moral foundations; how we prioritise and express six fundamental values. We feel close to people that we feel we share values with. But because the prioritisation and expression of values can vary so widely, it is easy to lose sight of the fact that almost all people and groups are moral, and share very similar moral foundations. Because we use moral similarity as a way of identifying in and out groups, and because humans have a social suite that includes in-group preference, it is a common mistake to think that people with different values from us belong to different groups and that people in different groups to us are less morally worthy or virtuous.

At the simplest level, when we find ourselves in disagreement with another person, we most benignly attribute this to the other person being factually incorrect or, more significantly, lacking the intelligence or skill to draw the correct conclusion from the facts or, most seriously, being morally compromised. The purpose of Rule 3 is to remind us to look for this benevolent explanation of difference, because often more conflict is caused by two good parties failing to apply Rule 3 to each other than is done by genuinely bad people with ill intent.

A few years ago, I took a ride on my bicycle down the Thames path. It was high tide and the river had burst its banks and stretches of the path were submerged by a few centimetres. I came across a long stretch of path covered by water. A few cyclists had gathered cautiously on the far side, halted by the tide. There were three restaurants looking out over the river, so there were a couple of hundred people sitting at tables looking at this scene. I decided to show the cyclists, and the people at the restaurants, how to ride through shallow water. I shot through the first part of it, but what I hadn't realised was that the cloudy water had obscured a slipway halfway along. Suddenly my front wheel dropped into deep water, I flew over my handlebars and disappeared headfirst into the river. I delayed my re-emergence as long as I could. I was expecting to surface and be met by pointing and laughing. When I did eventually pop up, I was surprised that the main sentiment from the crowd was for my wellbeing. One woman even ran down and retrieved the apple that had flown out of my backpack and was bobbing down the Thames. When I reflect on Rule 3, I am reminded of that occasion, and my surprise at how well treated I was by a large group of strangers.

Key principles:

Start by assuming that the other person is good
Keep an open mind, and be receptive to genuine warnings to
the contrary

If you are influenced by strong negative feelings about a person, seek to debunk confirmation bias and the fundamental attribution error

Unlike most of the rules, which play out in the course of a conversation, Rule 3 often involves talking to yourself or asking yourself questions, before you engage in dialogue. The professional world easily creates scenarios where people feel that they are in competition with each other. When I worked at the motor dealership, the used car department and the new car department competed on several fronts. One of them was a scramble each time a customer walked through the door as salespeople tried to sell them a new or a used car. When the dealer principal revamped the floor space on which the cars were displayed, it was inevitable that the head of new car sales and the head of used car sales both wanted prime position. Coming on top of a long history of competition, it was possible that this conflict could escalate into a personal one – that they could each come to see the other as greedy or unscrupulous. Before arguing with each other about competing for this and other resources, they would each need to remind themselves that some of the statements from the following list might be usefully applied to this specific situation:

Remember he is probably a good person – most people are.
Try to disprove your assumption that he is being deliberately or unnecessarily difficult.
It is too easy to look for more examples of difficult behaviour, and to think that he intended to be difficult, or to upset me.

> *Can I remember examples of him being kind and helpful towards me?*
>
> *I don't think his main objective is to damage my career, but I can see that we are competing for a finite resource. How can we make this a fair competition?*
>
> *Is his difficult behaviour just about him or me, or is it circumstantial?*
>
> *Could circumstances include my own behaviour?*
>
> *Are either of us feeling unnecessarily tribal or vengeful?*

Even after 27 years as a political prisoner, Nelson Mandela retained the ability to see goodness in other people. This was part of what made him an effective leader as South Africa negotiated its way to democracy. Mandela's book *The Long Walk to Freedom* illustrates his optimism about humanity, his willingness to challenge his own beliefs and his belief that hatred is circumstantial rather than innate.

In it, he describes how during the loneliness of his 27-year incarceration, he came to the belief that the freedom that he longed for was necessary not only for the oppressed, but for the oppressor also. He understood that a system that deprives some people of dignity actually deprives all people, even those who are advantaged, of their dignity. This belief was part of his determination not to pursue an agenda of revenge when he finally came to power – he did not want to be a prisoner of hatred.

Mandela talks specifically about being an optimist, and about believing the best about people. He acknowledges that this optimism can be shaken, and says that there were many times that his faith in humanity was tested, but says, 'I would not and could not give myself up to despair. That way lays defeat and death.'

The trajectory of South African politics was towards a civil war. Armed resistance to apartheid was opposed by the state military. People considered themselves enemies. Mandela said that in order to achieve peace, people had to partner with their enemies. They had to work together on a mutual goal. What happened along the way is that they became friends.

Despite being born into a system of racial prejudice, Mandela writes that 'nobody is born hating another person because of the colour of his skin, or his background, or his religion.' He says that what hatred does exist, exists because people have been taught to hate. His optimistic conclusion is that if people can be taught to hate, they can also be taught to love, and that this lesson will be learnt more readily, because 'love comes more naturally to the human heart than its opposite.'

RULE 4: TALK FAST AND SLOW

Tversky and Kahneman are Israeli-American psychologists who were pioneers in the field of behavioural economics. Behavioural economics established that human economic behaviour is not rational. We have predictable biases, which make predictable errors likely under particular circumstances. A thorough understanding of our biases can enable us to design influences, reminders, environments and social cues which make these potentially harmful errors less likely.

We can have better personal and public conversations if we understand how some of the predictable biases and errors that manifest most obviously in our economic decisions also manifest in the judgements we make about the people and the groups with whom we have personal and political relationships. When we understand these biases, we can design safeguards which can protect us personally and politically.

I was on a work team-building exercise once, and the facilitator told us that sometimes we needed to have what he called 'deep breath' conversations. What he meant is that occasions arise when we just need to pluck up courage and blurt out whatever it is that we have on our minds. But sometimes the reason something is difficult to say is that we're trying to say the wrong thing. We have arrived at an incorrect or incomplete judgement, and rather than being held back by a lack of courage, we're being held back by prudence. When we have calmed down or worked things through and arrived at a more reasoned and balanced position, talking is easier.

POWER IMBALANCE

In his book, Kahneman talks about the power of gossip to create change. Sometimes gossip is understood to describe our keen interest in discussing the minutia of our and other people's everyday life, often with emphasis on being disparaging or censorious towards someone who has acted outside of a social norm. In this sense it has the role of maintaining the status quo. Kahneman means that we should use gossip positively. If we maintain our interest in the details of ordinary life, and keep our keen eye for social transgressions, but turn our attention to errors of unwitting bias amongst ourselves, our family, neighbours and peers, we could use gossip to become conscious of costly but unnoticed errors of thinking, and that this can change the world for the better.

One of the difficult conversations that is worth having is about power imbalances.

At a personal level, one of the problems with abusive relationships is that they have volatility but also stability. The stability is based in the fact that the abuse is aimed at undermining the abused individual's ability to make accurate choices about the situation. Whether intuitively or deliberately, the abuser behaves effectively to create a false but powerful and dominant narrative about the relationship.

But relationships that involve abuses of power happen in the political realm also. When political systems allow those who are wealthy to also gain disproportionate political influence, economic inequality becomes a consequence of political decisions.

The World Inequality Lab publishes the 'World Inequality Report' every two years and maintains the World Inequality Database. It shows, for example, that in 1977, the richest 1 per cent of the US population owned 22 per cent of the total wealth of the country. In 2012 it was 40 per cent. By contrast, the middle 40 per cent owned a peak of 36 per cent of the country's wealth in 1985. By 2014 this was 27 per cent. The poorest 50 per cent of the US population have continued to own a negligible proportion of the country's total wealth.

These trends in inequality are present in less extreme forms in other Western countries, which have allowed taxation changes and lightly regulated markets to create a winner-takes-all economy in which the rich really do get richer. For the last 40 years, the economies of democratic countries have been becoming less equal. If I visited all the neighbours on my street who had a smaller house than me and proposed a scheme in which I doubled my wealth, but they all lost 9 per cent of theirs, I would expect a pretty vigorous conversation. It is a failure of democratic discourse that this actual wealth transfer between the middle 40 per cent and the top 1 per cent has not been presented to voters as a choice for them to discuss and agree to or reject.

Similarly, if I visited a single neighbour and proposed a personal relationship in which I would use the threat of anger and violence unpredictably and unreasonably to establish and maintain a relationship in which my wishes were prioritised, the neighbour was blamed for all of my transgressions, the worst of which I would promise convincingly but insincerely never to repeat, I think the neighbour would have quite a lot to say about it. It is a failure of our society that we do not gossip or talk more effectively about how to restrain abusers and help those who are abused.

Rule 4 is a reminder to be aware of our specific cognitive fault lines that allow conversations about anything from benign errors to entrenched personal and public inequality to be bypassed. Our worlds have a lot of information, so a lot of the time we need to think quickly just to keep up. Quick thinking is usually correct, but it is prone to predictable errors. Thinking slowly can help us to spot and then quickly gossip about these errors. This is necessary if we are to use talking as a way of consciously improving our and others' lives.

FAST OR SLOW?

As already discussed, Kahneman calls fast, automatic assumptions System 1 thinking. When we are operating at unconscious competence, we are making use of a well-trained System 1. Examples are a squash player deciding to fake a drive but instead play a drop shot; an experienced driver in a car flicking the indicator switch, or a television interviewer asking a question that has just come to mind. But when we operate at the level of unconscious incompetence, we are using System 1 also. A squash player who does not plant her feet correctly before striking the ball, the learner driver who ploughs through a pedestrian crossing without noticing it, the television interviewer who fails to respond to a lie that their interviewee has just told are also using System 1, but unless they realise the error as it is happening, they are in unconscious incompetence.

System 2 is slower, more effortful decision-making. When the squash player thinks about the angle of her shin before playing a drop shot, when the learner driver thinks through the correct sequence of checking his mirrors, when the interviewer reflects on what her subject has just told her and tests it against what she knows to be factually true or logical, they are in conscious competence. Slow thinking is often necessary to take the first step of skill development – to move from unconscious incompetence to conscious incompetence – it is necessary for us to become conscious of our errors.

System 1 and System 2 interact and inform each other. Fast System 1 thinking can superficially process a lot of information. A security guard watching a bank of CCTV screens would be using System 1 to monitor them. But if something anomalous were to happen, his System 1 would alert System 2 and he would study one particular screen more intently or go and investigate. System 1 is a filtering or triage system to guide us where and when to bring our more effortful System 2 to bear.

But even System 1 cannot pay attention to everything. If the security guard was at a shopping mall and one day had been told that a gang of pickpockets was operating, and another day was told that a gang of shoplifters was operating, he would use his System 2 to deliberately prime his System 1 to be more alert to particular cues on different days. He still would not have time to individually and painstakingly analyse each person who crossed his screen with System 2. But System 1 would be more alert to some warning signs than others.

One night I was driving home. It was late and raining. I saw an elderly man standing next to the road. Using System 1,

I instantly recognised him as blind because he had a white stick. But the image nagged at me for the next few seconds. Something was wrong. This is System 1 in action. I was thinking quickly and automatically, unconsciously comparing my image of this man to images of other people I have seen using white sticks. This man was not resting his stick on the ground, but at 45 degrees. I thought to myself, 'If he isn't using his stick, maybe he is lost.' This thought just popped into my head, which is how System 1 works, but once I became aware of the problem, I began to use System 2 to consider how to solve it. It was likely that he lived nearby. I consciously calculated a route that would allow me to drive back through the town and go past him again. I spoke to him. He had lost his bearings when getting off the bus, and I gave him a lift home which was just around the corner.

This interaction between System 1 and 2 is what makes gut feeling. It takes both systems.

TRUST YOUR GUT

Gut feel is when System 1 alerts us to an exception that warrants further attention or energy, which we then use System 2 to apply. When we say to ourselves, 'I should have listened to my gut!' it is because System 1 alerted us to an exception, but we did not successfully apply System 2 to the problem.

We know that there is something wrong with a society where some people get richer and more powerful, and everyone else gets poorer or stays poor. That is not fair for either relative or absolute definitions of poverty. This is a System 1 calculation. But the System 2 calculation is much more effortful – how do we engage with the complexity of this society to come to a measured decision about how to respond?

Those politicians who gain wide appeal with simple solutions to complex problems are holding their audience in System 1. The audience know that something is wrong but are enticed to make an automatic and simple judgement about a solution. This is an appealing choice, because we are easily overwhelmed by complexity and uncertainty. Kahneman says that when we operate in System 1, we are more agreeable, gullible and in a better mood than when we use System 2. Politicians are often understood as appealing to people's gut instincts, but gut instinct requires an interaction between System 1 and System 2. When politicians hold people in System 1, they are preventing, not facilitating, the use of gut instinct.

Peter Coleman says that political situations where gut instinct is suppressed are sometimes more volatile than they appear. When people do finally apply System 2 thinking to discomfort triggered by System 1, they can change their minds rapidly.

As with the example of the security guard, the other way that Systems 1 and 2 work together is when System 2 primes System 1 to pay particular attention to something. Indian Test cricketer Rahul Dravid once explained to me that to tell the difference between a short-and a full-pitched delivery, you have to watch for whether the bowler releases the ball early or late. System 1 intuits whether the ball is going to be short or full, but System 2 directs your attention to the timing of the release. It would be useful to know particular patterns of evasion or particular factual errors that a politician is prone to, and then use System 2 to prime System 1 to watch out for these.

Dr Steve Peters wrote a bestselling book called *The Chimp Paradox* which teaches mainly that we should replace 'chimp' thinking

(System 1) with 'human' thinking (System 2) in order to function better under stress. This has been the prevailing attitude to the idea of a split between fast and slow styles of thinking. In his title, and again in the concluding paragraph of the book, Peters hints at the 'paradox' that it's not always about replacing System 1 with System 2. Peters' use of the loaded terms 'chimp' and 'human' to replace the neutral terms System 1 and System 2 reflects an attitude that we should always strive to become more conscious and deliberate – who wants to ever think like a chimp? But although in many circumstances we default to System 1, sometimes to our detriment, there are situations when we are drawn to slow System 2 functioning when we should stay with fast System 1. These include high stakes, complex, fast-moving situations.

Another Indian Test cricketer, Shikhar Dhawan, told me that when he bats, he wants to 'express his inner beauty'. This is a profound and effective goal. It is effective because maintaining a System 2 awareness of his talent primes Shikhar to rely on System 1 even when the pressure is high, and other cricketers are tempted to start overthinking, trying too hard, or being pulled into System 2 dominance. Naming his automatic state 'inner beauty' instead of 'chimp' allows Shikhar to access it even when the situation is dragging him towards consciousness. Relying on System 2 is our natural inclination when we are trying to avoid error, but abandoning System 1 entirely can compromise performance in other ways. We observe situations where we are inclined to use System 2 but would be better off using System 1 most frequently in sport, but they occur in normal human interactions also. System 1 is where spontaneity, humour and empathy come from, and there are times when we need to protect and use this way of thinking and talking.

We do sometimes act as if our System 2 is the reliable system, and System 1 is error prone. For sure, System 1 does not check up on itself, but a well-trained System 1 allows Shikhar to cope with the speed and complexity of hitting a cricket ball. If our System 1 is well primed and trained, we can use and trust it to notice details and generate ideas even when we feel uneasy about a conversation or relationship. Then System 1 directs us to mobilise the effortful System 2 to investigate specific concerns. In normal life we also need to maintain a balance between System 1 and System 2. If we respond to pressure by becoming too deliberate, our thinking is slowed, and we are at risk of missing information. We may be thinking hard and deliberately about something, but we do this at the cost of a broader awareness.

We need to use System 2 to decide what to pay attention to in a democratic debate. We need to prepare System 1 to notice evasive answers to questions, a refusal to commit to specific goals that could be measured as successful or unsuccessful, and attractive but simple answers to complex problems.

And in relationships where there are some System 1 'gut feel' alarms, it would be useful to be primed to look for certain warning signs. Is anger unpredictable and excessive? Is the explanation for anger that the abuser was provoked? Are there repeated and unkept promises to change? Most people don't like conflict and communicate signs of regret or discomfort during arguments. But abusers are indifferent to this distress themselves and are encouraged by rather than sympathetic to the distress that conflict causes others. They signal during conflict that they are happy to prolong or escalate the argument. Being primed to detect these signs can help us avoid the 'false negative' test – not seeing an actual threat.

It is also useful to prime your own System 1 to be alert to the hard-to-spot common patterns that distort even normal healthy relationships and conversations. Sometimes in healthy relationships, we make the opposite error to that mentioned above – we make 'false positives' and detect problems, insults or injuries that are not there. These errors arise quickly and frequently in conversations, and rather than trying to train yourself or the people around you not to make them, which would take constant and expensive System 2 vigilance, it's easier to learn to use a primed System 1 to spot them early and reliably when they are committed, and then activate System 2 to correct them.

SPOTTING PATTERNS

When analysing your own or someone else's argument, it is helpful to use your System 2 to learn the patterns of common errors, and then prime your System 1 to be alert for them. One example is the familiar fundamental attribution error, where someone confuses intent and circumstance in a way that is favourable to themselves and unfavourable to someone else. I ran over the squirrel in the car many years ago, and I have told the story of my over-reaction to Claudia's subsequent comment many times. Hopefully the repeated tellings have by now primed me to spot more of my own 'false positives', when I make the fundamental attribution error and detect a threat that is not actually there. Other examples of System 1 errors which can complicate an actually healthy relationship include simplifications, where some or most of the causes of or solutions to a conflict are ignored (more of this in Rule 8: Use complexity), the use of extremes, where degree is ignored, and words like 'always', 'everything', 'definitely', 'impossible' and 'everyone' are used in ways which makes perceptions and conclusions more severe (more of this in Rule 6: Use resilience), and putting words in someone else's mouth, which can come about as a combination of the above three errors.

Making these errors gives a distorted view of the relationship. 'Claudia was trying to upset me' (fundamental attribution error), 'Claudia doesn't respect me' (simplification), 'Claudia is always like this' (extreme thinking), and 'So you're saying I'm a bad driver' (putting words into someone's mouth) would all be very difficult positions from which to begin a conversation. And if they were true, it would be necessary to have this difficult conversation. But if we have made a false positive, or have exaggerated the size of the problem, the conversation is actually an easier one. This is when rather than taking a deep breath and weighing in with your own opposing opinion, it can be better to be alert to common biases so that you can spot your own and other's small errors as they arise in the process of opinion formation. When, as Kahneman suggests, we gossip about breaches of correct thinking, we train ourselves to use both systems more effectively.

Part of our lived experience as humans is to have duality. Classically, this was a split into the soul and the physical. Another split is the emotional and the rational. Tversky and Kahneman used the labels 'System 1' and 'System 2' deliberately because they are neutral. This neutrality reflects the fact that one system is not superior to the other, or more correct than the other. Both systems are completely human, both are appropriate to different tasks and we use them both correctly and incorrectly. System 1 and System 2 do not correlate to the emotion/rationality split that has historically been used to understand the duality of human deductions. Emotions are used to assess rationality and correctly applied rationality allows us to derive accurate emotions. System 1 can operate unemotionally and rationally. A footballer who makes an intelligent pass, a squash player who plays a practised squash shot, and you, if you can still remember your times tables, are using System 1 in a way that transcends the rational/emotion split. Likewise, as my school maths teacher would be able to tell you, it is possible to make painstaking, careful, conscious System 2 calculations that are wrong.

Tversky and Kahneman also state that human beings have two ways of making decisions. This is the Econ/Human distinction. The 'Econ' is a rational decision-maker that acts in its own best interests. Traditionally, when people thought about human decision-making, they assumed that humans were Econs. This decision-maker, for example, would not be vulnerable to targeted advertising, because rational self-interest would lead it to make the right choices. Part of why the Econ explanation for our decisions is resilient is because we experience ourselves as rational even if we are not. It is easier to explain the past than it is to predict the future, and when we look back our choices seem explicable and hence rational.

We also have a flexible definition of 'self-interest'. In some ways, the Econ explanation should not be able to survive the fact that anyone at all – let alone majorities in some populations – smoke, abuse opioid painkillers, or eat unhealthy amounts of sugar. Instances where people are clearly not making rational self-interested decisions can be explained as consequences of people having but failing to apply rationality in their pursuit of self-interest. From this perspective, the failing is with the individual concerned. Because a failure to apply a skill that you possess is a failure for which you are culpable, the cases where human beings do not act as Econs, and make poor and harmful choices are not considered to be important exceptions to the general rule of rational self-interest.

YOU'RE BEING IRRATIONAL

It is appealing to think of ourselves as rational and incorruptible. This is partly the fundamental attribution error and partly what is called the Dunning Kruger effect (the less skilled or informed we are, the less able we are to recognise our inability or ignorance, which creates a paradoxical correlation between ignorance and confidence where the less we know, the more confident we are in our knowledge). But being more aware of our general vulnerability to influence is worthwhile because it makes us more likely to notice specific attempts to influence us. It seems like a contradiction to argue that we can become stronger by becoming more aware of our weaknesses, but being optimistic that conscious incompetence is preferable to unconscious incompetence allows us to develop our ability to use System 1 and System 2 in combination to reduce this vulnerability. To do this is to accept that we are humans, rather than expect ourselves to be Econs.

This is important because many conversations are about the distribution of responsibility. When political systems allow the enrichment of very few people at the expense of many, there are two justifications: either that consumers and voters are fully independent and rational and that these outcomes are their preferred outcomes, or at least trade-offs against some supposedly more important but undeclared benefit; or, that because the disadvantaged parties have the power of choice, but for some reason (moral failure) are just not exercising it, they deserve the negative outcomes. By this logic, the beneficiaries of economic or political systems are not responsible for the inequality because they are just being influenced by circumstances (including market forces, political lobbying, and the law of the jungle). But the disadvantaged groups are considered to be responsible for their misfortune. Their circumstances (including lack of opportunity, long, low-paid hours, and constant stress) are not considered to be significant influences on their behaviour and choices, and because they are not more hardworking or entrepreneurial, or do not exercise different political choices, they are held responsible for inequality.

Political conversations about inequality involve concepts of fairness and justice. Fairness is a common subject in our personal and professional lives also. These conversations will be more accurate and effective if we make correct judgements about the balance of influence and intent in influencing our and others' behaviour, and how this affects what we can and cannot be held responsible for.

One responsibility we do have to ourselves and each other is to be aware of our vulnerability to influence and error so that when circumstances mislead us, we are deliberately misled by self-interested individuals or organisations, or when we are unfair to others by presuming more intent and responsibility than was actually the case, we can think harder and more slowly in these situations, and gossip more quickly when we recognise others to be caught in them.

Tversky and Kahneman expanded our understanding of the complexity of how we come to form beliefs. They point out that we are rarely stumped. As comedian Dara O'Briain observes, we think we understand more about the world than medieval people did, but most of us can't explain refrigerators, television, electricity or the internet further than, 'You plug it into the wall.' We are excellent confabulators – we make up explanations as we go along and don't realise that we are doing it.

Some of the biases that Tversky and Kahneman documented include:

- Positive test strategies and confirmation bias – our tendency to seek to prove our ideas correct rather than test them by looking for contradictory evidence. To overcome confirmation bias we need to be able to answer questions like, 'What would change my mind?' and 'How would we know?'
- Our preference for plausibility over probability. We feel confident with familiar (repeatedly expressed), available (prominently communicated), established, simple, plausible beliefs. We have ignorance blindness – a lack of awareness of what we do not know.
- Our increased gullibility when we are tired or distracted.
- Denominator neglect, which is our tendency to fail to seek context; the anchoring effect, which describes our vulnerability to having our opinions excessively influenced by the first piece of information we come across, and the halo effect, which describes our vulnerability to assuming that what is true in one area will be true in many.
- The law of small numbers refers to our vulnerability to consider small samples as adequate evidence upon which to draw a conclusion. This can be a problem unless we anticipate that extreme outcomes are sometimes best explained by randomness.

When we seek reasons for why we disagree, familiarity with these biases can help us detect the errors that can set the formation of our opinions in different directions.

We can guard against these biases by deploying System 1 and System 2 together, which gives us gut feel and priming. Priming means consciously understanding the biases and their signs so as to direct and improve the accuracy of our alarm systems; gut feel means having the willingness and ability to investigate more rigorously when the alarm systems are triggered.

THE PARTICULAR AND THE GENERAL

Psychologists Nisbett and Borgida say that our unwillingness to deduce the particular from the general is only matched by our willingness to infer the general from the particular.[6] When we are watching a sports match, and the referee penalises our team, we may be unwilling to infer the particular from the general and consider this decision unbiased because referees are generally unbiased (if you disagree, the bias is probably yours). But we are eager to infer the general from the particular and consider all referees biased on the basis of a particular decision with which we disagree.

Most people who are looking for a partner can list attributes that are important to them. But often when people meet someone that they like, without realising it, they remake the list to conform to the person that they have just met. Similarly, while we all have

---

[6] *University of Michigan*: Richard E. Nisbett and Eugene Borgida, 'Attribution and the Psychology of Prediction,' *Journal of Personality and Social Psychology* 32 (1975): 932–43.

values, sometimes when we support a politician or other public figure, we remake our list of values to correspond to those which the public figure holds. This is deriving the general from the particular, which can cause us to be inconsistent in our preferences or values. We need to be more aware of this pattern, and more ready to step away from particular judgements or debates. When things seem important or urgent this can be harder to do, but as Rule 2 states, agreement deserves skill and effort. The general is less subject to bias than the particular, so we have more chance of agreement, and once we have established general agreement, we have more chance of particular agreement also.

When we draw conclusions, we prioritise representativeness and the plausible over the probable. But the best chance for agreement is for both parties to be correct. Ideally, we agree because we have a shared approach to collecting and using facts, applying reason, and being alert to typical errors, rather than relying on persuasion or coercion. If we have derived different opinions, often it is a worthwhile conversation to use negative test strategies and to look for common errors in each of our observation and deduction processes. By using Rule 4 to anticipate and reduce avoidable error in ourselves and other people, we can achieve agreement more often.

Errors complicate talking because they cause divergent views. Even errors with benign origins in a failure of accuracy rather than a bias in calibration are made more significant by the fundamental attribution error and our tendency towards in-group bias. Rather than seeing disagreement as benign and something that we can cooperate to solve, we can believe that the disagreement is a consequence of someone's desire to oppose us, or an inevitable conflict between different groups of people. These attributions make originally innocent disagreement more consequential and entrenched.

Some judgement errors enhance unequal power structures. Anchoring, or expectations, protect the status quo. CEOs are anchored on high salaries and large raises. Forty years ago, the average CEO earned 30 times as much as the average worker in his company; today it is 270 times. Conversations about inequality are made more difficult by the fact that the CEO and the worker are anchored on very different numbers. They have both become accustomed to their salaries, and change is considered relative to the 2020 disparity, not the 1980 disparity. The representativeness heuristic (which assumes that because someone looks typical of a group, they are part of that group) drives a self-fulfilling prophecy that tall, white, confident men become CEOs. The halo effect means we think if someone is good at one thing, we assume that they are also good at others, so the CEO who is good at projecting confidence (which is relatively easy if you are a tall, white, rich man) is assumed to be universally competent.

WINNING AND LOSING

Prospect theory states that we are more motivated to avoid loss than we are to achieve gains.[7] The switch from strong loss-aversion to weaker gain-seeking and back again happens disproportionately and quickly around a zero point. But we do not respond to equal prospects of gaining or losing with equal motivation. If I face the

---

[7] Tversky and Kahneman

prospect of winning or losing an equal amount of money on the flip of a coin, I will generally refuse because I am more motivated to avoid loss than I am to achieve gain. But the zero point against which I judge gain and loss can be arbitrarily set and is subject to narrow framing – considering only part of what is relevant. The zero point is typically relative to the status quo of what I have now, which is why territorial battles are usually won by the incumbent. The owner is normally more motivated to avoid loss than the challenger is to achieve gain.

The certainty effect refers to the fact that a small shift from a very high probability to a complete certainty is more tangible than a large shift from a medium to high probability. It is relevant to relationships. A highly honest person who is trusted by others is strongly disinclined to lie, because the shift from being completely trusted to being mostly trusted seems significant. On the other hand, Politician A, who is not always truthful, isn't too bothered whether he is considered mostly truthful or only occasionally untruthful, as the shift doesn't seem as important to him or his supporters.

The possibility effect operates at the other end of probability also. Small shifts from highly unlikely to impossible are more salient than they should be. This is why people buy lottery tickets – the difference between having no chance of winning the lottery when you haven't bought a ticket and the meaninglessly small chance of winning when you have still seems significant. Like the certainty effect, the possibility effect operates in broader judgements. Politician A, who doesn't care about lying sometimes, is still motivated to tell the truth often enough so that it is not considered an impossibility, and the abuser who is rarely nice is still motivated to avoid the conclusion that he is never nice. Being alert to the certainty effect and the possibility effect can help us appreciate shifts that are meaningful but not extreme. It is worth improving a good relationship even if it cannot be made perfect, as inequality can be lessened if not eliminated. This sensitivity will improve the insight and complexity of our conversations about change.

The interaction of the certainty and possibility effects and prospect theory creates a fourfold pattern. The fourfold pattern can be applied using System 2 to improve slow talking about inequality and power imbalances in personal and political relationships.

People are risk seeking at the extremes, when they perceive that they have (1) everything or (2) nothing. People who perceive that they have everything will double down on risk, accepting the chance of large losses to avoid the certainty of small losses, and people who perceive that they have nothing will take risks for small gains or small probabilities of gains.

People are risk averse when they perceive that they have something but not everything. They (3) fear large losses and so (4) reject small gains or small probabilities of gains.

This is why:

1. Some powerful people may take the risk of committing a larger crime or telling a larger lie to try to cover up the possibility but not certainty of being found guilty of a smaller indiscretion, and why some politicians are willing to risk economic or civic disruption to maintain power hierarchies that are preferential to them.
2. Some people will work for low wages in the very small but not impossible hope of a big promotion or even being CEO one day. This is essentially being paid in lottery tickets, and was the exact justification Jamie Dimon, the CEO of JP Morgan, gave for earning $31 million in a year while some of his employees earned less than the cost of living. People

who perceive themselves to be in this category might also vote for politicians who tell them that they are at the bottom of the social hierarchy but offer them the prospect of a step up. The prospect of a step up can be attractive even if it is only relative, and is achieved by forcing other groups into a step down.

3. People who perceive themselves to be broadly middle class, who may belong to a privileged class or race without being in a particular position of power, or who have some accumulated wealth, accept or 'put up with' unfavourable policies or flawed politicians because they have been induced to fear something that is actually unlikely, or

4. Accept continued losses, like the erosion of middle-class wealth over the last generation, and political norm violations, because they fear catastrophic change were they to oppose it.

This fourfold pattern is important for conversations about inequality partly because it introduces error into the process of making decisions about risk, and error creates the probability of disagreement. But it is also important because it gives insight into a new political phenomenon where partnerships develop across the wealth divide. Traditionally, politics were divided into left and right. The right has held power for longer than the left (since the days of the aristocracy). Rich people generally wanted to keep things the same and so were called conservatives, while poor people wanted freedom from traditional structures and so were called liberals. But more recently, alliances have emerged between rich elites and poor disenfranchised people.

It is a puzzle why economic inequality has grown for so long without becoming a central part of the political conversation.

Politicians pursue policies that favour the rich but are voted in by poor majorities. One explanation for this is given by Jonathan Haidt in his book *The Righteous Mind*. He says that because rich conservatives espouse authority, tradition, taboos and a particular brand of fairness, as well as economic policies disadvantageous to the poor, the best choice some poor people have is to vote with their moral interests but against their economic interest.

The fourfold pattern gives an additional insight into this phenomenon.

Those with power are not offering those without it fairness or equality. Risk-taking politicians are not committed to disrupting the current social hierarchy to the point that their own privilege could be threatened. But they have realised that dispossessed people will gamble for gains that are small, meaningless or unlikely, and they can use this risk-taking environment to pursue their own gambles at the other end of the advantage spectrum.

Because we are humans and not Econs, not only are we irrationally drawn to risk-seeking or risk-averse behaviour, we are not always rational and correct when we position ourselves on this spectrum. Different perspectives could cause people with similar wealth and opportunities to consider themselves to be at different positions of the spectrum. Part of the debate around inequality is about the difference between absolute and relative poverty. One perspective justifies growing inequality by highlighting the fact that absolute poverty is diminishing and that this fact trumps concerns about lack of social mobility for poor people, a diminished middle class, or an expanded billionaire class.[8]

---

[8] By contrast, 2019 Economics Nobel prize winners Abhijit Banerjee and Esther Duflo emphasise the centrality of human dignity to wellbeing.

Previously well-off voters troubled by relative losses of wealth or status experience a threat to their dignity. The zero point that they are referencing their current situation against is where they were financially and socially a generation ago, and they are motivated and prepared to take risks to reclaim what they see as rightfully theirs.

But previously poor voters troubled by lack of opportunities to gain wealth and status also experience a threat to their dignity. This group's zero point is not the extreme poverty that they suffered a generation earlier, their reference is the opportunities currently available to other groups that they perceive as being denied to them.

Some political parties in developed countries depend on a voter base that is energised by concerns about a loss of wealth, status or opportunity that is not absolute, but relative to what they had in the past. These concerns are prioritised over those of other groups who are still disadvantaged, with the justification that the other groups are no longer in absolute poverty and may even have experienced a relative improvement in circumstances. But it is not consistent to believe that some groups should be grateful for absolute gains and at the same time sympathise with other groups about relative losses.

Whether individual or political, abusive relationships are sometimes tragically stable. The fourfold pattern casts light on how abusive relationships of all kinds can endure. The abuser risks flouting social and legal norms to avoid losing the certainty of total control in the relationship, while the victim risks being harmed in the hope of the remote possibility that things will improve. They are united by hope – for the abuser that things will stay the same, and for the victim that things will change.

Understanding how we may be blind to power imbalances, or just error, improves the quality of conversation that we can have about these problems. Successful conversations are based on being correct rather than being persuasive and Rule 4 is a reminder to talk fast and slow about large and small real-world problems.

Key principles:

We need to talk fast (freely, automatically) and slow (deliberately, consciously, carefully)

Doing this helps us move through the stages of competence

Gut feel involves an interplay between fast thinking and slow thinking

Common conversational errors to detect with gut feel include:

Simplifications

Failure to use degree

Failure to use probability

Putting words in someone else's mouth

Awareness of potential for error can protect us from avoidable error

Gossip can train and alert us to the errors that are typical to us

In democratic societies, our decisions are shaped by political conversations. Better conversations mean more informed voters and better democracies. This transcript is of a political conversation between a journalist and a politician where the journalist tries to hold a politician to account for his position on an issue.

Journalist: [Politician B] has made some offensive comments. Have you defended them?

Politician A: I didn't defend [Politician B's] comments. I thought they were crass comments, they were horrible comments. But I don't agree with the idea that because you've been taped saying something in private that is objectionable, you should be driven out of public life. There is not a single person in Parliament who hasn't at some point in their lives in private said something they regretted terribly the next morning.

[This comment makes superficial sense. It is true. But it fails to appreciate that there are degrees of how objectionable a comment can be. There are not just two categories, objectionable and not. It is possible for a comment to be so highly objectionable that even if it were said in private it would disqualify someone from public life. But the politician's argument rests on there only being these two categories and that all objectionable comments are the same. The journalist fails to use System 1 to spot this logical error or to use System 2 to subject it to closer scrutiny.]

Journalist: Have you [ever said something you have regretted]?

Politician A: I've no idea, worse perhaps, in some cases. People say all sorts of things and goodness me, you know people on a Friday night out after a drink say all sorts of stupid things. And the idea that [Politician B] should not even be in office because he said it or that [Politician C] shouldn't be [a politician] because he has written some fruity articles, we're reaching levels here of political correctness that are frankly ludicrous.

[The politician has used exactly the same logic again, and the journalist still does not raise the matter of degree.]

Politician A: Isn't it amazing when a UK citizen goes to fight for ISIS in Syria, we are happy to kill them with drones, but when they come back to this country, we are legally constrained?

[By asking us to be 'amazed', the politician is appealing to plausibility, rather than probability. He is inviting us to draw conclusions based on 'amazement' and 'outrage'. This is System 1 thinking. It is deeply troubling and dangerous that some UK citizens fight foreign wars which are opposed to UK foreign policy, and then return home. But the 'amazement' argument relies on a prior assumption that this unsatisfactory arrangement could be simply solved, and only remains a problem because of a lack of competence or will on the part of the relevant decision-makers. These are superficial, evidence-free judgements, and are in contravention of Rule 2.]

There are 400 [UK citizens who fought for ISIS and have now returned to the UK] and I think that is an outrage. I think the fact there are 75 more people out there like [the man who just committed a terrorist attack inside the UK] who potentially could do us harm is something that has to be addressed. Do you know, of the six people who were in that plot, one has already been remanded, one has had his parole stopped because he'd breached the terms and one has committed murder. Do you honestly think we should allow 75 more people like that to be out there? I don't think so. I think we should act very quickly.

[Here the politician is explicitly calling for speed ('I think we should act very quickly'). Kahneman says that fast, System 1 thinking is associated with gullibility and optimism, and even though the politician is taking a stereotypically 'tough' position on crime, he is highly optimistic that his glib analysis and his simple suggested 'lock 'em up' solution will be an adequate response.]

Journalist: The victim's father has asked that the murder is not politicised.

Politician A: The victim's father can say what he likes and take whatever view he wants. He is being charitable and decent in what he says. But I promise you this, if we polled a thousand people now and asked, 'Are you happy these 75 are out on our streets?' I know what the answer is. It is something that should give us all pause for thought.

[The politician simplifies again. His dismissal of the victim's father is very glib. He does not take the opportunity to think more deeply about a different opinion. The politician then cites a hypothetical poll and assumes that it validates his opinion. The politician is making some fast logical leaps here. They may be correct. They may not. But the politician is skilled at talking so fast that the journalist does not have time to analyse what he is saying. She fails to get him to talk slowly or to talk slowly herself. Clearly nobody is happy about having dangerous people on the streets. But while strong emotion inclines us towards fast talking, solutions or improvements to complex situations are usually found with slow talking. The politician does eventually call for 'pause for thought'. But he uses this as a rhetorical device to confirm his own position, rather than to genuinely invite debate or analysis. He is inviting us to reflect on the emotion of the 1,000 imaginary people that he has just polled, rather than the complexity of the situation. The journalist misses the chance to ask, 'What should we be pausing to think about?']

RULE 5: KEEP THE CONVERSATION SAFE

On 18th June 2018 I was fired on a burning aeroplane. So as not to be unduly alarming, I will clarify that I was fired *on* a burning aeroplane, not *from* a burning aeroplane. And actually, I wasn't technically fired. It was more demoted or moved sideways from my position as sports psychologist to the Saudi national football team at the 2018 World Cup in Russia. And to be completely honest, the aeroplane wasn't on fire – not yet anyway.

In my day job, one of the things I do is work for a sports club. One day I was walking back to my office from the training pitch when I got a call from an old friend. 'The Saudis are looking for a sports psychologist to help them prepare for the World Cup. Are you interested?' I thought, 'This could be brilliant!' And it was. I went to Riyadh to negotiate my contract. When I worked with Olympic gold medallist Abhinav Bindra in 2008, I had neglected to stipulate a results-based bonus (which my wife has reminded me of from time to time), so this time I proposed a modest bonus if the team qualified for the knockout stages. Once I had the preliminary discussion with the president of the Saudi football association, I was taken to meet the minister of sport at his house in a secure compound on the outskirts of Riyadh. I was shown past his Ferrari and Bugatti, covered in desert dust in the driveway, on my way to an outbuilding waiting room.

There was a delay while the minister concluded a telephone call with the king, but eventually I was shown into his reception room. I was introduced and shown to my chair. The minister looked at me and got to his feet. 'Psychology is very important! It can make a big difference to the success of our national team! So if we qualify for the knockout stages of the tournament, Tim will receive a bonus of two million pounds!' This was about one hundred times higher than the figure I had proposed. The president of the football federation looked alarmed. This was going to be coming out of his budget. I stayed silent; things seemed to be going well without my involvement. The minister carried on, 'And if we win one of the knockout games, Tim will receive a bonus of 10 million pounds! And after the World Cup, Tim will work with the top football clubs in Saudi Arabia!'

And with that the contract was agreed, and we began the work. The team was made up of a wonderful group of young men. They were conscientious and supportive of each other. I wasn't under any illusions about their levels of talent or ability, so I wasn't going too crazy about the probability of the potential bonus, but I'd be lying if I said it wasn't on my mind, or the beautiful view from the lovely house I was going to buy with it. Our first match was the opening fixture of the World Cup against the home team, Russia, in front of the eyes of the world, and Prince Mohammed bin Salman, who sat watching seated next to Vladimir Putin.

We lost 5–0, the biggest defeat ever in the opening fixture of a World Cup. My unlikely bonus (and lovely house) evaporated in 90 minutes. Each of the five times that Russia scored, Putin turned to Salman with a big smile on his face and shook the prince's hand. After the match, players and officials were terrified. There was talk that players would be banished from the country or never be allowed to play football again. My view that the team had actually played quite well was not well received. What I was trying to say was that, given our relative ability, a 3–0 loss was actually a realistic result, and the last two goals in extra time (a crazy shot and a long-distance free kick) were unlucky and shouldn't be reflected in the evaluation of the performance. This is still my position. My argument didn't go down well.

I was approached by the team manager on the flight to our next match and told that I was going to be replaced in my role. At this stage of the flight we had suffered the initial engine failure, which was to lead to the fire, but although the plane was flying at a strange angle, there were no actual flames. I digested the news while sitting next to my friend Frans Hoek, the goalkeeper coach. The first bang happened 30 minutes into a 90-minute flight, but we soldiered on for another 60 before coming in to land. I was deep in conversation with Frans. The aeroplane began to vibrate severely as we descended. I didn't stop talking to Frans because I didn't want him to worry, but at the same time I was considering the possibility of another bang and a sudden plunge to earth. I wasn't sure whether Frans had noticed anything. At this point the engine lit up and we landed with flames coming off the starboard wing. Once we were on the ground I said to Frans, 'That was serious,' and he agreed. He had noticed but hadn't said anything because he hadn't wanted me to worry. I sent a message to a friend:

> Just landed in a plane with an engine on fire.
> *Happy to be alive? New lease on life?*
> Just annoyed really.
> *Well, for what it's worth I'm glad you're still around.*

Looking back, one remarkable part about it is that I was at least as upset, maybe more, about the firing as I was about the fire. Being exposed to the possibility of plunging to my death in a fireball has become an amusing anecdote, but being dismissed for the only time in my career still rankles.

I am not alone in this priority. Emotional safety is important to all of us. As human beings, we fear for our physical and emotional safety, and often of the two it is the emotional fear that grips us more strongly. This is why many teenagers drive recklessly or overdose on drugs at music festivals – because the fear of social rejection has more influence over their behaviour than the fear of physical danger. The universal need for emotional safety plays a significant enabling or disabling role in many conversations.

EMOTIONAL FEAR

In order for conversations to be safe we need mutual purpose and mutual respect. Mutual purpose is more attainable if you can move between the particular and the general. For example, this applies to conversations I have with my wife, Claudia, about what movie to watch. Sometimes Claudia and I find a movie that fits inside the narrow band of our overlapping preferences – time travel sci-fi with a romantic rather than an apocalyptic angle. In this case, mutual purpose already exists, and the conversation is easy. But when Claudia is scrolling through lists of noir detective mysteries and I am looking longingly for sports documentaries, we have to take it up a level and remember the more general purpose of spending the evening together.

Relationships affect conversations and conversations affect relationships. It's easier to talk when the relationship is good, and it's easier to have a good relationship when the talking is good, but it's deeper than that. Talking makes relationships, and relationships make talking. The depth of this interaction means we shouldn't be looking for tricks or techniques. We should be looking for principles.

Level shifting between the particular and the general often happens quite well at the personal level, but sometimes in public discourse protagonists are so invested in a single issue that they lose sight of the damage they are doing to the general framework of civil, honest, rigorous debate, and how useful and fragile this framework is. We can be quite tolerant of thwarted particular purpose as long as we feel that our general purpose is achievable, but if there is no hope for any level of purpose in a conversation, it collapses into conflict very quickly. Protagonists do need to protect each other's needs in the conversation. Sometimes we see thwarted purpose when it is not there. We feel incorrectly that someone is wantonly opposing us, or someone incorrectly feels that we are deliberately opposing them. While we need to be alert to situations where our needs are not respected, we also need to look out for these false positive situations which create alarm where it is not required.

This principle shows how Rule 1 (agree what you are talking for) has a role to play in the safety of the conversation. So does Rule 3 (remember most people are good, competent and worthy of respect), which establishes mutual respect. When we find ourselves in disagreement, the fundamental attribution error makes it easy for us to attribute this disagreement to something more significant than just that we have been exposed to a different set of observations. The most benign of these alternative explanations is that the person we are talking to has made a simple error. More significantly, we could attribute the disagreement to a lack of competence on the other person's part or, most seriously, to malign intent. Applying Rule 3 guards against this error as well as helping us observe Rule 5.

Human societies and many animal societies are hierarchical – some individuals have more status and privileges than others. The advantage of this system is that many altercations can be resolved by status rather than conflict. The pecking order in chickens, which is so well known that it serves as a name for all social ranking systems, is what makes mass chicken farming possible. Chickens are aggressive and predatory animals, but mass fights do not erupt in the huge commercial flocks because the pecking order makes it unnecessary – lower ranking birds mostly defer to higher ranking birds. The advantages of being high ranking are significant. Birds only have to engage in conflict at times and against opponents of their choosing, and get privileged access to food, mates and roosting spots.

If this sounds stark, consider that the difference in prospects for the highest and lowest ranking humans in our society and world is substantially greater than for chickens. Status is a matter of life and death and will be defended vigorously. Entrenched, steeply hierarchical societies develop elaborate accents, mannerisms and courtesies as ways of showing status. These can be used to signify in-group membership, and when the in-group is a privileged group the mannerisms are actually a way of expressing a status advantage. This is closely linked to contempt rather than the respect that real manners convey. But even in more shallow hierarchies, and in smaller and more intimate groups, respect is an important signifier of the desire to avoid conflict, and an awareness and sympathy for the needs and rights of another person. Its absence is a significant risk to our safety and wellbeing. We are highly sensitive to a lack of respect and are inclined to escalate conflict to insist that we receive it.

Because false positives can lead to unnecessary escalations of conflict, we need to apply System 2 error checking to our System 1 disrespect alerts. Like the surfer who sees a shark's dorsal fin in every choppy wave, or the tourist in a jungle who sees a snake in every tree, when we operate in societies or groups where hierarchies are steep or have high consequence, we become primed to detect disrespect, and prefer to make false positive identifications than false negatives.

Sometimes the alerts are accurate and then of course a proportionate response is required. I spent some time working at a school for troubled children in inner-city London, and I remember how primed these children were to detect disrespect and how quickly they would escalate conflict once they made a judgement. For these children, status was directly connected to wellbeing, safety and, ironically, conflict avoidance, so their vigorous defence of it had a purpose. For many of us, our more measured use of conflict escalation to protect respect is a 'there but for the grace of God go I' situation. We need respect just as much as the children, we just have the luxury of not having to fight for it as often.

Being aware of this tendency can remind us to recalibrate our detection systems, and so avoid unnecessary false positive escalations, while retaining the potential to defend ourselves if genuinely necessary. One day I was in the classroom early and I heard the children approaching. They were in a boisterously good mood and were not expecting me to have arrived before them. They jokingly called out to me using my first name. I have no problem with children addressing me by my first name, but in this context it was an act of disrespect. I de-escalated the situation by quietening and slowing things down. I reminded them of how respectfully I always spoke to them and that the convention of the school was that adults were addressed in a certain way. It was effective because I moved it to a System 2 situation and reminded them of how they also were beneficiaries of the respect system.

The following conversation is an example of an escalation of disrespect. A politician was on a radio show outlining his ideas for a political project that he wanted to implement. A doctor, who had previously been involved in determining the population health impact for the project, and had possibly legitimate concerns about it, phoned in.

Doctor: I was actually involved in drafting the plans of mitigation for [the project you are proposing]. And my question to you is what mortality rate are you willing to accept in the light of it going ahead?

[The psychologist and foremost authority on couple relationships John Gottman says that discussions tend to end as they start. This is an aggressive opening from the doctor, questioning

the politician's intent – the most serious form of accusation – above questioning his knowledge or his competence.]

Politician: I don't think there is any reason to suppose that [the project] should lead to a mortality rate.

[The politician responds with a non-rigorous statement: see Rule 7.]

Politician: I'm surprised that a doctor in your position would be fearmongering this way on public radio.

[The politician attacks the doctor's intent in turn. The conversation has become unsafe.]

Doctor: Can I remind you I wrote the plans of mitigation.

[The doctor is defending his competence, but it is actually his integrity which has been attacked.]

Politician: Well you didn't write very good plans if you hadn't worked out how to mitigate, had you?

[The politician takes the opportunity to attack the doctor's competence as well as his intent. This is also a non-rigorous statement, this one is illogical – if the risks of a project cannot be mitigated, it could be because mitigating planning is bad, or the project is bad.]

Politician: It's fortunate they are being written by other people now who are serious about mitigating rather than [derogatory term for political group] ... I think it's deeply irresponsible, Doctor, of you to call in and try to spread fear across the country. I think it's typical of [political group] campaigners and you should be quite ashamed, I'm afraid.

[The politician makes further attacks on the doctor's integrity, then makes an unfavourable comparison, and for good

measure, stereotypes him. The 'I'm afraid' phrase is not a genuine expression of regret, it is an in-group mannerism designed to cloak a personal attack in civility and express superior status, which heightens the contempt of the insults. The debating technique that this politician uses is so well used by a certain kind of politician that I call it the 'Eton one-two'. First, mount a pompous but evidence-free objection, second, make an irrelevant ad hominem *attack.]*

This conversation started badly and ended badly. It achieved nothing. The actual topic for discussion was not discussed at all, but would also have been a difficult one to resolve because integrity is hard to prove. This was an unusual and fraught conversation because the protagonists did have a prior disagreement (their political positions) but did not have a prior relationship. This made the conversation volatile. For the conversation to have succeeded, they needed to do more safety work.

When arguments become too heated, John Gottman, imposes 20-minute time-outs. He has found no better system than to get everyone to go away and only return once they have physically and emotionally calmed down. Where there is an existing relationship – unlike on the radio show – there is the opportunity to take a break from the argument and return to it under more agreeable conditions.

GATVOL

In South Africa we have a term, *gatvol*, which expresses the same sentiment as the English 'fed up' or 'had enough', but more pithily. 'Gat' means hole and 'vol' means full and . . . actually maybe there is no need for me to walk you through the literal meaning of the term. I have found it a useful one because it expresses that gradual build-up of discomfort which eventually reaches a point of being suddenly intolerable. Wilfred Bion's concept of the 'container-contained' relationship also describes this phenomenon. Bion says that we generate emotion internally, but also receive emotion that radiates from others.

We each have a certain capacity for containing emotion. When our emotion loads are substantially below our own capacities, it is easier to avoid radiating our own emotion and to sympathetically absorb the radiated emotion of others. When we accept the negative emotion of others, they experience the relief of having their emotional loads reduced, while we experience the effort of containing it. This work gets harder the closer we are to our own capacity.

In the years that I worked as a counselling psychologist, broad negative emotion was more frequently the medium of my work than the specific performance pressure that I work with now as a sports psychologist. A large part of my job was just containing the negative emotion that my clients couldn't contain and weren't having contained by the people around them. One of my clients once told another, 'Tim is really good. He doesn't do anything, but he's really good.' What I was doing was listening attentively and mostly without judgement or reaction.

My effectiveness in doing this emotional work for my clients, and the fact that I could sometimes do a better job of it than other people who were close to them, was based on at least three advantages designed into the therapy process. First, I was myself contained by the structure of therapy. It took place in a safe space that I was familiar with and it happened for a limited period of time. No matter how distressed my client, the session would end in an hour. This meant that I knew there was always a limit to the amount of emotional work that I would have to do and as a consequence I was more prepared to do it. Second, I was not emotionally invested in the issue being discussed. I was professionally interested in the problem being resolved, but the result would not affect me personally. This meant that I was not generating my own internal emotions and thus had more capacity to receive the emotions of my client. Third, the client was delivering the emotion to me in a mostly deliberate and controlled manner. We were talking.

In my personal life, it can be harder to contain even the less fraught negative emotions of friends and family. I am not protected by the therapeutic structure and my investment in our relationship means I often have less capacity to contain their emotion because I am already working to contain my own. Sometimes when I approach, and definitely once I reach my own capacity, I start to radiate emotion back to them, sometimes in ways that I am not aware or in control of.

My exposure to two different circumstances for containing gives me an awareness of how difficult containing in real life actually is. But difficult as it is, containing is critical to talking, because it is impossible for an uncontained conversation to be safe. So it must be done. As happens in a therapeutic conversation, it may be necessary to design structures into fraught real-life conversations that, by limiting potential exposure to negative emotion, encourage us to work with what difficulty is present. John Gottman's 20-minute time-outs are a simple structure that achieves this. Another is ensuring that the word count of each protagonist is roughly the same in the conversation. This makes it more likely that the exchange of emotion is also equivalent, and reduces the risk that one person will have to absorb too much emotion, and so become *gatvol*.[9]

While containing is a challenge, it is also an opportunity because, at a general level, sometimes the purpose of a conversation is simply to contain. Once, when I was working for a sports team before a major competition final, two star players confronted one of the senior members of management in a corridor. Emotions were already high because of the pressure of the competition, and they were upset that they had not been given enough tickets for the final to give to family and friends. The staff member listened to them sympathetically, then explained the process of ticket allocation, said that he believed the system was fair and expressed regret that he was unable to help them with this specific problem. Because the staff member gave the players no extra tickets, there was no explicit particular mutual purpose, but everybody left smiling because he had contained their emotion and shown them respect, which was a satisfactory general purpose.

PRINCIPLES OF RELATIONSHIPS

John Gottman says that while part of keeping a conversation safe has to do with that actual conversation, the foundation of a safe conversation is a safe relationship. The principles of a safe relationship are: know each other, admire each other, turn towards each other, be influenced by each other, solve solvable problems, overcome unsolvable problems, create meaning.

---

[9] Gottman says that, in his experience, men become more easily filled with and incapacitated by emotion than women. He calls it 'flooded' instead of *gatvol*.

Claudia and I had been happily married for about 14 years when we read the book for the first time, and it definitely improved our relationship. Some of the principles came quite naturally to us, but 'the turn towards each other' principle is one that was relevant to us. In times of stress, we had to learn to see each other as teammates rather than as competitors. I once counselled a couple who embodied a more extreme form of the necessity for this principle. They would verbally argue and physically fight. The wife was reasonably content because she won all of the arguments, and the husband was reasonably content because he won all of the fights, but neither seemed aware that each considered the other to be their main adversary or competitor in life.

I worked with other couples who didn't experience violence but were trapped in the same dynamic. Sibling rivalry, a competition for parental attention, is commonly recognised, but many spouses have rivalries also. They compete with each other for status and influence. Talking about who should have more status or influence is a very difficult conversation, which the 'turn towards' principle can make less charged or unnecessary. The world is a tough place and there is an abundance of people to compete with. There is no need to add our own family to that list.

The principles of solving solvable problems and overcoming unsolvable problems were really useful for me. Claudia and I talk well together, and we work away at arguments until we find a solution. I am probably a bit better than Claudia in this regard; she can get quite alarmed when we have these temporary arguments, and I'm the one who reminds both of us that the emotion will pass. But Claudia is better at the intractable issues. I can be a bit of an idealist, and sometimes the abiding flaws in Claudia and myself, and the consequent unsolvable problems and limitations in our relationship trouble me. Claudia's acceptance of these issues, and of my flawed self, calms me and helps me reciprocate. At both the personal and the public level, many disagreements which become fraught are actually about relationships and allegiances rather than the apparent topic.

THE FOUR HORSEMEN OF THE CONVERSATION APOCALYPSE

Four particularly damaging behaviours in a relationship are criticism, contempt, defensiveness and stonewalling.

Criticism is attacking someone's personality or character rather than complaining about their behaviour. Contempt is a more significant form of criticism, as it diminishes the other person in relation to yourself. It attacks their worthiness.[10] Some actions are wrong, and some people are bad, and in these situations, contempt is warranted. Some people are routinely contemptuous of others who do not deserve it. The recipients of persistent unwarranted contempt may eventually come to believe that it is justified. Defensiveness is shifting responsibility. It is the fundamental attribution error applied to ourselves – something bad happened, but it must have been circumstance rather than our own intent or failure. Stonewalling is withdrawal from the conversation. It happens when someone has become *gatvol* and is also called the silent treatment or passive aggression.

In animal and human societies with ritualised challenge, like sport or play-fighting, and when mercy is a feature of this conflict

---

[10] Gottman says that contempt alone is a strong predictor of divorce.

(the winner stops the fight when the loser gives up), individuals can respond to threat submissively, aggressively or assertively. Where there are not rituals of conflict and no mercy – for example, the fights to the death that happen between male lions, and in rare situations between human beings – there is no point in submission. Protagonists have their backs to the wall. But most human conflict is ritualised and has rules. Submission can make sense.

Submissive behaviour before or during a fight will be interpreted as acceptance of subordinate lower status. As many fights are about status and its associated privileges, when one protagonist submits, there is no need for either protagonist to risk continuing. The opposite reaction to submission is aggression, where a protagonist indicates willingness or eagerness to escalate the conflict, hopefully with the effect of persuading the opposing party to submit without conflict. The third response, assertiveness, indicates a willingness to engage.

In sport, different athletes can respond aggressively or submissively to different circumstances. These attitudes are deeply associated with body language. We can all picture an aggressive posture and a submissive posture. This body language is so universal we can use it with other species. When I studied baboons in the Drakensberg mountains in the 1990s, I used submissive body language to calm aggressive males when they felt I had infringed some social rule. The problem for athletes is that submissive body language weakens the core and aggressive body language tensions the wrists and makes the body upright, and so each interferes with skill execution. Only assertive body language allows our bodies to operate optimally.

Submission and aggression probably affect our thinking patterns also. Submission makes us excessively agreeable, and aggression makes us narrow minded and disinclined to change our minds. In conversation, the combination of an aggressive and a submissive protagonist can deliver a swift but poor quality agreement, and two aggressive protagonists are unlikely to make progress towards agreement. Submissive talking is safe in that it doesn't provoke open conflict, and aggressive talking is effective in that conclusions can sometimes be reached rapidly. But no conversations are safe without being effective, and no conversations are effective without being safe. We need to talk assertively and encourage the person to whom we are talking to do the same. When conversations have become unsafe for either or both protagonists, we need to recover them.

MAKE IT SAFE

The VitalSmarts team say that we recover unsafe conversations through apology, contrast, commitment and perspective.

Apology

Apologies have a compassion element and a responsibility element. Amongst black South Africans, the high compassion, no responsibility apology is used widely. If you see somebody incur a misfortune in which you played no part, it is still polite to say sorry. This apology isn't used as frequently in Western conversation, but we do use it sometimes, for example when we say to someone who is bereaved, 'I am very sorry to hear of your loss.' It is an apology with high compassion and without responsibility or involvement.

At the lower end of the responsibility continuum is the apology where you acknowledge the effect that your innocent action had on somebody else. In this apology, there is an acceptance of involvement, but not of responsibility. A use of this apology would happen in crowded public transport if you were bumped into and knocked into someone else. You would apologise to the person you had hit without acknowledging responsibility.

Sometimes with this kind of apology, there is an implication that the harm was caused by the other party's sensitivity rather than your own action. It is possible to apologise without acknowledging responsibility, if, as in the example mentioned above, the purpose of the apology should be to express compassion. When an apology is used to acknowledge harm, but shifts responsibility for the harm from the speaker to the person that was harmed, and also fails to express compassion, it actually has neither component necessary to qualify as a genuine apology. The 'I apologise if anybody took offence' apology is better categorised as an accusation.

Other apologies emphasise what the protagonist is *not* responsible for rather than what they *are* responsible for. If I stepped on your toe and said, 'I am sorry I stepped on your toe, but I was in a hurry and there was a crowd and I didn't see you,' it is quite a different apology from, 'I am sorry I stepped on your toe. I didn't mean to do it, but I realise I was a little clumsy.' These apologies acknowledge that your action caused the harm, but claim the intention was innocent.

Further up the continuum still is the apology that acknowledges action as well as mistaken intent. If you had stepped on my toe accidentally and I lost my temper and reciprocated, I would have to say something along the lines of, 'I am sorry I stepped on your toe and hurt you. I was angry because I thought you had stepped on my toe deliberately and I retaliated. I was mistaken in my assumption and wrong in my actions.' Acknowledging mistaken intent and wrong action is a full apology.

Often we are reluctant to apologise because we fear that it will be held as an acknowledgement of guilt. But compassion is not connected to responsibility. And an accurate and precise acknowledgement of responsibility – not apologising for too much, but not apologising for too little, either – can help quieten accusations and hurt feelings. It is a very effective way back into a conversation, and often the sooner it is deployed the less there is to apologise for.

Contrast

The contrast recovery does not have to include regret or compassion. The purpose is to contrast your intention with the impact of your actions on the other person.

The best application of the contrast is to establish the difference between what somebody thought you said (or how they interpreted what you said), and what you actually said (or what you actually meant). In this case, because you have clarified that while what you were perceived to have said would have caused offence, what you actually said should not have caused offence, the culpability for harm is dissolved by the clarification and there is no need for an apology. This contrast can also be used to distinguish between our actions and our intent. In 2007, I worked with a golfer who played in the Open Championship. He missed the cut, so I had two days to follow Tiger Woods around. On one hole, Woods hit a wayward approach shot which bounced off a woman's head. It sounded like a cricket shot. The woman fell to the ground. When Woods arrived he placed his hand on her shoulder and said in a stilted way, 'I didn't mean to hit you.' He was contrasting what had happened with what he had wanted to happen. It would have been more effective had he also acknowledged the impact on the woman. When somebody has been hurt through your actions but without your intent it is legitimate and important to use contrast. Making a good contrast allows us to express compassion without necessarily accepting responsibility, which would have allowed Tiger Woods to have come across as more human in the above interaction.

Commitment

The commitment route back into a conversation is to say something along the lines of, 'We don't seem to be making progress towards agreement right now. But I am committed to keep trying until we do.' Commitment establishes a general mutual purpose – to have a relationship and a method of communication that transcends the current dispute. The spouse who threatens to 'pack my bags' during an argument and the negotiator who threatens to walk away from the table are hoping that their threat will affect the balance of power and make a settlement that is favourable to them more likely. But this sacrifices the general purpose and intensifies the stakes of the conversation about the particular dispute. It assumes that the current dispute is also the final one, so there is no harm in damaging the potential for amicable resolution. The idea of commitment is that it facilitates a settlement that is particularly favourable by virtue of being generally fair, rather than being favourable to one party, or only a specific situation.

Perspective

The fourth route back into a conversation is perspective. While the purpose of contrast is to explain that a criticism or otherwise hurtful statement was not meant, perspective is meant to establish that it is not all-important. Perspective aims to clarify intent/culpability, frequency and significance. This concept will be dealt with at more length in the next chapter on Rule 6: Use resilience.

Gottman mentions a more fundamental recovery technique. He calls it a 'bid'. He says that when people argue, there is the opportunity for one of the parties to make a bid. This is a verbal or non-verbal gesture that indicates regret for the argument and hope that closeness and agreement can be restored. In parties that know each other well, bids can be established unique gestures. During an argument, one of the couple could reach out and gently touch the other in a particular way, or smile, or shrug. When the meaning of these gestures is understood by both parties, it can restore safety to the conversation even when nothing has explicitly been said or resolved. Gottman says that bids can become automatic, so they can be deployed easily and naturally. He also says that if a bid is made, but rejected, the implications for the relationship are severe.

When there is less intimacy or prior knowledge between parties there is not the potential for established or idiosyncratic bids, but the offer can still be made. Natural historian and broadcaster David Attenborough told a story of his party meeting a group of Papua New Guinean villagers on an expedition. There was a moment of tension between the two groups, but he caught a man's eye and flicked his head upwards slightly in a gesture of acknowledgement. The gesture was returned – the bid had been accepted.

Monty Python have a theory about the brontosaurus which is that it is thin at one end, much thicker in the middle, and thin at the other end. Conversation failures can have this pattern too – an initial phase during which emotions rise gradually, then a sudden dramatic escalation of emotions, which is followed by a long period as the consequences play out over time. When I was a university student in the early 1990s, I had a part-time job as a scuba-diving instructor. The other trainers and I felt that many accidents happened after a gradual progression of stressors led to a sudden escalation and panic. We were very interested in training people to detect and reverse the initial slow bit. Often these problems were quite easy to solve – the skill was in the detection. But once the escalation had begun, it was very difficult to stop. It is useful to learn not only to detect threats to your own emotional safety, but also to detect signs that the person you are talking to may be feeling protective of theirs. If you have the skill to do this early enough, often the solution is simple by comparison.

Key principles:

Maintain mutual respect and mutual purpose

Use slow thinking and talking to respond to what your fast thinking has judged to be disrespect

If a conversation gets too emotional, take a 20-minute time-out

Contain your and the other person's emotion

Avoid the four horsemen: criticism, contempt, defensiveness and stonewalling

Recover conversations with apology, contrast, commitment and perspective

In the early 2000s, I worked for a wellness company that provided healthy lifestyle counselling over the telephone. One of our telephone counsellors was compassionate and effective when she spoke to clients, but, relative to her peers, took a long time on each call, and so completed the fewest calls. I tried to help her line manager address this issue during a performance review.

Andile: Janet, we have been looking at your call records. You have the lowest number of calls out of all the counsellors.

Janet: Oh. Nobody told me that.

Tim: That's why we are telling you now.

Janet: I work very hard at my job.

[Janet immediately defends her competence and self-worth. This is a warning sign that Andile and I have not done a good enough job of establishing safety in the conversation before making a criticism. Mutual purpose could have been an agreement that we both want a profitable company with skilled, satisfied employees. Mutual respect would be that we value Janet as a person, for her role on the team and for the care that she takes with her clients.]

Andile: I know you do, Janet. I'm not saying you don't. But you don't make enough calls.

Janet: So what are you saying? I'm not good enough at my job?

Tim: Well . . . there are some things that you need to change. We are running a business.

[This is an opportunity for me to make a contrasting statement – that it is not my intention to say Janet is not good at her job, but that it is fair that anyone should accept feedback and try to improve where possible. I do not take this opportunity.]

Janet: I can't afford to lose this job. I just cannot afford to lose this job.

[Janet is now feeling highly emotional. The conversation we wanted to have was a detailed outline of call procedures. With this level of emotion, this conversation is no longer possible. I need to start having another conversation – about how to make this conversation safe again. But I fail to do so.]

Tim: Janet, you're not definitely going to lose your job. But we need you to make more calls.

[I fail to contain Janet's emotion and make an inadequate attempt at perspective. Committing to resolving Janet's insecurity and, over a longer time span, her call rates, would have been a better route back into this conversation.]

Janet: I can't believe you are saying this to me. You don't understand how hard I work. You don't know how much I care about the people I talk to. Why do you think I spend so long on the phone with them? [Rolls her eyes.] You people in management!

[Janet is now criticising us for not understanding her, and expressing contempt.]

At this point the conversation broke down. Janet was offended and anxious and Andile and I did not feel like we had got our message across. Over the next few days and weeks we managed to calm Janet's anger and anxiety, but this was mainly by sweeping the issue under the carpet. Her low call rates, and the new procedures which may have allowed her to increase them, went unaddressed.

RULE 6: USE RESILIENCE

When my friend Paulo was young, he dreamed of succeeding as a professional athlete. He lived in a small town and his parents did not have the time or money to pay much attention to his dreams. For him, getting to practice meant rushing home after school to switch his school bag to his sports bag and then rushing to catch the bus. If school ended late, he would have to cut across the playground and jump over the fence, and if it ended on time he would still have to run but would be able to leave via the school gate. Once he had switched bags, he would have to run up his street to catch the bus, and as he ran his friends would call to him, 'Paulo! Where are you going? Stay and play with us!' But he would pound his feet after the bus, saying to himself, 'I have to! I have to!' Paulo became a successful professional athlete, and when he goes back to his home town his friends talk about how well he has done, and how they failed in their efforts to persuade him to skip practice. They are proud of Paulo for having overcome disadvantaged circumstances.

In 2001, conflict in the Congo raised the possibility that the militaries of other African countries would be called to operate as peacekeepers. This created a scenario for the younger generation of South African servicemen and women of being exposed to hostile fire for the first time. One of the helicopter squadrons of the South African Air Force chose to run an escape and evasion camp at Hells Gate, the military base up the east coast of South Africa, and they asked me to assist with the training. My co-presenter was an ex-special forces soldier. I had worked with him before and, eventually, when he came to trust me, he told me the story of the bullet scars he had in his ankle and elbow.

During the Cold War, when Western powers covertly supported apartheid South Africa because they feared communist expansion into Africa, South African special forces would penetrate deep into other countries to report on military operations. These were deniable operations, meaning that if the soldiers got caught, the South African government would refuse to help them or even acknowledge their presence in the country.

On one mission, the soldier and his partner had set up a close observation point near a military training camp in another country. They had a small radio antenna set up in a clump of grass which was linked with a wire back to their hiding place. One day a patrol was walking around the camp and one of the soldiers was idly swinging a stick through the grass. He accidentally struck the antenna and was alerted to its presence. He picked it up, realised what it was and started pulling the wire, which betrayed the soldiers' hiding place. The patrol opened up on the two soldiers with AK47 fire. As they ran away, the soldier took one bullet through the ankle and another through the elbow, and his radio was shot off his hip. Without the radio, they had no chance of being evacuated, so he turned around and ran back into the fire to retrieve it. As he ran away again, he unobtrusively dropped a phosphorous grenade and the pursuers ran into the explosion, which stopped their chase.

The soldier and his partner had got away, but he had two bullet wounds and they discovered that the radio was irreparably damaged. Their only chance of survival was to trek through the night in the remote chance of meeting another two operatives who had been inserted into the country 30 kilometres away and who had not been compromised. The soldier said that his partner, who was uninjured, just wanted to give up and die. But he forced his partner to march through the night and they found the other two who were able to radio for a helicopter extraction. When I asked the soldier what had kept him going he said to me, 'You *have* to!'

This isn't an explanation of what made him different from his partner – or most of us. But it is exactly the same as the phrase that my friend Paulo used.

The soldier and I were teaching the aircrew how to cope psychologically with escape and evasion, and the soldier made many interesting points. One of them was that if you are captured, even if you are wounded and tortured, no matter how long and badly you are tortured for, at some point your interrogators will get tired and leave the room. The soldier told us, 'That is your opportunity to relax. You must take it.' I was wondering who would have the presence of mind to remember to relax in those circumstances, but I have used the advice myself in less extreme but still stressful situations.

Eighteen years later, I still don't know what makes some people as resilient as the soldier, or the young Paulo. People like this are like diamonds – they are made better under pressure. But not everybody survives extreme adversity. It is not always true that what does not kill you makes you stronger. Other possibilities are to be scarred or injured. While stories like Paulo's are often what we imagine when we think of resilience, exposing people to extreme pressure is not the strategy I would recommend as a way of building toughness.

A more common way to build resilience is through experiencing success and then learning optimism by seeing that success is repeatable and generalisable.

Rule 6 is an examination of the skills we can develop and the processes we can use to become more resilient. Resilience is a relevant chapter in a book about talking because we need to use it while we are talking. Disagreement is stressful, and the better we can contain our and others' emotions, the more likely we are to have a successful conversation. Also, even if the conversation itself is not stressful, often we talk to other people about what distresses us and what we might want them to change. If we are more resilient, these conversations will be less weighty and more likely to succeed.

In Joseph Heller's novel *Catch 22,* the main character, Yossarian, is a US Air Force flight crew on a bomber flying operations during the Second World War. In one scene Yossarian watches his friend Orr fiddle interminably with the components of a faucet. Yossarian is already distressed by the missions that he has to fly, but becomes so frustrated by Orr's patience and preoccupation with detail that he contemplates murdering him with a hunting knife. Yossarian's generally depleted resilience makes the particular situation more difficult to cope with than it would otherwise be. He is so agitated, that the task of getting Orr to stop irritating him seems overwhelming, and so he contemplates murdering Orr rather than talking to him. This is one scenario where resilience benefits talking – we can let minor or insignificant irritations pass and save our conversations for things that really matter. Later in the story, Yossarian eventually realises that he has been so distracted that he has missed an important but subtle signal that Orr had been trying to communicate. In difficult conversations, resilience can help us keep access to the skills and sensitivity that are more necessary but also more difficult to deploy than they are in less charged situations, and it is only when Yossarian becomes resilient that he is able to receive Orr's message.

In some ways, Rule 6 is a simple companion to Rule 5. Safety is about how to keep a conversation safe and resilience is about how to keep yourself safe. But in other ways, resilience is a broader issue.

Some people are drawn to the idea that we can choose to be resilient or make ourselves resilient. At the music festival Glastonbury in 2019, the singer Lizzo took this popular position on resilience when she told the crowd:

> I want you to know that I love you very much and I'm very proud of you. And I want you to know that if you can love me, you can love your goddamn self. I want you to go home tonight and look in the mirror and say, 'I love you, you are beautiful, and you can do anything!'

The popular position conflates self-confidence and self-esteem with resilience. Self-confidence is a generalised belief in one's probable success in a range of fields including health, finance, career, family, sport, social and romance. Self-esteem is a belief in one's right to acceptance, love, respect and influence. The popular position believes that both are affected by individual choice and self-directed action; that we make ourselves successful.

Resilience is also a political issue. We can use skills to become more resilient and cope with more pressure. But how should we split our energies between being resilient in a stressful world and trying or asking to change that stressful world? If we see somebody struggling with pressure, should we expect them to cope with that pressure, or should we try to change their circumstances? This debate has acquired a terminology: triggers, snowflakes and trolls. If triggers are situations that distress us, and snowflakes are people who are distressed, do we need fewer triggers or fewer snowflakes? Are trolls using free speech to trigger and expose snowflakes for their individual limitations, or are they using hate speech to hurt people?

It is easier to be resilient about one challenge when other challenges like financial stress or systemic disadvantage have not left you close to your emotional limit. It is also easier to be resilient when social, financial and reputational safety nets have already lowered the costs of risk and failure. When we are required to operate at the upper end of how resilient human beings can be, the solution is not only an individual responsibility.

One component of resilience is accuracy. We need to accurately assess the level of threat or opportunity that we are facing, as well as the level of skills and resources that we can bring to bear in response. When we feel that the challenge and resources balance each other, we feel that we can cope, we feel resilient. When we feel over-resourced for a challenge, we can feel bored or complacent, and when we feel under-resourced, we feel anxious or afraid. Resilience is not about dismissing genuine threats. This is sometimes considered to be a form of toughness, but actually it leaves us unprepared for those challenges which cannot just be wished away. Resilience is also not about excessively anticipating trouble, which is sometimes considered a form of prudence or preparedness, because this error will leave us depleted and unprepared for the real challenges which will come. Resilience is not the absence or abundance of negative emotion, but accurate quantity and quality of emotion.

When one of my sons was five, I took him to a swimming pool with four friends, three of whom were triplets and operated as a sometimes domineering group. The four friends had learnt to swim, but my son had not. They jumped in and left my son on the side. When they realised he hadn't followed, they turned around to mock him for not being able to swim. My son was immediately incensed. Looking down at them from the pool deck, he eviscerated each of the boys in turn with an articulate stream of threats and insults. As his father I thought, 'This boy is not going to have a problem with being bullied.' My son had responded to a challenge with aggression. But is this resilience?

A few months ago, I spent an evening with Thierry Henry. Thierry is statistically one of the greatest footballers of the last 20 years, and if he did occasionally mention this fact during the evening, he did not bother to also assert that he was considered one of the most creative, elegant and charismatic footballers of his generation as well. The conversation turned to tactics, and Thierry suddenly asked me, 'So if I'm striker, and you are centre half, and I pull to the left, what do you do?' The correct answer, I know now, is to call for my fullback to drop back and cover, but I was stuck and said, 'I would move wide to cover you.' Thierry scoffed. 'You? You would go 1v1 with me? With my speed?' I was a tiny bit hurt. I know obviously that Thierry is faster than the *real* me, but the only version of me that would ever be playing football against Thierry Henry would be the imaginary me. If I could imagine myself into a professional football match, why couldn't I also imagine myself a few extra yards of pace? How could Thierry assume that he is so fast that he would also be faster than my imaginary self? Thierry was showing tremendous self-confidence. But is this resilience?

An abundance of aggression or confidence are commonly considered to be forms of resilience. But a more detailed examination shows that resilience is about accuracy rather than excess.

There are two parts to resilience. First, the ability to gauge the level of threat, and second, the ability to respond to it effectively and appropriately.

PART 1. GAUGING THREATS

The ability to accurately gauge and then appropriately measure a response to threats involves three concepts. These are: probability – how likely something is to happen; degree – how much of a big deal that occurrence would be; and intent – whether someone is trying to make it happen. Most of the time these are System 1 calculations. But sometimes we calculate incorrectly and so it is useful to use System 2 to improve the reliability and accuracy of our responses.

When I was a scuba-diving instructor in the early 1990s, we would get a new intake of students every month. One month, two of the students were men in their sixties. They were friends, Brian and Angelo. I was 21. For some reason, Angelo took it upon himself to wind me up, constantly questioning my competence and intentions as an instructor. He was relentless, and I got angrier and angrier. Eventually I was struggling to resist the urge to punch my own customer in the face. Fortunately, during one exchange Brian saw my suppressed fury. He started to laugh and said to me, 'Don't rise to him.' Brian's comment was very helpful to me, and I have used it many times since. By the end of the course Angelo and I were good friends, even though he hadn't stopped teasing me.

Brian had helped me make a more accurate judgement of probability, degree and intent. What was the probability that Angelo's behaviour would harm me in some way? How much would it affect me? Was he intending to produce the negative emotions that I was experiencing? My initial System 1 calculation to these questions was: high probability that his insubordination would hurt my instructor status, a high degree of problem if he did, and high intent, in that he meant to do it. But when Brian laughed about the situation, I shifted perspective. Maybe it was low probability that Angelo's teasing would make anyone think less of me, low degree of personal cost if this one course went less than perfectly, and low intent, in that he was actually trying to tease me rather than hurt me. Having this perspective made it easier to follow Brian's advice, 'Don't rise to him.' When Angelo got a muted or no verbal response from me, it gave him less to work with.

There is a classic cognitive behavioural therapy technique called ABC – adversity, belief, consequence. The idea is that when we face an adversity, it is our beliefs about that adversity that determine the emotional consequence. While we often process these beliefs automatically, sometimes the beliefs are incorrect, leading to unnecessary or inaccurate emotional consequences. Each negative emotion has a belief that underpins it. Fear and anxiety are linked to the belief that we face a future threat. Sadness is linked to a belief that we have lost something. Embarrassment and shame are linked to the belief that we are being unfavourably compared to someone else. Anger is linked to the belief that our rights or status are being threatened in some way. Guilt is linked to the belief that we have violated someone else's rights or status.

Even when I had processed Brian's comment, I had still felt some annoyance and anxiety about Angelo's teasing. I think this is fair enough – I did have to work hard as a 21-year-old instructor to keep the respect of the group, and Angelo was making this more difficult for me. So, the quality of emotion may have been correct. What Brian's comment helped me with was the quantity of emotion. Emotions can only be accurate if you have the right emotion in the right amount. Here, annoyance and anxiety were appropriate, but only in such small amounts that they could be laughed off. This is the objective of teasing, to deliver a negative stimulus in a tolerable quantity. Teasing becomes bullying as the quantity of the stimulus gets closer to or crosses the limit of each individual's ability to cope. The quality of the stimulus matters also, as we have lower thresholds for nastier stimuli. Brian helped me be resilient by improving my judgement about the quality and quantity of the personal threat that I faced.

The resilience debate becomes political when people argue publicly about the quality and quantity of threat that individuals and groups do, and should, face. Is any given case a small deal (i.e. low quality and low quantity of threat), in which case the individual or group should be able to cope without support? Or is it a big deal (i.e. high quality and high quantity of threat), in which case they deserve our support?

TRIGGERS, TROLLS AND SNOWFLAKES

One of the arenas where this debate plays out is on university and college campuses in the USA. In 2015 at Yale, some students were distressed at Halloween because other students were wearing costumes that mimicked traditional dress from other cultures. Erika Christakis, who was the associate master of a Yale college, wrote an email to students expressing a position: Christakis argued for more freedom of choice, and less sensitivity, writing:

> Is there no room anymore for a child or young person to be a little bit obnoxious . . . a little bit inappropriate or provocative or, yes, offensive? . . . Have we lost faith in young people's capacity . . . to exercise self-censure, through social norming, and also in your capacity to ignore or reject things that trouble you?[11]

This email caused a strong negative reaction. Some students felt that this was not a situation that they should have to cope with individually. They felt that Erika Christakis was wrong and that it was the college's responsibility to protect them from this situation. Christakis's husband, Nicholas Christakis, was also associate master of the same college. He held a meeting to discuss his wife's email with a group of students. In the video, which is on YouTube, there is a charged atmosphere and, while everybody is civil, some students are in tears. Erika Christakis ended up leaving Yale as a consequence and the

---

[11] Published in thefire.org on October 30 2015 (https://www.thefire.org/email-from-erika-christakis-dressing-yourselves-email-to-silliman-college-yale-students-on-halloween-costumes/)

broader disagreement became emblematic of the tension between resilience and safety, and rights and freedoms.

If a student wears a Halloween costume appropriating or stereotyping dress from another culture, is this a trigger? Is the student wearing the costume a troll? If somebody is offended by the costume, is this person a snowflake? Was Erika Christakis standing up for resilience, or was she standing up for trolls? How would we know?

To start with a simpler example, when I got so upset after Claudia criticised me for running over the squirrel, in retrospect, I was probably being a bit of a snowflake. People are snowflakes when they meet two conditions. First, they can't contain their emotion, and second, the emotion that they do feel is not justified. If, when Claudia had criticised me, I had been angry but calm, that is not enough to be a snowflake. I would just be mistaken. If I had said something like, 'I don't think it's fair for you to criticise me,' but stayed calm enough to listen to Claudia's point of view and keep the conversation safe (Rule 5), I would have given her the opportunity to say something like, 'I didn't mean to criticise you or your driving. You couldn't have known what the squirrel would do. I exclaimed because I got a shock and because I regretted that your choice turned out to be the wrong one.' My composure would have kept the conversation safe. Measured dialogue is not snowflake behaviour.

On the other hand, had my anger been accurate and justified, even if I hadn't managed to contain it, it would not have been snowflake behaviour. If, for example, Claudia had said something like, 'You shouldn't have swerved! Deliberately running over that squirrel is a typical example of your prodigious cruelty and incompetence,' *that* would have constituted unfair criticism, violating my right to fair treatment and threatening my status, and getting angry would have been an accurate and fair response. Justified or righteous anger is not snowflake behaviour. It is only when we are unwilling or unable to contain negative emotions that are qualitatively or quantitatively inaccurate that we are being snowflakes. Being emotionally mistaken and being uncontained are individually both such common experiences that were we to label people who experienced either independently as snowflakes, the insult would become so common as to lose its impact.

We can also define trolls. It is not trolling to deliberately pressurise or challenge someone. This could be a motivational technique, or it could be controlled teasing. It is also not trolling to flood someone with emotion. When we are distressed, sometimes we pass it on without intending to. But to deliberately try to flood someone is trolling. Snowflakes lack resilience and trolls overload resilience.

The Yale students who contained their emotion, regardless of whether it was justified or not, cannot be accused of being snowflakes. They were just expressing a philosophical or moral point of view. But some students were flooded with emotion that they could not contain and so met the first condition. Did they also meet the second, that this emotion was qualitatively or quantitatively inaccurate? Emotions can be qualitatively evaluated by checking the accuracy of their underlying beliefs. For anger, was a right or status violated? For sadness, was there loss? For anxiety, is there threat? For embarrassment, is there unfavourable comparison? For guilt, is there violation of another's rights?

Emotions can be quantitatively evaluated by determining the scale of the violation, loss, threat, or unfavourable comparison. Scale is determined by asking three questions:

Was the impact intended? Is it frequent? Is it significant?

High intent, highly frequent and highly significant violations, losses, threats or unfavourable comparisons are more important than those which are not, and so would justify a higher quantity of emotion. For example, had Claudia intended to criticise me, or had Erika Christakis intended to upset the students, this would be more of a big deal than if they hadn't. If Claudia frequently criticised me, or Christakis frequently upset students, this would be more of a big deal that if they didn't. And if Claudia's criticism was significant, if she was criticising my character or competence, it would be more of a big deal than if she was criticising my driving or my decision. This is relevant in how the students responded to Christakis.

Intent, frequency and significance – the three determinants of scale or quantity of emotion – can be assessed systematically. Legal culpability is assessed by asking to what extent an outcome was foreseen, desired and actioned/caused. This checklist works quite well for intent also. If Claudia had anticipated that her remark would upset me, desired it to upset me, and actually said the words that upset me, the scale of her intent would be high. If she had not foreseen, desired and caused my emotion, the scale of her intent would be less. But the emotional significance of intent is not only determined by the degree of intent. The importance of that intent matters also.

Claudia is a very important person to me, so her intent matters. This is possibly why I over-interpret her intent sometimes, because I am quite dependent on it. On the other hand, the intent of a passer-by who I will not see again should matter less to me. When I became upset about Claudia's comment, I was incorrect because I saw intent where there was none. On the other hand, one day when I became very angry about a driver who was tailgating me, this emotion was inaccurate because his intent was not important. What mattered was my safety, which I could have managed by pulling over to the side of the road and letting him past, rather than attempting to manage his intent by getting out of the car and confronting him.

Frequency is assessed by choosing an appropriate sample time period. Often, we think that things are more frequent than they are, because we are recalling only the recent past. Although at the moment of my anger Claudia had criticised my driving exactly once in the last 60 seconds, which is quite a high rate, if I considered how often this happened in a month, or a year or over the duration of our relationship, I would have got a more accurate idea of frequency.

Significance is determined by evaluating the impact on my general wellbeing. Protecting wellbeing is fundamental to resilience, so it warrants some examination.

PROTECTING YOUR WELLBEING

Martin Seligman is a professor of psychology at the University of Pennsylvania. He was a founding influence in the field of positive psychology, which examines the constituents of a good life. Seligman interviewed thousands of people from all over the world, asking them to describe their lives and evaluate their general life satisfaction. He found that people who reported high levels of life satisfaction described their lives as having high levels of positive emotion, engagement, relationships, meaning and accomplishment. Seligman called this PERMA.

Psychologist Barbara Fredrickson argues that understanding ten key positive emotions (amusement, awe, interest, inspiration, joy, pride, hope, gratitude, serenity and love) gives a deeper appreciation of wellbeing than using the concept of 'happiness'. It's a nice exercise to take some time to think about your experience of each of them. When did you last feel each of them? When do you anticipate next experiencing this emotion? Where do you experience it, and what are you doing when you feel it? We are inclined to give more time and attention to negative emotion than we do to positive emotion, but when I run resilience workshops, it strikes me that there is often humour and laughter as we discuss failure and frustration, but these positive emotions are discussed directly and solemnly. When we do take the time, we are serious about positivity.

Engagement is experienced when you are involved in something that you are good at. We can be engaged in conversations, skills, experiences, music, art, reading, dance, sport, exercise and in relationships. When we are engaged, we are less aware of time or outside distractions, motivated by the experience rather than the outcome, and focused on the activity rather than ourselves.

Relationships were described in Rule 5. Relationships contribute to our wellbeing if they meet John Gottman's criteria outlined previously, where he describes good relationships as involving knowing each other, admiring each other, turning towards each other, influencing each other, solving solvable problems, overcoming unsolvable problems, and creating meaning. More relationships with more of these qualities improve our wellbeing. Seligman was awarded a contract with the US Army to teach resilience skills. A few years ago, I went to Philadelphia to sit in on one of the courses. He told me that as part of the course he had administered a questionnaire to the members of the US Army. A very small percentage of those people died from suicide the following year. Because of the scale of the project, inadvertently, Seligman had ended up gaining a unique insight into people at risk of suicide. He said that it was 'low meaning' and 'low accomplishment' that were the dangers.

We obtain a sense of meaning from belonging to something larger or more important than ourselves – a family, a community, a religion, a nation, a political movement, a set of values, or even a sports team. We also obtain meaning from confirming an aspect of our own identities. If I have an identity as someone who works hard, it is meaningful for me to work hard, if I see myself as someone kind, or strong, I obtain meaning by behaving consistently with that identity.

When I was in private practice working with children who struggled to concentrate in the classroom, often I would get sent boys who had been labelled as naughty. This became a problem when the boys absorbed naughtiness as part of their own identities, because it then became meaningful for them to be naughty. The meaningfulness of manifesting identity can help explain why some people are motivated to behave in ways that are cruel or antisocial. Once an identity has been conferred, even if this is a negative identity, there is a private reward for confirming it.

When we are appreciated, and come to see ourselves as good, it is meaningful for us to help others. When I was working mainly with children, I never had to answer any existential questions of myself at the end of the day because I felt that as long as I had slightly helped at least one of them, my day had been worthwhile. Seligman's insight into how important meaning is to our wellbeing explains some of the passion and determination with which we pursue meaning through different interpretations of belonging, confirming and helping.

When I was a young sports psychologist, the first person I knew who broke through to the highest level of competition was a surfer who I had worked with since he was 13. When he was 19, he qualified for the World Championship tour, which was only open to the top 44 surfers in the world. Just after he had made it, he came to see me, and we sat and just stared at each other in silence for a while. Eventually I said to him, 'So dreams do come true.' But I was wrong. This accomplishment was not to bring him lasting happiness. The next year he lost his place on the tour, and he gave up competitive surfing soon after.

I have had the experience of sitting with athletes who have won the biggest trophies on the biggest stages and who are not fulfilled by this success. But this is a testament to the complexity of achievement, not its lack of importance. We gain a sense of accomplishment from achieving something challenging through effort. It is more rewarding to walk to the top of a large hill than a small one, but we need a constant diet of accomplishment. In some ways, the difficulty that the high achieving athletes found was that their single massive accomplishment caused them to overlook the constant smaller daily or weekly accomplishments that are necessary for our wellbeing.

'WHY ARE YOU SO UPSET?'

To return to the Yale Halloween confrontation between Erika Christakis and her students, was Christakis being a troll? Did she mean to cause uncontainable levels of emotional distress to the students? And if she did not mean it, does this mean that the distressed students were snowflakes? Some students were flooded with emotion. But were they wrong to be upset? The students were upset by what they considered to be cultural appropriation and also by what they considered to be an authority figure's support for that appropriation. Arguing that the students were wrong to feel any degree of sadness or anger would require demonstrating that there is no loss or violation attached to cultural appropriation, or that there was no inappropriate institutional support for cultural appropriation. Arguing that the students experienced an excessive amount of emotion would require showing that they had overestimated the intent, frequency or significance of appropriation.

When I was a young boy in the 1970s, I was delighted to receive a representation of a Native American costume for my sixth birthday. I whooped around the garden in a feathered headdress waving a rubber tomahawk. I now know that Native Americans prefer people not to casually wear feathered headdresses. But at the time my intention was not to be disrespectful and I have not worn the costume since. So, in my case of 1970s appropriation, intent and frequency were low. But what if I was an adult instead of a child and had worn the costume in spite of a request not to? What if I or someone from a similarly privileged demographic wore the costume every Halloween? Were the students at Yale really overestimating intent and frequency?

Noticing that someone is flooded with emotion is easy. But judging them to be inappropriately flooded is harder. The problem is that somebody with an already high emotional load can be flooded by a small additional amount – the straw that broke the camel's back. We have all had the experience of being flooded by something which would be easily contained by someone different, or by ourselves in different circumstances. The fundamental attribution error biases us towards overestimating the role of circumstances in our own distress and overestimating the role of emotional fragility in other people's distress. We have to remind ourselves that when we see somebody who is uncontained, it does not automatically mean that they are generally unable to contain emotion or cannot usually contain emotion from this specific circumstance. This is where the saying of 'walking a mile in their shoes' comes from. Correctly judging someone to be experiencing uncontained emotion that is also of an inaccurate quality or quantity, and that they are thus a genuine snowflake, requires levels of perspective, evidence and deduction that are quite difficult to achieve. Being aware of the difficulty of this judgement should make us cautious about labelling distressed people snowflakes.

But it is true that often we do overestimate risk. Daniel Kahneman says that nothing is ever as important as it feels at the moment that we are thinking about it (because we are unaware in that moment of all the other important things that would create perspective).

This does mean that a significant element of resilience is correcting ourselves when we are unduly alarmed. When we go through the intent, frequency, significance assessment, the result is often that we are either experiencing the wrong emotion or the right emotion in the wrong amount. Making this correction makes talking easier because it means that some things do not need to be discussed at all, while others can be discussed less emotionally or with less reliance on achieving agreement because they are not as significant as they initially appeared. John Gottman says that many couples in successful long-term relationships are able to overcome some abiding problems just because they have realised that the problems, while unsolved and possibly intractable, are not that important.

PART 2. RESPONDING TO THREATS
Genuine danger or false alarm?

When I was a boy in the 1980s, I lived with my family in a small rural town called Empangeni on the east coast of South Africa. I had chickens in a coop at the bottom of the garden and it was one of my daily tasks to feed them. Sometimes I would procrastinate this task and I would have to go and feed them in the evening. I would then face a long walk through the dark garden back to the house. Sometimes I would become convinced that I was being stalked by a wolf. I would manage to banish the fear by reminding myself that there are no wolves in South Africa, but sometimes the fear would overcome me, and I would start to run. Running only magnified the fear – it seemed to make sense that if I were running, the wolf must be real.

When I ran from the wolf, I was confusing one kind of alarm for another. Sometimes we experience fear because our alarm system has accurately detected a genuine danger. This is a danger problem. Other times when we experience fear it is a false alarm. This is an alarm problem. It is important to be able to distinguish between the two because, while they feel similar while we are experiencing them, each problem has a solution that does not work with the other.

When I was at university, we had a project in a game reserve where we investigated the impact of the grazing habits of elephants and rhinoceroses on the vegetation of the reserve. Once, we were in a car and came upon a rhino sleeping in a dust pool with his back to us. For some reason I thought it would be funny to get out of the car and creep up behind the rhino to see how close I could get. At some point of my stalk the rhino heard me and, with a speed and agility that I had completely underestimated, sprung to its feet and turned to face me. The fleetness of foot that I had used to escape imaginary wolves was nothing compared to how fast I now found myself sprinting back to the car.

I had started by treating a danger problem as an alarm problem. I thought that if only I could quell my fear, everything would work out OK. Once the rhino turned to face me and I realised that this was in fact a danger problem, I responded correctly by running away. But with the wolf, there was no danger. I was responding incorrectly to an alarm problem. This error made things worse, because the running made me feel more afraid and also made the imaginary wolves feel more real.

Many people have minor rituals that they perform that do not actually influence an outcome, but because the outcome is rare or hard to measure, they do not get definitive feedback that the action has no effect and so become increasingly attached to it the more they repeat it. Someone who does not step on cracks in the pavement for fear of causing an aeroplane crash can persist in this belief because if they only rarely step on cracks, and aeroplanes only rarely crash, there is a strong connection between not stepping and not crashing.

Sometimes people ask if there is anything wrong with using ticks, rituals or compulsions to manage minor anxieties if they make the person feel better. One of the questions athletes get asked most often by fans is what superstitions and rituals they use to protect themselves from the anxiety of performance. But there is a problem with treating imaginary solutions and imaginary problems as if they are real. First, solving imaginary problems with imaginary solutions can take a lot of time. This is real time in your real life, and you don't have an infinite supply of it.

Second, when you face a real problem rather than an imaginary one, it cannot be solved by ticks and rituals, so it is not a good idea to become too practised at imaginary solutions.

Fear never solved the wolf problem (it just wasted my breath) but fearlessness in front of the rhino was not a good strategy either. Now that I am 47, I am no longer afraid of the dark: I have fixed that alarm problem. But I am still afraid of rhinos and will use this fear to keep myself inside the car the next time I come upon one.

The second part of resilience is responding to threat. The required scale of the response is determined by two factors: probability and impact. If something is high probability and high impact, like the danger from the rhinoceros was, it warrants full attention. If something is low probability but high impact, it warrants a lower level of attention. While an aeroplane crash is high impact, it is also low probability. This is why you do not take the time to get your affairs in order and say goodbye to all your friends and family every time you go to the airport. And if something is high probability, but lower impact, like catching a cold from a sneezing colleague, it warrants a different level of attention again – you're probably going to keep your distance but stop short of wearing a biohazard suit. And now that coronavirus has become a reality, we have to judge our response to a virus that is more contagious and more deadly than the flu – we have to gauge our response to an illness with an increased probability and impact.

When you have determined the level of response, this energy has to be invested in two directions. The first direction is avoiding the threat. The second is planning on how to mitigate it. So, to avoid catching the cold, you might take the effort to avoid your sneezing colleague and wash your hands when you get home. But you might also plan for the possibility of catching a cold by stocking up on tissues and remedies.

Some threats are physical, like car crashes, diabetes or lung cancer. These threats need to be managed by adapting our own behaviour. Other threats, like exam pressure or relationship problems, may also require a change in behaviour. Adapting behaviour requires motivation. Rule 2 (accept that agreement takes skill and effort) described my motivation theory: Motivation = Reward/Task x Confidence. Here we will discuss two other theories of motivation.

THE SIX SOURCES OF INFLUENCE

Some behavioural scientists say that it is the influence of circumstances rather than willpower that mainly drives behaviour.[12] VitalSmarts say that the best way to change is by designing the personal, social and environmental cues that influence our behaviour. Some influences affect our motivation, and other influences affect our ability to do something:

1. Personal influences on my motivation, like personal goals, or parts of my own identity that I want to live up to.
   - If I wanted to improve my study routine for an exam, I would influence my personal motivation by reminding myself why I wanted to do well in the exam, and how doing well is something that matters to me
2. Social influences on my motivation, like a peer group that share my interests, or a friend who holds me to account.
   - I would arrange to study with classmates, or tell a friend what topics I plan to study today, and arrange for them to check to see if I had succeeded

---

[12] Like the VitalSmarts team in their book *Change Anything*.

3. Environmental or situational influences on my motivation, like a gym that I enjoy going to or a sports league that I participate in.
   - Going to the library, or finding a place without distractions
4. Personal ability makes it more likely that I will get something done. When I know exactly what to do and how to do it, it makes it more likely that I will succeed.
   - I have a schedule for when I will study and a plan for what material I need to cover
5. Social ability refers to the resources that I can reach out to
   - I have a teacher or a study partner who can help me learn to do a task, or help me complete it
6. Situational or environmental ability means designing our worlds in a way to make our tasks easier.
   - A classic exercise trick is laying out your sports gear the night before you go running in the morning. When you wake up, it's so much easier to get going

These are the six sources of influence in which change is designed rather than demanded. If in order to be more resilient I need to manage the probability or impact of risk by managing someone else's behaviour rather than my own, using these six sources of influence is a good way to structure the conversation. My two oldest sons are drivers now and fit into the demographic of young male drivers who hold 1.5 per cent of the driving licences in the country but suffer 9 per cent of the serious and fatal driving accidents. This is a real risk and my worry about it warrants real attention. My most effective and resilient way of talking about it with them is to strategise together about how we could use the six sources to influence their and their peers' willingness and ability to drive safely. The temptation is just to communicate my anxiety, but this is an imaginary rather than a real solution to a real problem.

INSTANT INFLUENCE

Michael Pantalon offers a strategic approach to behaviour change in his book *Instant Influence*. He says that you should ask six questions. (1) Why might someone (not you specifically) want to make this change? (2) On a scale of one to ten, how motivated are you to make this change? (3) Why not *less*? (4) What would the benefits of this change be? (5) Why are these benefits important to you? (6) What's the first step to making this change?

This technique has some effective features. It counterintuitively asks someone why they are not *less* motivated to change – this encourages people to list the reasons why they *are* motivated. If I was to ask my son, 'Why are you only 4/10 motivated to drive carefully?' it would encourage him to answer along the lines of, 'Speed is fun, it's not that dangerous and my friends think I am a racing driver.' On the other hand, if I had asked him, 'Why are you 4/10 motivated and not 1/10 motivated?' he might answer, 'Because I don't want to die young, and I'm not as silly as other people who think they are invulnerable.'

Another effective feature of the technique is that it connects benefits to meaning. Outcomes like reduced insurance pay-outs, reduced risk and a longer life are all benefits, but they have more impact on behaviour when they are connected to things that would be meaningful to my son (like caring for himself and his friends, and freedom to pursue life goals in the future).

Reinhold Niebuhr is credited with creating the serenity prayer, which goes: 'God grant me the serenity to accept the things I cannot change, courage to change the things I can, and the wisdom to know the difference.'

Part of resilience is changing that which can be changed. Part of it is mitigating the impact of that which cannot be changed. We can get into intractable conflicts at home, at work or in the public sphere, we and our parents grow old, our children develop priorities other than our interests or face problems that we are not the arbiters of. In these cases, we need the serenity to accept the things that we cannot change. Part of the reason intractable problems seem so threatening is that they threaten our wellbeing by threatening our PERMA structures. We spend a lifetime building adequate sources of positive emotion, engagement, relationships, meaning and accomplishment, and change can threaten this supply. If I fall ill with a chronic disease, if I fail an exam or if my son crashes his car and I have to visit him in hospital with a broken leg, it all reduces an existing supply of PERMA. The serenity part of resilience is to accept that my current sources of PERMA are not my only potential sources. If a work project had brought me engagement and meaning, when it is over, where else can I find this? As my friends disperse and my children move out of home, how can I adapt my relationships or find new ones?

The quality of emotion is determined by the correctness of beliefs about the adversity – is this a loss, threat, comparison or violation? If it is, our consequential emotion of sadness, anxiety, embarrassment, anger or guilt is correct. But for the emotion to be accurate, it needs to have the right quantity also, and for this we need to determine intent, frequency and significance. Resilience is not about having less negative emotion; it is about having accurate emotion. Emotion is a spur to action, and when we face negative circumstances emotions motivate us to act in ways that are meant to change those circumstances. Insufficient emotion leaves us complacent and wastes genuine opportunities for change, and excess or incorrect emotion wastes time and effort on actions that do not make meaningful differences to our wellbeing.

It is possible to learn to be more resilient in the face of adversity. And becoming more resilient ourselves is not a political betrayal of those who are more distressed than us – to cope with a situation is not necessarily to condone it. And when we successfully deploy resilience, we may need to temper our expectation that others should be similarly successful. At times, we may be most useful to others by demanding that they are more resilient, at other times it may be more effective to accept that they are not. As with our judgements about our own resilience, effective judgements about others depend more on accurate qualitative and quantitative assessments of specific threats and resources, than on political and popular expectations about what we and others should or should not be able to cope with.

Key principles:

The world is a safer and more forgiving place for some people than it is for others. Because of this, personal resilience has a political element

Between adversity and the consequence lies belief. Beliefs moderate the emotional consequence of adversity

We derive beliefs by gauging the intent, probability and degree of a threat. Making an accurate assessment allows us to respond accurately and proportionately

Wellbeing comes from PERMA – positive emotion, engagement, relationships, meaning and accomplishment

Resilience is improved when we have secure and diverse sources of PERMA

When we feel afraid or anxious, determine whether there is a genuine threat or if our alarm system is overactive

Use strategic motivation to change behaviours

A friend of mine had this conversation with his 11-year-old daughter during the drive home after he picked her up from school one day.

Ismail: How was your day, Nina?

Nina: Bad.

Ismail: Sorry. [pause] What happened?

Nina: Nobody likes me.

Ismail: Oh?

Nina: It was a terrible day.

Ismail: I'm sorry you had a bad time.

Nina: I don't want to go to school tomorrow.

Ismail: That's understandable.

Nina: [silence]

Ismail: What actually happened today?

Nina: You won't understand.

[Nina is not using degree to assess the threat. When she tells Ismail that he won't understand, Ismail does not respond to her doubt as if it is an intended insult. This means

that he can keep the comment in perspective, and not overreact.]

Ismail: Maybe I won't understand everything. But I might understand some of it.

Nina: It's Frankie. She's a bully. She is always having a go at me. She won't leave me alone.

[By saying 'She is always . . .' Nina is failing to use probability or frequency to moderate her beliefs about the threat that Frankie poses.]

Ismail: What does she do that you don't like?

Nina: She calls me Norman. And she doesn't let me sit in her group.

Ismail: She calls you Norman?

Nina: Yes.

Ismail: And you don't like it?

Nina: No.

Ismail: I understand. It's not respectful. That is a problem that we need to sort out. I can think of three responses. You can talk to her directly, you can talk to your teacher, or I can talk to your teacher. Do you have a preference?

[Ismail agrees that name-calling is form of disrespect that warrants action. He suggests some practical actions.]

Nina: I will talk to my teacher. If that doesn't fix it, you can talk to my teacher.

Ismail: OK, deal. What about her not letting you sit in her group?

Nina: I don't like that either.

Ismail: It's never nice to be excluded. But is her group the only group that you can sit with?

Nina: No. But some of the girls in the group are my friends.

Ismail: Do you have friends who sit in other groups?

[Ismail suggests an alternate source of relationship PERMA.]

Nina: Yes. Maybe I'll sit with them instead.

RULE 7: USE RIGOR

My mother-in-law, Clara, and I had a rocky start to our relationship, but once we had forgiven each other for being or not being Italian, we came to love each other dearly. Clara was a devoted mother and grandmother, a skilled graphic designer and a successful businesswoman. I would not want anyone to draw too strong a connection between the strength of our relationship and this next point, but she was also an astonishingly good cook.

I have eaten no meal that compares to the consistent excellence that Clara produced in every meal that she cooked. Claudia says that the only cook that compares to Clara was Clara's mother, Amelia, whose food I sadly never tasted. Clara, Amelia (and fortunately for me, Claudia) are part of a lineage of Italian cooks that belong to one of the great cuisines of the world. Clara had exceptional range in her cooking. My own favourites were her soups, broths and stews, but the roasts and risottos were also incredible, and, unusually for an Italian, Clara also made exceptional custard. I was also fascinated by *how* Clara cooked – she never weighed or timed anything. Even when we had pasta boiling, she would suddenly just shout, 'Pasta's ready!' and would serve without testing it and get it right every time. Her recipes show this measurement-free approach, for example:

Fillet: brown thickly sliced fillet pieces in a pot. Add garlic and parsley and brown. Add a few mushrooms and wine and allow to simmer, retaining all the gravy. Later, add a little flour to thicken the gravy.

'A few', 'later' and 'a little' are terms that require interpretation.

Clara used this licence to cook fast, creatively and parsimoniously, producing high quality meals with very little waste. Her immersion in her culinary lineage, the range of ingredients she used, her delicate sense of taste and the nature of the meals that she cooked mean that she did not rely on rigor to produce high quality meals.

Like Clara, I am also not a rigorous cook. To my own tastes, I am perfectly adequate, with generous portion sizes and occasional if rare highlights. Claudia, however, might suggest that I lack range beyond soups and stews cooked in a single pot, show little planning for the meal apart from raiding the fridge and cupboard, and still need to discover an optimum quantity for garlic somewhere between nothing and too much. Clara's depth of knowledge and subtlety of judgement allowed her to cook without the rigor that would be useful for me.

That rigor is more broadly useful in some circumstances but not in others is reflected in its dictionary definition, where interpretations of the word's meaning range from *harsh inflexibility, austerity, severity, cruelty, challenge,* to *precision, exactness,* and *logic.*

In the 1980s a paint-by-numbers craze swept South Africa. My cousin loved it, and to my untutored eye his paintings looked like fantastic works of art, but not everybody shared my appreciation. 'Painting-by-numbers' has become a metaphor for situations in which rigor subtracts something from the process and the outcome. But in other areas, rigor is so critical that its presence is taken for granted. We expect that airliners, bridges and skyscrapers are built with rigor, and we expect that surgery, air traffic control and legal arguments are performed with a precise methodology.

Rule 7 is about those circumstances in which rigor is useful for talking, situations where intuition, folk knowledge, and adaptability are not preferable to measurement, timing and method. The most obvious of these examples come from the professional world.

Virginia Apgar was an obstetrical anaesthesiologist who was once asked by a student how to assess the health of a newborn baby. She said, 'You evaluate heart rate, respiration, colour, muscle tone, and reflex irritability.' That became the Apgar score, where each of the above are scored as 0, 1 or 2, and totalled out of 10. The Apgar score is now used worldwide and is credited with saving the lives of countless babies by accurately and systematically identifying those who need extra care.

Other experts also use checklists. When US Airways flight 1549 hit a flock of geese on take-off, lost both engines and made a successful emergency landing in the Hudson River, the pilot, Chesley Sullenberger, received a lot of credit. But also crucial to the landing was the first officer, Jeff Skiles, who worked methodically through procedural manuals and checklists to guide Sullenberger as he was flying the plane.

But rigor is not universally applied professionally. When Jonathan Levav, an associate professor at Columbia University, found that, regardless of the merits of the case, judges consistently gave more favourable rulings to prisoners after lunch, we were surprised rather than vindicated to discover a lack of process to guard against human unevenness.

And even in less formal settings, rigor has a role. When we talk to each other, dialogue happens extremely quickly. We cope with this speed by using incomplete sentences and using our imaginations to fill in the gaps of what has actually been said. This makes talking a fast and effective way of exchanging ideas, but when I read transcripts of conversations that I have been in, I am often surprised to see what I have missed. Applying rigor to talking doesn't require a transcript, but if you are prepared to follow Rule 2, slowing talking down has advantages. This is particularly the case when we disagree, and are tempted to speed up the conversation, and rely more heavily on intuition and opinion. Rigor allows us to talk more generally – about how to work something out, and exactly what it is that we want to know, and so is often useful even in personal conversations.

You don't have to be so good at rigor as to be able to apply it at full speed. Rigor is best applied consciously and deliberately. This methodical application means that it is more accessible to the beginner than might be expected, and it is possible to make significant improvements to conversations by applying basic rigor with a basic methodology. Conscious competence can suffice. Painting-by-numbers may have been mocked, but it produced a lot of paintings that would never have been painted without it. When we find ourselves in disagreement, we should be looking for a pragmatic solution, and talking-by-numbers can help us to achieve this.

Rigor is critical to talking in two circumstances: when we agree and when we disagree. Rigor is important when we agree because of the danger of groupthink. It forces us to double check ourselves when we don't have the 'devil's advocate' dissenting voice that can cause us to double check our processes or conclusions. Rigor is important when we disagree because it provides a depersonalised route to a solution. If you and I are stuck in disagreement, one way of handling this is for one of us to prevail, either by using our own power or by recruiting the support of others. This is the 'politics' which is spoken of so disparagingly yet used so frequently in the workplace: when one uses their position in the hierarchy, or convinces someone powerful, to overrule an opponent.

Some people speak of 'your truth' and 'my truth' as if truth is relative to perspective. But this interpretation of truth does not distinguish between what we believe to be true and what is real, which is a distinction that obviously exists and is useful to appreciate. We are all frequently mistaken and being respectful and sympathetic to those in error should be easier than it is. But if this sympathy extends to calling your opponent's opinion 'their truth' you have lost the opportunity of agreement through rigor. Rigor overcomes disagreement not by getting Person A to agree with Person B's point of view, or vice versa, but by using an objective process to lead both to a third point of view – the truth, or its closest approximation.

The ambition with rigor is that we agree with the truth rather than with each other.

In real politics, people often use metaphor and superlatives to address disagreement. In one instance, a politician who disagreed with the outcome of a negotiation accused one of the negotiating parties as having come to the table 'holding a fluttering white flag'. Rigor would have required the accuser to have articulated which concessions he disagreed with and why he disagreed with them, but the metaphor was a shortcut to expressing his disapproval, and possibly to forming it also. Once an opinion is formed, politicians often support it with superlatives rather than evidence. They use words like 'deplorable', 'egregious' and 'opprobrium', which come across as pompous because the speaker is trying to convince us with style rather than substance.

This chapter is about seven concepts: precision, accuracy, evidence, method, verifiability, meaningfulness and inference. These concepts can be used as a test for rigor and to check or improve the quality of forecasts, questions, trust judgements and opinions.

THE SEVEN SIGNS OF RIGOR
Precision

Precision has two components: clarity and detail. Clarity means saying exactly what you mean without leaving room for interpretation. Because we are excellent confabulators (filling in the gaps in our knowledge without realising we are doing so), we often do not detect imprecision until it is too late. A good test for precision is if the statement contains non-rounded numbers. 'It might rain tomorrow' is not precise, neither is 'There is a 50 per cent chance of rain tomorrow', but 'There is a 53 per cent chance of rain between 11am and 1pm tomorrow' is a precise statement.

Accuracy

Accuracy also has two components: calibration and spread. Calibration refers to whether there is a consistent bias. On the rare occasions when I do follow a recipe, I tend to be over-calibrated – I am always tempted to add just a little more of whatever ingredient the recipe suggests and then to cook it all for a little longer than directed. I am consistently inaccurate in one direction. Weather forecasters tend to be over-calibrated for rain, because people get angrier about it raining when they thought the sun would shine than they do if the sun shines when they thought it would rain. Spread refers to how consistently close to the target you are getting. The two components of accuracy can be independent of each other – a referee can be inaccurate without being biased if he makes a lot of wrong decisions without favouring one team over another, and he could also have a very low spread and get almost all the decisions right but still be biased because a small number of decisions consistently favoured one team.

Evidence

Evidence is 'knowing that' and is easily misused. An argument that uses correct evidence without a correct method is not a rigorous argument. It is true, for example, that when Neil Armstrong and Buzz Aldrin planted a flag on the moon, the fabric of the flag moved. This is an observation. To conclude that the only explanation for this movement is a breeze and that therefore the astronauts were not in an atmosphere-free environment and that therefore the moon landings were faked is a non-rigorous argument because of its selective use of evidence.

We misuse evidence in two particular ways. First, like a horse wearing blinkers, we can be unaware of that which we cannot see. We are content to draw conclusions from evidence without any awareness of how complete our evidence is. The classic example of this was the old European belief that all swans are white. They made the argument, 'I know that all swans are white because

I have seen many swans and they are all white [observation] so I believe that all the swans that I have not seen are white also [conclusion].' Black swans were discovered in Australia in 1697. 'Black swan' has become a metaphor for our human tendency to be unaware of our ignorance, and so to draw confident conclusions from the evidence that is available to us. The second way that we misuse evidence is that we have a tendency to positive test, rather than negative test. This means that we look for reasons why our beliefs are true rather than why they may be false. This tempts us to revisit the evidence in places that we have already seen instead of looking for new evidence in new places that we have not seen.

Method

The point of evidence is not to use it to 'trump' other evidence or select it to confirm an opinion; it must be used methodically and include the following steps:

- suspend opinion while gathering all available evidence (so opinion does not bias selection of evidence)
- rate the credibility and completeness of the evidence (so weak evidence does not outweigh strong evidence)
- propose one or more precise, verifiable, probabilistic explanations that accommodate all, not just part of the evidence
- formulate additional queries and tests that could uncover new evidence or new explanations that could falsify or fail to falsify your explanation. The question, 'What would change my mind?' is a useful check for this

These four steps describe the scientific method. Evidence is 'knowing that', so method is 'knowing how'. The scientific method is our best way of 'knowing how'. Many public arguments are about evidence when a more fruitful topic of discussion (Rule 1) may be method. Our public debates are often quite 'method blind' – politicians are frequently grilled on their facts and opinions without undergoing any questioning about the methods by which they derived those opinions. This is a pity, because often method is our best chance of agreement. We are better at designing unbiased tests than holding unbiased opinions because we can see methods from a general rather than a particular point of view. When we disagree, it is useful to ask the question, 'How would we know?' A useful starting response to disagreement is to collaborate to design an agreed, valid test. The measure of tests is that they are reliable and valid. Reliable tests give the same result each time they are applied by the same tester; valid tests give the same result even when they are applied by a different tester.

In this conversation between a politician and an interviewer, they argue over crime rates in the city that the politician had been responsible for and the causes of a reduction in crime.

Politician: The last time I was asked to fight crime here in this city, what we did in getting it down by, I think, about 20 per cent overall, the murder rate down by about 50 per cent.

Interviewer: How much did it go down at the same time in the rest of the country?

Politician: Well, you know.

Interviewer: Twenty-six per cent.

Politician: Well, look at the murder rate.

Interviewer: That fell in the rest of the country too, so you were behind the rest of the country.

Politician: No, the murder rate. I don't believe the murder rate in the rest of the country went down by 50 per cent. Did it?

Interviewer: Overall, crime went down faster in the rest of the country. The murder rate was roughly similar as it fell, yes. So you didn't outpace the country.

Politician: I don't agree.

Interviewer: You were part of a national trend.

Politician: If you look at what we did in [city], we had a murder rate when I came in running at about 160 a year, something like that. Look at the graph. We got it down over four or five years to fewer than a hundred murders. That was a remarkable achievement, and that was because we had some very robust policing, and we backed the police to go out and do their job, and the particular problem we had was with knife crime and gang crime, and we backed the police to do stop and search.

They could resolve this argument by agreeing a method to determine crime rates and establishing a method to investigate what really causes crime to drop. This argument is meant to sound rigorous because it contains a lot of numbers, but they are not being used methodically to draw a valid conclusion.

Verifiability

Verifiability is making a statement that can be tested. The statement, 'The moon is made of green cheese' is verifiable because it can be tested.

When we are questioned, it is normal to distinguish between those questions we know the answer to and those that we do not know the answer to. But we get this distinction wrong more often than we realise – our confidence in our knowledge is not a good predictor of its accuracy. A better distinction is to divide questions into those that are answerable and those that are not. When searching for agreement, rather than arguing about the answer to a question, it is better to identify if a question could be answered and then collaborate to find a method for answering it.

Two scientific-sounding arguments that are used frequently in explanations of human behaviour are brain science and evolutionary psychology. Some behavioural quirk, adaptation or mistake will be explained as having originated from a particular part of the brain or from a behavioural practice common amongst our distant ancestors. The explanations could be true. They could be false. It is just that there is no way to tell. Even though talking about the brain sounds scientific, in everyday life, the brain cannot be observed. Science depends upon observation. While words, thoughts and behaviour do not have material existence they can be observed and measured, and theories about them can be scientific. By contrast, theories about how the brain and its component regions influence complex daily behaviour cannot be observed or measured and so lack verifiability and rigor. The use of 'brain science' theories of behaviour and other 'science-y' arguments rely on a patina of rigor, which should serve as a warning to examine the actual rigor of the argument more deeply.

Meaningfulness

Meaningfulness requires that statements be more than precise, accurate, evidenced and verifiable. It needs them to also be relevant.

For example, in 2017, the White House responded to the US Global Change Research Programme's statement on climate change by saying, 'The climate has changed and is always changing'. This statement is verifiably true (if imprecise) but it is meaningless because it says nothing about the direction, rate and cause of change, which are the crucial elements in the debate.

Politicians make true but contextually meaningless statements when they wish to obfuscate their way out of a difficult topic or question. One politician's catchphrase on being asked a question that she couldn't or didn't want to answer was to announce, 'What's important is . . .' and then say something that may even have been precise, accurate and verifiable, but wasn't relevant to the question that had been asked.

Inference

Inference is drawing a conclusion from observations or prior opinions. This is the process that we refer to with the words 'logic' and 'reason'. We infer in two ways: deduction and induction.

Deduction is moving from the general to the particular, applying an established principle to an observation. If (as Rule 3 says) most people are good, I deduce that a new person that I meet is likely to be good also. Induction is moving from the particular to the general, deriving principles, opinions or theories from observations. If I meet a lot of good people, I could induce that most people are good.

There are three kinds of inference errors.

The first are logical flaws. 'Most people are good, therefore this person I have just met is likely to be *bad*' is a logical error. But we are quite good at inferring logically and are open to being corrected when logical errors are pointed out to us – we do have a strong drive to see ourselves and be seen by others as logical or reasonable.

The more common and insidious inference errors draw logically correct deductions from incorrect theories and make logically correct inductions from inadequate observations.

One of the problems of living in a country like South Africa with a high crime rate was that we inferred from the specific to the general. This person stole my car, so most people are bad. This isn't an illogical statement; the error is to use a relatively small number of car thieves as representative of a larger number of people who are not car thieves. The deductive error would be to meet an individual and conclude that he was likely a bad person because most people are bad. This also isn't illogical, but it is drawn from an incorrect premise.

I only corrected this inductive/deductive error in my own head after I had lived in the United Kingdom and came to realise that it was obviously wrong, but its manifestation that I feel most embarrassed and guilty about happened when I still lived in South Africa. I was standing outside a mall taking a break from shopping. After a while, I was joined by a South African man of Asian ancestry, who was also waiting for his family, and we began to chat. After some time, one of my sons (who was extremely young) saw me in conversation with the man and rushed up to me and said in a loud stage whisper, 'Dad! Don't speak to black people!'

I was so horrified that I had no capacity to reflect on how hurtful it must have been for the man that I was talking to. I panicked and tried to pretend that the whisper had been inaudible. I failed to apologise to the man, explain my son's error, or correct my son. I was imagining what the man was thinking: *the boy made a racist statement . . . the boy is too young to have independently developed racist views . . . he must have got them from his father . . . the father is a racist and the fact that he is talking to me is a sham.* This inference is logically correct and is highly plausible. Out of respect to the man, and the many people who have suffered similar insults, rather than challenge this argument, I will focus on the inference errors that my son was making.

First, South African people of Asian ancestry would usually refer to themselves as 'Indian'. During apartheid, some Indian people referred to themselves as 'black' to undermine the apartheid government's attempt to establish 'different but equal' populations, but in the early 2000s, 'black' was usually used to refer to people of African ancestry. My son was making the error that because people referred to as black have brown skin and this man had brown skin, he could be referred to as black.[13]

Second, my son had picked up that most incidences of criminal activity or violence that we had been engaged in involved a black person. The most serious involved two white men, but my son did not know about this incident. This was an error of induction, or a sampling error, that because all the criminals we had met were black, all criminals are black. It was also an error of logic, that because all criminals are black, all black people are criminals.

---

[13] He was logically wrong, but not much more wrong than the original idea to refer to anyone as black, or white, given no human being has a skin colour anywhere close to either shade. Now the terms have acquired meaning unrelated to their descriptive qualities, so although they are problematic in several ways, it does make some sense to use them.

The third error was an error of deduction, moving from an incorrect premise to an incorrect conclusion – that because all black people are criminals, this man was a criminal also.

While I had not coached my son in racist ideology, I had clearly failed to correct the perceptions and deductions that led to the comment. At the time, my son did see me being friendly to black people, but only some black people – those I knew, and black women, children and old people who were obviously not a physical threat. My default position to strange young black men was suspicion and hostility. I inferred from their reciprocal hostility that my initial attitude was justified.

There is an old computing term, GIGO: garbage in, garbage out. It is true of induction and deduction also, as we are better at the logical processes of formulating (induction) and applying (deduction) theories than we are at determining whether the evidence on which these theories rests has been collected with an adequate methodology. Because we have confirmation bias – once we believe something to be true we seek to confirm the belief rather than disprove it – we can get trapped in a loop of selecting evidence that confirms our theories and interpreting our observations and adjusting our theories to fit the facts that we select. This is a common source of error and a fruitful area to investigate when we find ourselves in disagreement.

A RIGOR CHECKLIST

These seven concepts can be used to assess rigor similarly to how heart rate, respiration, colour, muscle tone and reflex irritability can be used to assess newborn health in an Apgar test. Opinions can be appraised for rigor by rating each concept on a scale of 0 to 2 and giving a total score.

	Results 1 NASA (total: 14/14)	Results 2 The Heartland Institute (total: 1/14)
Precision *(clarity and detail)*	• Score: 2/2 • Reports on global temperature rise and warming oceans are reported in decimal points of a degree (e.g. 'The planet's average surface temperature has risen about 1.62 degrees Fahrenheit (0.9 degrees Celsius) since the late 19th century') • Reports of shrinking ice sheets expressed as a non-rounded number of billion tons ('Greenland lost an average of 286 billion tons of ice per year between 1993 and 2016') • Time periods used for sampling expressed precisely • Report covers global temperature rise, warming oceans, shrinking ice sheets, glacial retreat, decreased snow cover, and sea level rise	• Score: 0/2 • The article doesn't use numbers
Accuracy *(bias and spread)*	• Score: 2/2 • Reports that its key theme, that human activity is causing the warming trend, is more than 95 per cent likely to be true. • Multiple independent studies corroborate similar figures	• Score: 0/2 • The article incorrectly disputes that 97 per cent of climate scientists agree that human activity is causing a warming trend in climate change. • The article incorrectly claims that 'every forecast made using these models since 1990 has been wrong – with actual temperatures getting further from predictions with every passing year'

Continued

	Results 1 **NASA (total: 14/14)**	**Results 2** **The Heartland Institute** **(total: 1/14)**
Evidence *(quality and completeness)*	• Score: 2/2 • Heavily referenced article citing multiple extensive studies carried out by credible organisations	• Score: 0/2 • The article has no references and uses no scientific studies. • The article relies on reporting opinions, like those of investigative reporter Elaine Dewar
Method *(follows scientific method)*	• Score: 2/2 • Article uses references published in multiple credible, peer-reviewed papers • Conclusions in above papers derived from research according to credible and documented methods	• Score: 0/2 • The article shows no methodological approach to knowledge acquisition or opinion formation
Verifiability *(testable)*	• Score: 2/2 • Because conclusions are reported precisely (with clarity and detail), the reports are falsifiable	• Score: 1/2 • The article does make some verifiable statements (which are verifiably false)
Meaningful-ness *(relevance)*	• Score: 2/2 • The reports on global temperature rise, warming oceans, shrinking ice sheets, glacial retreat, decreased snow cover and sea level rise are directly relevant to the broader topic of climate change	• Score: 0/2 • One of the article's main points is that while many people speak of 'carbon emissions', carbon is a solid and what is actually emitted is CO_2, which is a gas. This is true, but irrelevant to the broader debate. • Another point is that CO_2 is a trace atmospheric gas that makes life on earth possible. Also true, but irrelevant to the debate about whether we have too much of it

Continued

	Results 1 NASA (total: 14/14)	Results 2 The Heartland Institute (total: 1/14)
Inference *(induction and deduction)*	• Score: 2/2 • The article induces from long-term observations about temperatures and variables dependent on temperature (glaciers, sea levels) that there is a warming trend • The article induces from long-term observations about CO_2 levels that there is an increase in atmospheric CO_2 • The article reasons that because CO_2 is a greenhouse gas, rising CO_2 levels are causing the warming trend, and that because human activity is causing rising CO_2, human activity is causing the warming trend	• Score: 0/2 • The article argues incorrectly that because politicians use the term 'carbon' to refer to 'CO_2', they cannot be correct about climate change. • A related incorrect argument not made in this article is that because there are a variety of terms to describe the phenomenon of human-caused rising CO_2 levels causing a warming trend with a range of global effects, the use of several terms shows that there is a lack of consensus or certainty in the science. • The article argues that because CO_2 makes life on earth possible, it cannot also be a 'pollutant'

For example, I selected two articles on climate change. First there is 'Climate Change: How Do We Know?' published by NASA, and second, 'Global Warming: Fake News from the Start', published by The Heartland Institute. These are both available online.

The Heartland Institute's article doesn't rate well. I did not cherry-pick it for its poor rigor, it was the highest ranked article sceptical of climate change that came up on Google when I searched for 'climate change hoax proof'. It is easy to get frustrated when confronted by the paradox of how bad some arguments are and yet how faithfully some people accept them. It is so easy for people to generate non-rigorous opinions that the task of contesting each one rigorously can seem overwhelming. A more effective response may be to criticise the provenance of the opinion – to criticise the rigor with which it was formed rather than the opinion itself. While people have contrasting opinions, few contest the elements of rigor and their application. And if they do, the checklist is still useful, because if you differ on this point you would be wasting your time talking about anything else.

RIGOR VERSUS PLAUSIBILITY

One of the competitors of rigor is plausibility. Stories and opinions seem plausible when they have a coherent internal logic. Because we are better at detecting logical flaws than we are at detecting inference flaws (logically correct theories derived from incorrect or incomplete observations, and logically correct conclusions drawn from incorrect theories), narratives that are heavy in logic but light in evidence and method still appear plausible to us. Whether or not the man's judgement that I was a racist was correct, it was highly plausible. Less plausible was my son's judgement that the man was a criminal, but my son was still using plausibility rather than rigor as a proxy for truth. Another advantage that plausibility has over rigor is that we detect it mostly with System 1, so judgements are fast and easy to make.

Testing for rigor is more difficult; it needs to be done itself in a rigorous way. Establishing the methodology for a rigor test is one way of managing this difficulty. Another is priming or training your automatic System 1 to detect common violations of rigor: for example, checking for statements that include 'always', 'everything', and 'everywhere' (possible violations of precision and accuracy), 'evidence for' (possible violation of method), the use of untestable or irrelevant statements and glib inferences. We are so easily seduced by plausibility that it is worth priming your System 1 to sound an alarm at any highly plausible explanation.

An example of an incorrect but plausible explanation is that of how improvement after low performance and deterioration after good performance is attributed to paradoxical feedback. Daniel Kahneman recounts how Israeli Air Force instructors insisted that student pilots improved performance after reprimands and deteriorated after compliments because of the reprimands and compliments rather than because of reversion to the mean. You can demonstrate this fallacy with dice. If you throw a dice a number of times, and every time you throw a five or a six, say approvingly, 'Good dice!' and every time you throw a one or two, say angrily, 'Bad dice!' you will find that after you congratulate the dice it tends to return a lower score and after you criticise the dice it tends to return a higher score. Human nature is biased towards false positive detection of causality and intent and so even though we know that there is no way our words could be affecting the dice, the idea that they are remains beguilingly plausible.

Many sports fans and players believe that confidence causes good performances. This causality is so plausible it is almost universally accepted. I once had a conversation with Clive Woodward, the coach of the England team that won the 2003 Rugby World Cup. He said that England's confidence had been crucial to their success. I said to him that I thought it was more likely that the success had been caused by his coaching, Martin Johnson's captaincy and Jonny Wilkinson's play, and that the confidence had been caused by knowing that they had these luminous talents in these positions. The post hoc fallacy is *after this, because of this*. Because after success, or after capability, came confidence, it seemed as if the confidence caused the success or the capability. The plausibility of the post hoc fallacy is why many people find politicians compelling when they call for optimism, even when the optimism is not based on a rigorous assessment of the consequences of the choice being proposed.

OPINION FORMATION

Rigor is critical to opinion formation. One category of opinions is 'knowing that' – for example, knowing that human activity causes elevated CO_2 levels that cause a planetary warming trend, or knowing that the earth is not flat, or that vaccines do not cause autism, and that people did land on the moon. But many of us do not come to these opinions through rigor.

I believe these things because other people's beliefs make this plausible. I don't have time to methodically test the rigor of these statements, so I take the shortcut to opinion formation and trust the opinions of others. In this, I am no different to a conspiracy theorist.

There is a difference between trusting someone's intentions or loyalty and trusting their judgements or intentions. It is possible to accurately trust someone's loyalty and mistakenly expand this into trusting all of their opinions. This error allows incorrect opinions to spread quickly through closely connected groups.

The way to manage this dependency is to make accurate trust judgements. If I can accurately decide whether to trust NASA or The Heartland Institute on climate change, I can take a shortcut to rigorous beliefs.

People are trustworthy when they are willing to be trustworthy and able to be trustworthy. When I judge who to trust, I need to consider these two aspects. But I also need to consider what is at stake. If I am going to be wrong, would it be better to be too trusting or not trusting enough? Why should I raise the trust threshold, and why should I lower it?

My two older sons are currently in their late teens and early twenties. When friends offer them lifts, they have to make judgements about whether to trust the driver. This judgement will need to factor in the driver's *willingness* to drive safely (versus his motivation to drive to impress or thrill), and his *ability* to drive safely (knowledge of rules of the road and car control). They also have to consider what is at stake. Car crashes are a matter of life and death and the extra effort of walking or taking the train is not. Concern about the effects of a crash would cause them to raise the trust threshold, but the desire to get somewhere might lower their trust threshold.

These four judgements can be made rigorously:

- the willingness of someone to be trustworthy
- the ability of someone to be trustworthy
- the costs of trust being betrayed
- the benefits of trust being fulfilled

Is NASA willing to be trustworthy on climate change? What accurate, precise evidence is available on NASA's agenda? Can I methodically collect and infer from this evidence to produce a verifiable opinion?

Is NASA able to be trustworthy? In order to make a rigorous judgement, I would need to methodically collect accurate precise evidence on the institution's expertise and resources and infer a verifiable opinion. But once I have this information, my decision to trust NASA is also based on the risks and opportunities of trusting or not. My concern for the effects of climate change on my children and grandchildren is such that I am willing to trust NASA's opinion that we should take action, even if I do not have 100 per cent faith in NASA or am not 100 per cent convinced by the climate science. (I am highly confident in NASA and highly convinced by climate science, but not 100 per cent.)

This logic is similar to my logic in taking out fire insurance for my house even if I am not 100 per cent certain that my house will burn down, or wearing a seatbelt even if I am not 100 per cent convinced that I will have a crash. I have rigorously examined NASA's willingness and ability to be trusted and have also applied a low threshold to trust, because I believe that, in addition to the probabilities, the costs of a false positive (acting to halt non-existent climate change) are higher than the costs of a false negative (doing nothing about a real warming trend).

People do not trust the climate change consensus for one or two reasons. The first reason is that they have not made a rigorous trust judgement and are trusting the wrong people. The second reason is that they belong to that small part of the population for whom the costs of a false positive are personally higher than the costs of a false negative – those people who are so rich from fossil fuels and related industries that they and their children can afford to escape the worst effects of climate change, and can't countenance the possibility of losing their positions of wealth and status.

While a very small number of people can rationally discount climate change, these people are trusted by many people even though their different position on the risk of cost and the chance of benefits means that their agendas are opposed. We should always be rigorous about assessing the trustworthiness of people who claim to represent us, but for whom circumstance has created a situation where their agenda is opposed to our own.

FORECASTING

Another component of 'knowing that', or opinion formation, is developing opinions about the future, or forecasting. The authority in this field is Philip Tetlock, professor at the University of Pennsylvania and director of The Good Judgement project.

The method that Tetlock demonstrated outperforms all other tested forecasting methods.

First step: Unpacking the question

First, understand which questions need to be answered to provide the foundation of knowledge with which to answer the main question. So many political debates are actually competitions between different forecasts. The question, 'Should the country take X position or Y position?' is an attempt to answer whether X or Y will deliver a better future. In order to have a quality political debate, this question needs to be broken into component parts. How will X or Y affect the health, community, security, economy, identity, moral and international standing and education of the country?

We must also attempt to discover the limits of our knowledge. To use Donald Rumsfeld's phrase, 'There are known unknowns; that is to say we know there are some things we do not know. But there are also unknown unknowns.' A known unknown would be knowing that we do not have information on a topic, and an unknown unknown is something that could be crucial to the forecast, but just hasn't been thought of.

We have to invest awareness and effort to reduce our exposure to unknown unknowns.

To unpack a question we should also decide if it has been formulated precisely, meaningfully and verifiably. Political forecasts are rarely formulated precisely, meaningfully and verifiably, and when this step is omitted, debates rage on interminably because lots of people are each claiming to have correctly answered a different question.

Second step: The three views

The three views are the inside, outside and the others' view. The inside view refers to privileged information that is only learnt through select channels or known to a restricted group. If I run a small business and I realise that political choice X or Y will affect me in a particular way, that is an inside view, because I know things about my business that nobody else does. The outside view refers to data, statistics and base rates. A base rate is what we would expect without any extra or special conditions. If we want to decide how rainy February will be, the base rate refers to how rainy February normally is. If you are trying to predict your child's performance in their next exam, the base rate refers to how well they normally do in exams. The base rate does not take into account additional information, like how cloudy it is, or how hard your child has been studying. The outside view of the economic, political or security effects of X or Y are obtained by objectively looking for precedent. What other countries have taken this route, or at what other points in history have we done something similar, and what happened? The others' view is another or expert opinion apart from our own. What do my political opponents think? What do the economic, security, educational and health experts think?

Third step: Deliver an answer

The answer must be a synthesis of the three views. How much should I weight my inside view against the base rate, against expert opinion? This is a significant and nuanced judgement. Then I need to express the answer in a way that is precise and verifiable. This will allow me to check on the accuracy (spread and bias) of my answer. Is my spread too large and are my answers too random? Or is my spread small and my answers close to the truth? Am I biased and do I tend to overestimate or underestimate, or are my answers spread evenly? Politicians prefer imprecise unverifiable forecasts so that they cannot be proved wrong or held to account. It is our role to demand precision and verifiability from them.

The final part of delivering an answer is updating that answer. When forecasting methodology allows updating, accuracy and relevance are improved, and the temptation to defend a position is reduced.

It would be lovely to be able to talk as intuitively and skilfully as my mother-in-law cooked. And, in fact, most of the time, we can.

In those exceptional situations when rigor is called for, we can feel reluctant to comply, as if we are being forced to paint-by-numbers instead of expressing our impressions.

When we find ourselves in debate or disagreement it is tempting to break Rule 1 and oppose opinions rather than collaborating on methodology. Or, to break Rule 3, and assume that the reason for the difference is someone else's wrong headedness. Then it is easy to break Rule 2 and seek a quick or simple solution.

Rule 7, using rigor, is normally hard work. Being painstaking pushes us into slower System 2 thinking. But there is an advantage to this process. While it would have taken me a lifetime or more to learn to cook with Clara's flair and judgement, I can follow a recipe. Being rigorous is conscious competence, painstaking and by-numbers, but this quality of rigor should encourage rather than discourage us from using it. The more practised we become at rigor, the easier it is to apply. Rigor is not always fast or easy, but when we are in disagreement it may be the fastest, easiest option that we have, as well as the best.

Key principles:

The objective with rigor is that we both agree with reality, and hence each other

You don't need to be so good at rigor that you can apply it at full talking speed

We are easily seduced by plausibility – something that sounds as if it should be right

The seven signs of rigor are:

Precision

Accuracy

Evidence
Method
Verifiability
Meaningfulness
Inference

In this conversation, a journalist and a political commentator discuss the issue of gun control in the US.

Journalist: So why am I off the rails, Mr A?

Commentator: You know, honestly, B, you've kind of been a bully on this issue, because what you do, and I've seen it repeatedly on your show, is you tend to demonise people who differ from you politically by standing on the graves of the children from Sandy Hook, saying they don't care enough about the dead kids, if they cared more they would agree with you on policy. I think we can have a rational political conversation about balancing rights and risks and rewards of all of these different policies, but I don't think what we need to do is demonise people on the other side as being unfeeling about what happened.

[Because the statement 'standing on the graves of children' is contentious, offensive and not rigorous, it reduces the chance that the conversation will be a productive one. There is no way to determine whether the insult is deserved. The commentator is correct to say that the journalist is wrong when he infers that people who are not aligned with him on the gun issue do not care about dead children. But his request for a 'rational political conversation' is undermined by his own irrational opening.]

Journalist: How dare you accuse me of standing on the graves of children that died? How dare you?

Commentator: I have seen you do it repeatedly.

Journalist: Like I say, how dare you?

[What would have been more effective than repeating 'How dare you' would be for the journalist to have asked the commentator for accuracy and precision in what he actually means. 'Standing on the graves of children' is a strong term, but it is imprecise.]

Commentator: Well you can keep saying that, but you have done it repeatedly. You keep saying to folks that if they disagree with you politically, then somehow this is a violation of what happened in Sandy Hook. And I would really like to hear your policy prescriptions for what we should do about guns, because you say that you respect the Second Amendment, and I have brought this here for you so that you can read it, it's the Constitution, and I would really like for you to explain to me what you would do about guns that would have prevented what happened in Sandy Hook. If you want to do what you do in the UK, all right, which is ban virtually all guns, that is at least a fair argument, and we can have a discussion about whether that's something that we ought to do.

[This is the commentator's second mention of rigor ('reason' and 'fair'). Rigor, though, must be used rigorously. It cannot be applied in parts.]

Journalist: I have made it very clear what I want to do, which is exactly what MK wants to do, and rather than address your comments to me about standing on the graves of children of Sandy Hook, you can address them to MK, because he agrees with everything that I have been saying, because he feels the same way, as does his wife. They are gun owners, they both respect the Second Amendment of the constitution, they don't want to take away anybody's right to defend themselves with guns.

Commentator: They want to take away certain types of guns.

Journalist: They want to take away assault weapons which are capable, with magazines, that we saw at Sandy Hook, of unleashing ridiculous amount of bullets.

[The measure 'ridiculous amounts of bullets' is imprecise. The argument loses strength as a consequence.]

Commentator: The vast majority of murders that are committed in this country with guns are not committed with assault weapons, they are committed with handguns. So are you willing to ban handguns in this country?

Journalist: That's not what I am asking for.

Commentator: Why not? Don't you care about the kids that are being killed in Chicago as much as the kids in Sandy Hook?

Journalist: Yes I do.

Commentator: Then why don't you care about banning handguns in Chicago?

Journalist: We'll come to that. Let me ask you this. What was the weapon used at A?

[By saying, 'We'll come to that', the journalist deflects this comment. He is refusing to consider all of the evidence. This weakens his ability to make a judgement on the entire issue of guns in the US.]

Commentator: It was an assault rifle.

Journalist: What was the weapon used in the incident around Christmas when the firemen were lured to their deaths?

Commentator: That was an assault rifle.

[This is a misuse of evidence. Everything the journalist is saying is true, but he is still ignoring the gun deaths that are caused by handguns.]

Journalist: Right. So the last four mass shootings in America have all been with an assault rifle. That is the reason, Mr A, and you can smirk at me, and you can laugh at me . . .

Commentator: I'm not smirking . . .

[Suddenly they are arguing about whether the commentator is smirking at the journalist. This is another example of an argument that cannot be resolved because it lacks rigor. How do you measure a smirk? There is no point in having the argument.]

Journalist: That is the reason that people like me, and MK, and GG, want to have assault rifles like that removed from civilian hands.

Commentator: Your passion on the issue doesn't really justify your rationale.

[This is true. Feeling strongly about something doesn't make you right.]

Journalist: You don't understand why we want to remove the preferred method of choice, these killing machines, from the hands of deranged young men?

[The journalist responds to criticism of his passion by stating his position even more strongly. He may not have understood the commentator's point.]

Commentator: I want to ask you to be philosophically consistent. If what you are worried about is the removal of killing machines from the hands of deranged young people, then maybe we should talk about a blanket gun ban, and let's get to what the left really wants here, and you say that you're for the Second Amendment, but . . .

[The commentator appeals for the journalist to be 'philosophically consistent'. This is a fair request. But having asked for 'reason' and 'fairness', it is not philosophically consistent for the commentator to then make the imprecise, evidence-free, and possibly inaccurate claim that the left does not respect the Second Amendment.]

Journalist: Why is this about left or right, because in Britain it never is about left or right, this issue, so why is it here?

[It could be argued that Britain's position on guns is not relevant or meaningful to this debate.]

Commentator: Well, we can talk about Britain in a second. I think the reason it's about left and right here is that, fundamentally, the right believe that the basis for the Second Amendment, and they believe in the Second Amendment, is not really about self-defence, and it's not about hunting, it's about resistance to tyranny, that's what the founders said, and that's what the right believes in this country.

[This is a verifiable statement. This makes it a useful addition to this debate. A rigorous response to the statement firming up its precision (is this a universal, unmitigated

belief amongst the right?), and then using a sound method-ology to find evidence could allow a rigorous judgement of its accuracy.]

Journalist: Which tyranny are you fearing yourself?

[The journalist does none of this. He allows the commentator to speak as the spokesperson for the entire right.]

Commentator: I fear the possibility of a tyranny arising in this country over the next 50 to 100 years. Let me tell you something, the fact that my [Jewish] grandparents and great grandparents didn't fear that in Europe, is why they are now ashes in Europe. So this kind of leftist revisionist history, where there is never any fear of a democracy going usurpa-tious or tyrannical is just that, it's fictitious.

[Having argued that the passion that the journalist feels about the dead children is irrelevant or meaningless to his philo-sophical point, the commentator invokes the Holocaust. He also seems to be saying that the reason that the general public should be allowed to own assault rifles is to guard against the potential of tyranny from their own government in the next 50 to 100 years.

This idea relies on at least three assumptions. First, that a gov-ernment with access to the military technology available to it in 2070 or 2120 could be tempered by people armed only with assault rifles. Second, that if a citizenry is armed (either with only assault rifles or also with heavier weaponry) to the point that it could resist its own government, that this would make democracy more rather than less likely. And third, that the combined probability of (a) a US government turning tyran-nical, (b) an armed citizenry effectively resisting this tyranny, and (c) nothing else going wrong in the next 100 years with such a heavily armed citizenry, is worth the fear and loss of lives incurred in mass shootings in the US.

These ideas cannot be definitively tested, but Tetlock's forecasting method could allow them to be exposed to more rigor than it seems they currently have.]

RULE 8: USE COMPLEXITY

Riding a bicycle is simple and yet complex. The task is simple in that there are only so many component skills – you have to manage forward motion, balance and steering, but complex in that these requirements are nuanced and interact. This is the basic test for complexity – a system with multiple subtle interacting parts.

Beginner cyclists try to manage these parts separately. They turn to steer without leaning, balance without steering and want to pedal without rocking. Sometimes even experienced cyclists abandon complexity – just before crashing, it is common for cyclists to become rigid and upright, as if they are hoping that the interaction of grip, speed and centrifugal forces can be ignored or overcome with a massive focus on being vertical. This is a basic feature of our relationship with complexity: beyond a certain point we are tempted to abandon it.

Rule 8: Use complexity is about how, when we are talking about complex issues, it is better to engage with this complexity, even though it can become tempting to ignore it.

My youngest son, who is a freestyle 'first-person view' drone pilot (he wears goggles which show video streamed from a camera on the drone), and my middle son, who is a newly licensed car driver, like to argue about which task is more skilled. There are literally more dimensions to flying an FPV drone. Like a car, you have left/right and backwards/forwards, but you also have up/down, and roll, pitch and yaw – and these dimensions interact. But my youngest son flies his drone in an empty field. My car-driving son has to interact with other moving objects. In addition to needing to operate the accelerator, brake and clutch independently, he has had to learn the interaction between them too. He has to adjust his direction and speed in response to other vehicles, he has to interpret the intentions of other drivers and when he becomes part of the traffic, he becomes part of a larger system.

Many dictionaries consider the words 'complicated' and 'complex' to be synonyms, but they also get used to describe two distinct concepts. 'Complicated' refers to something with many dimensions; 'complex' refers to a system with interactions between those dimensions.

Complexity has three components: multidimensionality, degree and interactivity.

Multiple dimensions:

Asking the question, 'What affects this system?' helps us describe the dimensions. This results in a list, which we are quite good at creating. The list resulting from the question, 'What affects traffic?' would include things like type and number of cars, weather, people, time of day, roads and rules.

Degree:

We are not as good at describing degree. We prefer binary to nuance: the traffic is either good or bad, it is or isn't raining. If pushed, sometimes we only acknowledge one further degree, a middle option. So we would grant that the traffic is good, bad or OK. But the world does not necessarily organise itself into the categories that we find easy to comprehend, and there are times when it is worth making the effort to use subtlety. If you are driving a car through a speed trap, you will be interested in quite subtle variations in speed, and if you are a farmer, you will be interested in quite subtle variations in rainfall.

Degree can describe a quantity – how much speed, traffic or rain – but it can also describe a probability – how likely it is to rain, or how likely it is that there will be a traffic jam. Like quantities, probabilities are sometimes best expressed subtly. There are more categories of probability than definitely, maybe and definitely not.

Quantity and probability interact: in a given month it may be most likely to receive a certain amount of rainfall, with increasing or decreasing amounts decreasingly probable. This creates a range of probabilities which could be shaped like a bell curve (for example, when describing the probability of various quantities of rain) or a more simple curve (for example, when describing the probability of a car crashing on a corner, against the speed the car is driving around that corner).

Interactions:

Describing interactivity is the most cognitively challenging task of complexity. In complex systems, dimensions might interact linearly, so turning a car decreases forward speed. But dimensions also interact in loops. If I am in an argument, my emotion may affect the emotion of the person that I am talking to, which in turn could affect me.

Complex systems:

In winter evenings in parts of Europe, large flocks of starlings fly together before roosting. The phenomenon is called a murmuration. Videos show how the flock rapidly and continuously changes direction, shape and density. The flock is a system; its dynamism and coherence are emergent properties. The shapes are the consequence of tens of thousands of birds all following the same three rules with high degrees of accuracy: fly close, don't bump, follow your neighbours. The flock is complex because it has many dimensions – tens of thousands of birds all following three rules. It has degree – birds have to fly exactly close enough to maintain an acceptably low probability of bumping. There is interactivity – as one bird adjusts its position to respond to the position of others, this movement creates a ripple effect which will eventually come back to affect the same bird again.

Understanding linear and looped interactions are crucial to understanding complexity and are a powerful skill to use when talking. When human beings interact, it forms a level of complexity that is almost as hard for us to understand as it would be for a starling to understand the dynamics of its own flock. As situations become more complex, people are tempted to turn to increasingly simple explanations.

An example of complexity at an individual level is Martin Seligman's idea of wellbeing, which has five dimensions: positive emotion, engagement, relationships, meaning and accomplishment. Each of these dimensions can also interact – positive emotions and relationships loop together – as well as containing further nested dimensions. The first dimension, positive emotion, contains the dimensions of: amusement, awe, interest, inspiration, joy, pride, hope, serenity, gratitude and love. Within this, pride, hope and inspiration may also loop or ripple together. Complex systems are hard to change with a single point of intervention, or with a one-off action. Wellbeing is better affected with multiple efforts, applied consistently, and continuously adapted according to feedback from how the complex system responds. By contrast, the 'happiness' industry defines wellbeing in a much simpler way. There is no nuance in its adopted symbol of a circular yellow smiley face, and its suggested interventions are made less effective for their failure to appreciate the complexity of human needs and how we satisfy them.

COMPLEX CONVERSATIONS

One day when my boys were younger, I took them to a crowded shopping mall. I was walking slowly, holding each of the older boys by the hand while my younger son trailed slightly behind. I gradually became aware that the people walking towards me were behaving unusually; they seemed to be drawn to and delighted by something happening just behind me. My youngest son must have smiled cherubically at someone and received a smile in return. This broadened his smile, which increased the positivity of the response of the next person that he smiled at. This positive feedback loop must have gone on for a couple of minutes. By the time I turned around, my son was strolling down the passage like a prince, radiating happiness like the sun, beaming at every person he saw and receiving the focused joy of a crowd of people in return.

Some loops of interaction can operate in more complex ways, and some are short and simple like the one described above. In this transcribed conversation, two friends of mine use complexity to better understand one of the difficult topics of conversation in their marriage. I was present at the conversation, but like the best couple therapy sessions, they spent most of the time talking to each other.

Lucas: You turned around to me the other day and you said, 'It's OK that you go out and work, because you earn money.' You were saying that even though work is hard for me, it's balanced by the fact that I get paid for it, but the hard work that you do running the home, you don't get paid for it, and that's not fair.

Ava: Why don't we do the money conversation then?

Lucas: I don't feel necessarily safe about that. (laughs)

Ava: No, I don't either, but then that's why we avoid it.

Lucas: This is where the rules come in, isn't it? The rules give you a framework in order to be safe during most conversations, normal conversations.

Ava: Safe enough to facilitate the conversation, rather than avoid it, or fight over it.

Lucas: This conversation, about money – it's for feeling that we both contribute to the house. I think Ava has a strong sense of, everything needs to be fair. I grew up in a family of boys and nothing was fair (laughter).

[Lucas has simplified here by failing to appreciate degree. He says 'everything needs to be fair' and 'nothing was fair'. This is a binary statement.]

Lucas: I think right at the root of the problem is this idea of fairness. I commute 10 hours a week.

[When Lucas talks about the problem having a 'root', he is looking for a linear explanation.]

Lucas: I get nothing for commuting. However, Ava feels really bad if she doesn't get thanked for doing the laundry, right?

Ava: It's not quite like that.

[Ava wants a more complex explanation here.]

Lucas: Then, it sort of rolls into things like money. Ava turned around to me the other day and said, 'But you earn money.' I was going, 'It's not mine. It's for everyone to use.' But at the end of every month I add it all up to make sure we're not wasting any. I think that puts an undue amount of stress and tension on Ava, because Ava spends a lot. Therefore, she feels that she's responsible.

Ava: You do the majority of the earning and I do the majority of the spending.

Lucas: I think it would be really great to get us to a point where we both acknowledge the fact that we both contribute massively.

[Lucas adds complexity to Ava's 'you earn, I spend' statement. This prompts a useful reflection from Ava . . .]

Ava: I'll feel guilty for spending the money. Especially if I'm spending on myself, or on the kids. Then, I think that raises the tension in the conversation. The guilt kind of veils my insight, my emotions get really heightened, I feel anxious. I've always felt a little bit like it was a bit of a witch hunt, even though I know that Lucas is not the perpetrator.

[Ava describes interaction; guilt – emotion – veiled insight – feeling persecuted by Lucas.]

Ava: In those conversations, that's how I've felt. I think that it's probably fair to say that Lucas wants to ameliorate that uncomfortable negative emotion, and then that becomes the focus, rather than coming to some kind of agreement on the money issue.

[Ava describes another interaction; heightened emotion – conversation loses its original focus. Rule 1 would be useful here.]

Lucas: Do you feel guilty for spending the money?

Ava: Yes, I do. Not on groceries.

Lucas: So, what right have you violated that makes you feel guilty for spending the money?

Ava: The right for us to choose to do things as a family that has been prevented by my spending.

Lucas: So, you spend something on yourself when we should have been spending it on the family?

Ava: Yes.

Lucas: So, your value is money for the family, rather than money for yourself?

Ava: I guess my notional value would be money for the family, but my actual value is to spend it on myself. I feel guilty straight away and I feel physically ill afterwards. So, then, the question I've been asking myself is, what am I trying to ameliorate by that spending? I feel really, really challenged by that.

[Ava is trying to understand a pattern.]

Lucas: But it's good to have this conversation, right? This is getting into it.

[Lucas embraces complexity, and Ava responds.]

Ava: Yes, I really want to have it. I need to be more resilient in this conversation, otherwise it heightens my anxiety and my emotion.

Lucas: Do you think that this value on spending on family over yourself is correct, is it right?

Ava: I think it needs to be in balance . . .

[Lucas is using the concept of right/wrong, which is binary, Ava asks for balance, which is degree.]

Ava: . . . but I think it would be helpful if I could address that balance and get it more in line with our family values, which is to manage to pay the school fees without feeling stressed. But I'm not able to do that, because I have this emotional need that's demanding something.

[Ava introduces a new dimension to the conversation – her own emotional need.]

Lucas: I feel resentment when we throw out stuff.

[Lucas does not acknowledge Ava's new dimension, and introduces a new dimension himself, resentment.]

Lucas: So, to me, it's OK to spend, but if we spend well we keep it and we use it to completion. So, the waste is the thing that kills me.

Ava: I would defend the black bags of clothes that we give to charity shops and say that the majority of those are clothes that the kids have actually grown out of.

Lucas: Sure, and then I look at the rooms, and even in the rooms after the bags have gone there is still truckloads of clothing.

[Ava uses 'majority' to describe unwanted clothes, Lucas uses 'truckloads'. A more precise appreciation of degree would improve this conversation.]

Ava: We need to be careful to keep bringing us back to the spending rather than the clothing.

Lucas: Sure, OK. The thing about the adding up at the end of the month is we very rarely gain. We're not one of those families that exceeds their spending. But my real frustration is that we seldom seem to make any kind of headway financially in terms of saving money. It's just unbelievable, you know? I just don't feel like we get ahead, and this is the time of life when we've really got to save for our retirement.

Ava: So, in conversations that we've had in the past, at this point we would probably start saying, 'Well, what strategies can we come up with?'

Lucas: We think of a few things.

Ava: I'm the one who implements the strategies, because I'm the one who does the spending of the family, right?

Lucas: Yes.

Ava: Then, the fact is that I then don't implement them, do I? So, they're, what? Unrealistic strategies?

Lucas: We need consistent execution.

Ava: Yes, or I'm unable to execute that, so why?

Lucas: Do you buy into them?

Ava: Well, notionally, I do, yes. I mean, I want to do all of that, but then . . .

Lucas: One thing that you did say once is that whenever your mother felt hard done by your father, she would go shopping.

[Lucas proposes a linear interaction.]

Ava: I don't remember saying that. Maybe I said it, but it doesn't resonate with me at the moment.

[Ava rejects it.]

Ava: I googled 'Why do I shop?'. A lot of it is, 'it makes me feel loved', 'it makes me feel like I'm caring for myself', 'it makes me feel comfort'.

Lucas: A dopamine hit.

[Ava lists 'love', 'caring' and 'comfort' as dimensions in the system of what compels her to spend money. Lucas says, 'a dopamine hit'. If he is summarising Ava's emotions as 'a dopamine hit', this would be a simplification. If he is proposing an additional dimension to consider, alongside the emotions that Ava has listed, this would allow the complexity of the conversation to develop.]

Ava: I don't know what the chemical is, but I know what the emotion is, but it very quickly turns into a mild form of self-loathing, disappointment, irritation, a complete acknowledgement that that thing I bought isn't going to bring me a lasting sense of comfort. We could just take away the credit cards, but that's not actually going to address the emotional needs, is it?

[Ava rejects the dopamine dimension. She proposes a linear explanation of the spending. Like Lucas's original explanation, it also looks for a 'root cause'. Ava suggests that the root cause is an unmet emotional need.]

Lucas: Those emotional needs, what are they? To feel loved?

[Lucas accepts the additional dimensions that Ava has introduced to the conversation and invites her to explore them.]

Ava: Yes . . . We both know that we are actually loved and cared for.

Lucas: So maybe it's not as deep as your childhood. Maybe it's an early onset addiction, to the dopamine hit?

[The idea that current emotional, relationship or existential difficulties are rooted in unmet, often childhood, emotional needs, is pervasive in psychology. But they are unverifiable.

Also, while it appears to be a 'deep' explanation, it is a mostly linear and actually quite simple explanation (this caused that). But there may also be a complex explanation, that compulsive behaviour contains reinforcing loops that are hard to see or break. In this case, understanding current loops may empower change in a way that understanding lines which lead back to the distant past, does not.]

Ava: We have different ways of phrasing that, because you phrase it with brain chemistry and I with emotion.

Lucas: I think the brain chemistry and the emotion relate.

[Here, Lucas proposes a loop of interaction.]

Lucas: So the way I shop, and I know it's eternally frustrating for you, is that I don't want to waste money, so I spend an awful amount of time researching.

['Eternally' is binary, and 'an awful amount' is imprecise.]

Ava: Yes, sorry, but I would say that that's procrastinating the decision because you don't want to spend the money.

Lucas: I know that's what you're saying, but I'm telling you it's not. It's me, it's the fear . ...

Ava: You watched your father go bankrupt when you were a teen and that really affected your family.

[Ava proposes a linear 'root cause' explanation. These explanations are often beguilingly plausible.]

Lucas: Sure, but to me it's about using the money effectively. I hate it when I buy something and it's rubbish. That, to me, it's an abject failure on my part.

[Lucas does not engage with Ava's root cause explanation. He uses more binary concepts, 'hate', 'rubbish', 'abject failure'.]

Lucas: So we've got very fundamental, different approaches to how we spend money, and there's going to be conflict, because I look at the way you spend money, your judgements, and I'm saying to myself, you're not actually getting enough detail to make a proper purchase decision.

[Lucas makes the point that purchase decisions should be informed by complexity.]

Ava: When you question my judgement on what I buy, that sends me over, because I do use my judgement. Some people are better at spending and some people are better at saving, and saving is not to be valued more highly than spending, because we live in a world where we have to spend money. I do make a good judgement about buying. I ask, 'Is it value for money?', 'Am I going to use it?', 'Is it fit for purpose?' I am using my judgement in those things. I'm just bypassing the question, 'Is it necessary?' (Laughter).

[Ava argues that she does use complexity in making purchasing decisions, and lists the dimensions that she uses – value, usefulness and fit for purpose. But then she sees that without considering the dimension of whether or not the purchase is necessary, even though the purchase decision is complex, it is not sufficiently complex.]

Lucas: That's the thing to understand your point and the rule here about complexity, is that we should be really wary about the terms saver and spender, because there's infinite complexity.

Ava: Or thinking that saving is good and spending is bad.

Lucas: No, but there's infinite complexity in both positions, and as human beings we love stereotyping. It's the only way we cope with our lives is to stereotype each other, and if I put my stereotype on you as being a spender, and you put your stereotype on me as being a saver, then straight away we don't understand each other.

Ava: No, I bypass the, 'Is it necessary?'

Lucas: Correct. You bypass that one little filter which is absolutely key.

Ava: Intentionally.

Lucas: And I'm the saver, but I do sometimes spend.

[The conversation is now a good conversation. Ava and Lucas have both embraced complexity, and this is helping them feel curious about each other and optimistic about being understood. They start to joke about a purchase that didn't work

out. By joking, Lucas has abandoned his prior simplification
that a poor purchase is an 'abject failure'.]

Lucas: But inside these decisions is infinite complexity. If we
want to understand them we have to unpack that complexity.

Ava: I think it's a good point, yes. Well, this is the most
positive conversation we've had about all of this in probably
about eight or nine years.

There were three breakthroughs in this conversation. One was
Ava and Lucas's willingness to use complexity. Another was their
list of the dimensions under which difficult conversations were
more likely to be successful. And a third was Ava's insight that
while her spending decisions were complex, they were not sufficiently complex.

Conversations cannot have infinite scope, and Ava and Lucas
did well to mostly follow Rule 1 and keep the conversation
focused. But given their optimism about future conversations,
I would suggest two topics which could be further explored.

One would be Lucas's use of binary rather than subtle judgements – 'truckloads' and 'abject failure'. He often alleviates these
judgements with humour (sometimes the exaggerations are com-
ical), but nuance is often a better mitigation than humour for the
threats that these extreme judgements can pose to a conversation.

The other would be to explore an alternative to the linear explanation that Ava buys compulsively because of an unmet emotional need. Lucas hints at this when he talks about the interaction
between reward systems and emotion, and Ava hints at it when
she describes cascades of emotions, but neither of them quite close
the loop of how negative emotions can contribute to simplistic

thinking, which can cause the short-term reward of a purchase to be prioritised over the longer term value of family needs, and how repeated priority failures can heighten negative emotions, which clouds insight into the system, but also completes the loop and reinforces the habit.

A COMPLEX WORLD

When we are overwhelmed by complexity we are tempted to switch to simplicity. Multiple dimensions, degrees and interactions are difficult to comprehend, especially under emotional duress. Instead of trying to understand a sequence of events that loops back on itself, we can try to understand the problem in the most simple way possible. Lucas and Ava kept looking for a 'strategy' for their spending problems. They also looked for a simple root cause 'trigger' that trumped every other influence in the system.

Because we struggle with the concepts of randomness and influence, we seek to replace them with something we are all too good at detecting – intent. It is too easy for Lucas and Ava to understand the problem as a failure of Ava's intent. She is not trying hard enough not to spend. This shifts the debate to a moral debate, which is easy to understand, but is not the best way to analyse the system, and it does not take much for a moral debate to get charged and become difficult.

Ideally, we should maintain an understanding of the world that is complex, coherent and without contradiction. A complex, multidimensional set of beliefs and values allows me to understand more of the world that I see.

A coherent view of the world builds logically from established observations or principles. If, for example, we believe in a world based on moral foundations, the society that we try to build should be a logical expression of these values. Human rights are coherent with freedom and fairness. Social norms and rules, and police and the justice system are coherent with authority/social order. Welfare systems and charity are consistent with care. We are driven to establish a morally coherent world.

We also want to understand the world in a way free of contradiction. Sometimes new factual information can challenge us to change our minds. When Greek mathematician Eratosthenes measured different shadow angles from the sun at different locations around the world, this observation contradicted what he would have expected to see had the world been flat. In order to maintain a contradiction-free view of the world, he had to change his belief from that it was flat to that it was round. But sometimes it is difficult to maintain this contradiction-free perspective, particularly with more complex beliefs. If I believe that both freedom and fairness are important, I have to find a way of implementing these values so that my efforts to deliver fairness do not contradict freedom, and my efforts to deliver freedom do not contradict fairness.

Seeing the world in a complex, multidimensional way that is also coherent and free of contradiction is hard work, and sometimes not possible. Life does contain contradictions. Rather than finding the best fit between complexity, coherence and non-contradiction, it is tempting to radically compromise one or more of these. Conspiracy theories work by maintaining coherence and non-contradiction but reducing complexity. They only consider some of the dimensions of the system. By objecting to the contradiction between a moving flag and an atmosphere-free environment, they posit a more coherent explanation, but one which is based on a very limited set of facts. Many of our lesser disagreements follow this same pattern – we each defend an opinion that makes complete sense from an incomplete or simplified perspective.

We do get tired and bored with complexity. Some politicians take advantage of this fatigue by abandoning complexity, coherence and non-contradiction altogether. Even their simple statements can contradict each other or be incoherent. It seems exhausting to have to build a rigorous complex rebuttal to every spuriously generated comment, and so the temptation is to surrender and believe or accept the simplified political message.

To guard against being beguiled by simplicity, we must prime ourselves to quickly observe violations of complexity – insufficient dimensions, absolutes rather than degree and triggers rather than loops. We can respond to these alarm bells and do our best to restore complexity to our thinking.

Losing touch with complexity, coherence and non-contradiction becomes a loop in which blind faith plays a part, where we rely on the judgements of our leaders and peers. Once we feel that we have lost mastery of a topic, we can place inordinate faith in the opinions of others. But using complexity, coherence and non-contradiction positively is also a loop. Mr Hall, my old maths teacher, had a phrase 'faint but pursuing', which expressed that partial understanding is still better than none. Doubt and ignorance are uncomfortable because they challenge our desire to be masters of our subjects. Too often we try to achieve mastery by understanding only part of the world – we achieve coherence and non-contradiction at the expense of complexity. But the world is a big place, and our understanding of it may approximate reality more closely if we accept that it contains contradiction and is not always coherent, and so accept these difficulties, rather than sacrificing complexity.

We want to be intellectually independent, and we want our understanding of the world to be purposeful – that is, we want to be able to influence the world, not just describe it. Complexity is an effort, but this effort is rewarded. The world is an interesting place, and it is a joy to explore it.

Key principles:

When appreciating the complexity of an issue:
    See multiple dimensions
    Use degree
    See how the dimensions interact
    Interactions happen in:
        Lines
        Loops
        Ripples
Try to understand the world in a way that is coherent and free from contradiction. It is tempting to sacrifice complexity to do this

RULE 9: LISTEN

Sometimes listening is easy. When my sons come home at the end of the day, I love to listen to them talk about what they have done. When things are going well for them and their stories are of success, it is easy for me to use all the right listening techniques. I give them my full attention, I am physically still, I mirror them, I remember the details of their stories, I allow them to talk without interrupting and I question them when their stories slow. But I have to temper my enthusiasm also. They have had long days, and even if they are inclined to talk as they come through the front door, the stories are often not as long or the details as complete as I would wish. The answer to my question, 'How was your day?' is all too often, 'Fine.' I do not ask expecting to be overwhelmed with detail or their emotion.

And when they do talk, I have to be careful not to launch into some eager advice giving. Their experience of listening to me giving advice would be quite different to my experience of listening to them tell stories. Particularly at a moment when they are not eager to receive it, and just as I am able to use a range of signals to communicate that their stories are welcome, they are able to subtly communicate those moments when they do not want to listen to me.

This is a transcript of a conversation I had with my youngest son, Lawrence, when he was 14 years old. Lawrence had saved up money for years and wanted to buy a computer.

Tim: OK, so, what are we talking about?

Lawrence: Whether I should get a PC or not and if I'm allowed to get one.

Tim: What is involved in that decision?

Lawrence: If there's enough space for a new PC, if I have enough money to get one that I'm satisfied by, if I really need a new PC, or if I really need my own PC.

Tim: OK, so, I suppose on the one side you've got the costs, which are space and money. On the other side you've got the usefulness of it. So, what is your feeling about the usefulness of it?

Lawrence: Well, I feel having two PCs would mean that I have clearer file space and I can use the PC when I need it, so if my brother needs to do homework, we can both do it on separate PCs.

Tim: How much of a problem is that at the moment?

Lawrence: Not a large problem, but if he does start playing games or when he goes back to college and starts needing to do homework again, it will become a problem. But then another positive, kind of, would be . . . I forgot what I was going to say. I'll think of it later.

[My questioning at this point is quite direct. I am trying to bring rigor to the conversation. But Lawrence's answers are

quite short, and he forgets what he was going to say, which
sometimes happens when we don't feel listened to.]

Tim: So, are you saying we should buy a new computer . . .

Lawrence: Me buy a new computer, myself, as an investment.

Tim: Just to clarify, the reason you're suggesting is that you
can play computer games while Cameron does homework?

[Lawrence has corrected me that he is proposing buying the
computer himself, not have his parents buy it for him. I don't
acknowledge this distinction. Instead I ask quite a critical
question.]

Lawrence: No, it's to have a clearer file space to make a You-
Tube channel.

Tim: What is that?

Lawrence: A YouTube channel?

[Lawrence asks me if I know what a YouTube channel is.
I do know what a YouTube channel is, and he knows that
I know, because we have one together, which chronicles some
of his drone-flying adventures. But at this point he isn't feeling
understood, and this manifests as an assumption that I am
ignorant about his world.]

Tim: No, file space.

Lawrence: Oh, well, at the moment the PC's pretty messy
and I feel having my own PC where everything would be
mine and seeing a file or a document, I'll know exactly what
that is rather than having to look through files and files of
Mom's paperwork and Cameron's homework.

Tim: So, it sounds like you're really saying we should buy a
new PC because the existing PC is a bit messy.

Lawrence: I suppose that is, yes.

Tim: It sounds like there are two problems at the moment that a new PC would overcome, the one is that you would be able to use it when Cameron is using the PC and the second reason is that you would have your own space on the PC. So, I'm guessing we could tidy up the files and I'm guessing that would eliminate the messiness problem. Does that make sense?

[Saying 'does this make sense?' is often really an instruction – 'listen to me!' At this point Lawrence's answers are becoming shorter and shorter.]

Lawrence: Yes.

Tim: It sounds to me like a new PC is something you would really like.

Lawrence: Yes.

Tim: It also kind of sounds to me like we haven't quite got to the bottom of why you would like a PC.

[Finally I am getting somewhere with this conversation. I have listened to how he is listening to me.]

Lawrence: Yes.

Tim: Because those two reasons alone are not really strong, strong reasons. So, what else is there?

[I am applying Rule 3 (most people are good, competent and worthy) here. What I now do successfully is assume that even though Lawrence isn't making sense to me, his reasoning is probably sensible. This enables me to successfully apply Rule 9 (listen) and ask 'what else is there?' Lawrence now does feel listened to and this gives him the motivation and confidence to articulate his ideas.]

Lawrence: Well, there's always the novelty of building a PC, which I've always fancied, since I was little. And having the novelty of something that I spend a lot of time on, that I spend my own money on and that is mine. I've been collecting money ever since I started getting birthday money and working in the garden.

Tim: So, I think one of the difficult things here is that in some ways there's a difference between the practical reasons for buying a PC . . .

Lawrence: Not needing it, but actually just wanting one.

[This is an honest and important distinction that requires confidence to make.]

Tim: Yes, and the emotional reasons for buying it. If we were to upgrade our PC, you won't have the experience of building a computer and that is something that you . . .

Lawrence: Fantasise about.

[This is a strong expression, and shows that through my questioning and listening I have helped him to find his voice.]

Tim: That you would like to build a computer and have your own computer. I do know you don't ask for a lot, you know, you're not a materialistic person, so it's not like this is just one more thing that you're asking for.

[Rule 3 again.]

Lawrence: Yes, and it isn't even like if I'm really asking for it, I'm asking for permission and a small investment, but mainly permission.

Tim: Because would having your own PC feel like sort of having your own space?

Lawrence: Yes.

Tim: Is it almost like having your own room or something?

Lawrence: Yes, it's sort of having my own space in the virtual world. It would be like a little independent zone just for me, that nobody else goes on.

[Lawrence had been talking about the computer for weeks, so I thought I was familiar with the details, but I definitely felt like I learnt something from this conversation, even though the learning only started happening part way through.]

ASSIMILATION AND ACCOMMODATION

The Swiss psychologist Jean Piaget explained learning as an inter-action between assimilation and accommodation. Assimilation is the process of taking in new information and accommodation is adjusting what we currently believe to contain the new informa-tion while maintaining a complex, coherent and non-contradictory view of the world.

When I listen to my sons at the end of their days, the listening is usually easy, and I can use good listening techniques because the work of assimilation and accommodation is light. I can assimilate because I know that my sons are unlikely to overwhelm me with too much content, and I can accommodate because I expect that their stories will be mostly happy ones. We are all good at listen-ing to small amounts of good news.

When I was working as a psychologist, I was also a good lis-tener. I was confident that I could assimilate the amount of con-tent because the interaction was limited by time. Sometimes the nature of the content was extremely distressing, and it was hard work to take this in. I found it difficult to listen to the stories of people who had been affected by crime. It is not easy to listen to a father describe the emotion of having a gun in his back while somebody forces him to unlock the front door to the house that contains his children, or to hear secrets of childhood trauma.

But I hope that I listened to my clients well, by giving them my full attention, using non-verbal cues to indicate my receptiveness, respecting the ebb and flow of their narrative, prompting with appropriate questions and remembering the details of their story from one session to the next. I did this work because I was paid to do it, and also because I cared for my clients and my profession. But I also did it because it was made possible by the boundaries of my work. I knew that the volume of content was finite and, if the nature of the content was sometimes difficult to take in, accommodating it was made possible by the training that I have received. When I heard stories about human frailty or hostility, I was often able to accommodate this information within my existing ideas about the world. This made it less threatening than if I was having to continually revise my understanding of human nature.

This is a transcript from a conversation I had with two friends, Raoul and Puneet. We are discussing wealth inequality in society. They both say things that I disagree with. The first time, I manage to keep listening . . .

Tim: I don't think concern about slackers should affect how we design a social safety net.

Raoul: I don't know how many scroungers there are. I don't know how much more waste the system can bear.

Tim: I think that's a good question, worth unpacking. What do we mean by waste? And what do we mean by the system?

Raoul: Yes, I don't mean all social support is waste. We can clarify that.

[Even though I disagreed with Raoul's general opinion, I managed to keep listening and this led to some clarifications and distinctions which allowed us to move closer to agreement.]

Puneet: That's the natural law. Inequality is nature. As you look at the law of the jungle, it is exactly that.

Tim: But is that what you want?

Puneet: We are effectively animals.

[By asking a binary (and arguably irrelevant) question that communicates my disagreement, I provoke Puneet to disagree with me even more strongly and simplify and entrench his position. We lose the opportunity to unpack the question and find points of agreement.]

We all know how to listen. It's easy to listen when the listening is easy. But these conditions don't always hold, and at these times it can be useful to understand the threats to listening and to see if there are ways to avoid or manage them.

THREATS TO LISTENING

If I am being presented with information that is negative (like criticism or disagreement), difficult (like a maths lesson) or upsetting (like someone talking about their distress), I am less likely to be motivated to assimilate it. And if I do assimilate what I hear, I may still refuse to accommodate it. I could criticise the criticism and disagree with the disagreement. When I listen in this style, I am not listening to learn. I am assimilating but not with the intention of learning or accommodating anything, only with the intention of detecting opportunities to attack the account that I am listening to. I am looking to move my interlocutor, rather than be moved by them.

'Accommodate' doesn't mean replacing one simple worldview with another. It means filtering new information, taking in that which is of good quality and is relevant and working out how to improve our understanding of the world by accommodating the new information within our broader existing view. This new view will probably be more complex, and possibly more contradictory and less coherent than the one that it replaces.

Accurate assimilation and rigorous accommodation include hard System 2 work, and like all System 2 work, we need to be persuaded to do it. Sometimes when my sons decline my advice, they are making a fair call. It may not be the time or the place, and I may not be fully informed about the situation. But it is also possible that there are times when their rejection is in error. I have discussed this with other parents, including world-class athletes whose own children find it difficult to be coached by them and the owner of a prestigious fashion company whose son found it difficult to listen to his advice – on fashion. Part of the job of being a teenager is to become independent. Receiving advice from a parent contradicts this notion of independence and can also introduce an element of complexity that is not always welcome.

The other category of difficult listening is listening to accounts of emotional distress. As with listening to something that challenges our belief, this content has to be assimilated and accommodated in order for effective listening to take place. But the process of listening to and containing this emotion is different from the classic System 2 work of adding to or adjusting a worldview.

When I was a young psychologist in my late twenties, I saw a woman who was older than me. She had not come to discuss her father, but she mentioned him as part of a conversational thread about something else and thinking about him interrupted her train of thought. She paused, sitting straight up in her chair. I wasn't expecting what came next – she said, 'He died 10 years ago, and I still miss him *so* much!' and, still looking at me, her face suddenly crumpled and tears sprung silently from her open eyes and zigzagged down the creases in her cheeks. I was surprised because I hadn't expected her grief to be so deep or fresh from a bereavement that had occurred 10 years previously. But I was a young man and hadn't yet suffered an intimate loss myself. Now, 18 years after the death of my own father, I understand her emotion better. But, despite my naivety, it was still my job to listen to her. I had to accept her grief. This meant allowing her to express her grief fully, by giving her time and attention to show my respect for her tears, words and silent reflections. I had to listen attentively to her words and observe her sadness.

But my attention alone wasn't enough, I needed to allow her emotion to change me, I had to share her grief. I had to feel sad also. How was this possible for a young man who had not lost a parent? I was not mourning her father, but I cared about her and I was mourning that she had suffered loss. It should be obvious, even though we often act as if it isn't, that for her to share her emotion with me I needed to receive it, and this meant feeling it also. I became sad because she was sad. I had to grieve for her grief.

In the early years of my practice, I saw some young women who found eating difficult and complex. For one young woman, eating evoked fears, emotions and associations that meant that the need to taste, fuel, and replenish her body were far from her only considerations about food. This complexity was wearying for her, and her preoccupation with this difficulty distracted her from other challenges and opportunities in her life, so in addition to being pained by how difficult it was for her to eat, she was saddened and angered by the awareness that this problem was costing her more broadly. During one session, she became overwhelmed and wept, grieving for the potential of a young life that she did not know how to realise. I knew no better, and so all I could do was listen respectfully to her grief and try to share it with her. At the end of the hour, she looked at me and said, 'I have never cried so much.' I said to her, 'And you are still here.'

I was trying to show that I had observed and felt her emotion – I had done the work of assimilation and accommodation – but I had also survived. I was using my resilience to cope with her emotion. Accommodating her distress was possible because I was housing it within a larger system of relationships, emotions, ambitions and beliefs. Her distress changed this system, but it didn't destroy it. By accepting her emotion I could make it more possible for her to accept it. It was a long way from a solution, but it may have helped, and it created the possibility for us to continue to talk without avoiding difficult topics or always being overwhelmed by emotion.

The longer I worked as a therapist, the more complex and rich my experiences became. This is one of the privileges of being a therapist – you partake in many more intimate and important conversations than ordinary life would normally provide. If you can avoid becoming calloused to emotion, or overwhelmed by it, you have the opportunity to build a deep and complex acceptance of emotion and life, and this gives you the resilience to accept and absorb emotions and stories that are difficult because you have heard and survived difficult stories before.

I have only cried twice in my professional career. On one occasion I was working with a boy who had broken his neck after someone had tackled him with a foul tackle on the rugby field, and in an instant was permanently paralysed from the neck down. I had attended a case meeting with his parents, his doctor and a neurosurgeon. It was incredibly sad to consider how life had changed for this boy. We all had tears in our eyes, but nobody cried, not even his parents. I got home and put my oldest son, who was a baby at the time, into the bath. I could no longer contain my emotion and I wept. I remember my son's sensitive reaction. He had possibly never seen an adult cry before. He was used to the full-throated wails of the young, not this strange sobbing. He mimicked my intakes of breath, trying to understand what was going on. It is obviously not the job of a baby to contain the emotion of a parent and I recovered to pay him my full attention, but I remember his response as something precious.

The other time I cried as a psychologist was during my training. We were visiting an orphanage and we went to the infant ward. At the time, South Africa was suffering from an HIV/AIDS epidemic which was orphaning thousands of children each year. The ward had two rows of cots, about 30 in total, and each one contained a crying baby. The case worker explained that the infants were mostly HIV positive because they would have been infected during pregnancy and they would die within a couple of years.

There were not enough staff to hold them, and they would spend most of their lives alone in a cot.

Glimpses of some of the sadness of the world could be hard to take in. But if I could survive my job, I would be enriched by its complexity. If I could tolerate stories which didn't make sense or which contradicted a previous belief, and if I could contain the emotion that my clients shared with me, I would be able to listen to them, which, the longer I did it the more I realised, was the major part of what they wanted from me and also the foundation of whatever else it was that I had to offer.

Sometimes it is hard to listen because we are reluctant to handle complexity, and sometimes it is hard because the person who is talking to us is sharing difficult or persistent emotions. But sometimes it is hard because what we are hearing evokes difficult emotions in us. These situations include finding ourselves in error, disagreement or realising that we have something to learn.

In her book, *Being Wrong: Adventures in the Margins of Error,* Kathryn Schulz makes the lovely point that the feeling of being wrong is exactly the same as the feeling of being right. Because when we are wrong, we don't know that we are wrong. We think we are right. It is the discovery or the exposure of error that is the difficult part. This is the bit that is hard to listen to. Being wrong is a test of our resilience.

In chapter 1, when I ran over the squirrel, it was quite difficult for me to assimilate the message from Claudia that I shouldn't have swerved or to accommodate the idea that it had been the wrong decision. As it happened, I had recently seen a YouTube video where a squirrel does escape death by running between the wheels of a car. While there were some similarities between the situations, a key difference is that the person in the video was driving a Lamborghini and I was in a Peugeot 307. The shock of killing the squirrel and my sense of some culpability combined with an unwelcome comparison to a Lamborghini driver produced emotions in me that made it harder for me to listen to Claudia's comment. My resilience was tested. I was saddened, embarrassed and guilty about killing the squirrel. In the moment, these emotions seemed significant, justifying a significant quantity of emotion. The error seemed to lie with me – my decision to swerve, and that I didn't own a Lamborghini. It seemed abiding – while I don't often run over squirrels, I do sometimes make unconventional decisions, and the non-ownership of Lamborghinis is a fairly fixed state of affairs.

Because we are poor at deriving the particular from the general, it is difficult to reason, 'Like all humans I make occasional errors, so it is possible for me to be wrong in this particular situation.' But because we are inclined to derive the general from the particular, we are tempted to reason, 'If I am wrong in this situation it means I could be wrong in many situations.' This general and particular reasoning bias can leave us both unable to detect and unwilling to admit error. So, while I am able to generally acknowledge that I am not a perfect driver, I still need to remind myself to hear advice from the passenger seat for what it is – information – rather than a more general comment upon myself. When I remember this, it is easier for me to listen.

HEARING MORE THAN IS SAID

When I was studying to be a psychologist, the predominant theory that we were trained in was psychodynamic theory – the theories of Freud, Klein, Winnicott and Bion. Freud presented psychoanalysis as a science. Bion said that, 'It is very important to be aware that you may never be satisfied with your analytic career if you feel that you are restricted to what is narrowly called a 'scientific' approach. You will have to be able to have a chance of feeling that the interpretation you give is a beautiful one, or that you get a beautiful response from the patient. This aesthetic element of beauty makes a very difficult situation tolerable.' This idea was very attractive to us as young psychologists. It sounds as if Bion is saying that we need to use System 1 as well as System 2 in our listening, and when we comment on what we have heard, we will be able to observe if we are correct by the response of the person that we are listening to.

But there is a danger to this approach – hearing that which has not been said. The psychoanalyst Melanie Klein was talking to her own son who told her of his wish to be able to walk along the telegraph lines above the streets all the way to school. Klein explained this wish with an elaborate psychoanalytic theory, but given that they were German Jews and this was just before the Second World War, a more prosaic explanation is that the boy wanted to avoid antisemitic bullying.

As young psychologists, we were enthralled by the explanatory power of psychoanalytic theories. What we did not think of is that predictive power and the power to create change are both more important than the power to explain, and there are psychological theories that do a better job of the former two than psychoanalysis. We were not aware, when we interpreted what it was that our clients were saying, that our explanations failed Rule 7 in that they were unverifiable – there was no way to tell whether or not they were correct. We were taught that sometimes when our clients objected to our explanations that this was emotional resistance to the truth, rather than our own error.

Bion also said, 'The purest form of listening is to listen without memory or desire.' In our counselling, it was important for us to learn to hear all of what was being said, but no more.

This imperative exists for everyday conversations also. It is easy for us to put words into the mouths of people that we are listening to. Warning signs that this is happening are statements like, 'So what you are saying is . . .', 'What you are really telling me is . . .'. As with a therapist in a counselling session, in everyday conversations we are required to consider and evaluate what it is that we have been told, but this can only properly happen after we have understood what the other person has actually said.

LISTENING AND LEARNING

Carol Dweck's growth/fixed mindset theory, outlined in *Mindset*, offers what has become one of the most important perspectives into learning. Dweck says that those people who explain success as being a consequence of learning (growth mindset) behave differently from those people who explain success as being a consequence of talent (fixed mindset). People with growth mindsets seek challenges, want to learn, are prepared to invest effort, use criticism constructively and are inspired by the success of others. Failure is not intimidating for them because they don't see it as defining and believe it can be solved through effort. People with fixed mindsets avoid challenge and are less motivated to learn because they explain success as being a consequence of inborn talent, so they don't see the value of effort. They take criticism more personally and can be jealous of the success of others.

A few months ago, I went to India to visit a professional cricket team. Ishant Sharma is one of the senior established members of this franchise team as well as the Indian national team. He is a 1.95m-tall fast bowler and, as we assembled for dinner, he waved a long arm at me and invited me to come and sit at his table. He then spent the evening grilling me on sports psychology and listening intently and critically to my answers.

Some elite athletes shut up shop. They consider themselves to have reached their best level and intend to keep doing what they already do for as long as possible before they run out of road. These athletes have nothing to receive from me. Others, even highly successful athletes, want to keep learning. Ishant has a growth mindset. He wasn't an uncritical listener. Much of what I said didn't fit with his own ideas. But he considered everything that I said and accommodated some of it within the performance philosophy that he continually develops.

But the fact that Ishant is an eager and also critical listener meant that I had to be on my game. I had to listen to him also. We were talking just before a major tournament, so he didn't want to have to accommodate major shifts in his mental approach. He was looking for subtle suggestions to help him improve something that he was already very good at. So I had to listen to him to understand what he already knew and what he wanted to know. If I could successfully listen to how he was listening to me, I could reduce the quantity and improve the quality of my own suggestions and make them more palatable. This way, I could tell when I was starting to talk too much or when I was telling him something that he didn't need or wasn't interested in. I could then moderate my own message and make it easier and more useful for him to listen to me. In this way, I was using Ishant's disagreement to try to effectively adapt my behaviour. But disagreement is not always this easy to manage. Often the relationships or the issues are more charged, which makes the disagreement harder to handle. Once during a therapy session I was surprised to find myself in such strong disagreement with my client that I was lost for words. Durban is a multicultural city with a large Muslim population. The Muslim community there has a strong family focus and many of my clients were Muslim children.

One day in a therapy session, a boy I worked with was playing with some building blocks as we talked. In a pause in the conversation, he realised that he had built two adjacent towers of similar height. He said, 'Hey, the Twin Towers!' and laughed and knocked them down. I was left without words. The boy was clearly making a reference to 9/11, and what shocked me was that for the boy it appeared to be a positive reference.

I had never considered meeting someone who held this stance. What made it more difficult to continue to listen was that I did not have the option of disliking or rejecting the boy. I knew him and his family well. On one occasion I had watched the boy play a football match on a hot morning. On that day, this boy was fasting voluntarily for Ramadan. He had planned to only watch the match himself, but when one of the scheduled players did not arrive, he offered to play. He showed selflessness, courage and discipline to play a full match in the blazing sun and then go the rest of the day without a drink. I admired him for that. And I didn't just have positive emotions towards him, I had a professional obligation to him. His parents were paying me to help him gain a specific skill, and I was morally bound to do my best to help him. How could I cope with this disagreement?

Initially it felt as if this disagreement would define our relationship – he was apparently in favour of something I stood vehemently against. What troubled me next was that it seemed certain that he must have inherited this belief from his family. I was using the same logic as the man in the shopping mall might have when my son told me not to talk to black people: the child holds X belief. He is too young to have developed the belief independently. The parent must hold X belief even more strongly and simply than the child.

Part of staying willing and able to listen was realising that the extent of our disagreement may have been less than I first assumed. Possibly the Twin Towers comment did not reveal a complete and implacable opposition between his family's allegiances and mine. My initial assumption may have been wrong in quality (maybe the boy and his family didn't actually celebrate 9/11) or in quantity (the position of the boy and his family may have been more nuanced than just being 'against' America). The boy's chance comment had seemed to give me a sudden moment of insight. I initially felt that I disagreed with him profoundly, but when I thought about it more carefully, actually there was a lot that I did not know. I needed to listen to him more, not less.

Using this realisation allowed me to consider that my disagreement with him could have come from a place other than irreconcilable differences. I only saw the boy once a week, so I had time to process my own emotions and thoughts and by the time I saw him next, I was able to start listening to him again.

When I consider the people that I am closest to and rely on the most, the fact that they listen to me is a big part of the relationship. When John Gottman says relationships depend on knowing, admiring, turning towards, influencing, solving, overcoming, and creating meaning, the people who listen to me build each of these dimensions in our relationship through their listening. Understanding the challenges to listening, that assimilating or accommodating can for many reasons be difficult or threatening, can make us more able to listen. Understanding the benefits of listening, that it can give us the ability to conduct nuanced, problem-solving discussions like the one I held with Ishant Sharma, or deepen the relationships that we rely on by enriching every dimension of those relationships, can make us more willing to listen.

My friend Eddie is a great listener. When I am with Eddie I become a better talker. Eddie makes me become funnier and more erudite than I normally am. When we are together, we create a system in which talking and listening both improve each other. When I am listened to, I talk better, but I listen better also. These situations are rare. They illustrate the value and pleasure of good listening and are worth trying to find or create more often.

Key principles:

We indicate our willingness to listen by:
Being physically attentive
Reflecting on what has been said
Asking for more detail
Responding precisely to what we hear
Listening involves assimilating (taking in) and accommodating (adjusting our worldview to accept) new information
Listening is not always easy. It can be harder when we are presented with complex information, information that challenges our beliefs or an emotionally challenging message

Having a growth– rather than fixed – mindset makes listening
more possible

We should try to hear all that is said, but not more than what
has been said

This is a conversation between an Amazon customer and an
Amazon call centre assistant.

Customer: I ordered an item from you – a collector's edi-
tion Gods of War figurine. But it turned up with stickers all
over the actual item itself rather than in a box. I went into
the website to try and arrange a replacement, but it was sold
out. So then I rang you and I was offered a discount, but,
you know, that was no use to me, because I want the item as
I ordered it.

Then I was told that I could send it back for a refund. But
sending it back for a refund isn't going to solve my issue
either, because I want the item. The third option I was given
was that I could buy it from Amazon Marketplace, but
that you wouldn't be prepared to refund me the difference
in price.

But the item is in stock with Amazon sellers whose orders
are fulfilled by Amazon, so it's actually stocked by you. So
you could actually replace this item. Why is it when you've
actually got them in your warehouse, you're not prepared to
send a replacement out for me?

Customer Service: The three options sir, I cannot do anything other than what you have already been offered – that is
a discount or a return. We cannot refund you the difference
in price from another seller, that is not our policy, which

was available to you before you bought the item. We cannot replace the item because we do not have it in stock. It is stocked by a seller that is independent from us.

[There is quite a lot of information in this opening statement and the customer service agent has done quite a good job of assimilating the facts.]

Customer: It says here that it's stored, packed and dispatched by Amazon. So it's actually in your warehouse.

Customer Service: I am able to see that, sir, but that's coming from a different seller.

Customer: OK. But what I don't understand is, given that you've got access to it and you were the people who failed to send me an item in good condition, why you can't actually source this for me and replace it with this? I know there's a difference in price, but that's not my problem, is it? That was the situation that was created by you.

[The customer is assimilating information – he has heard that the item is stocked by an independent seller. But he is not accommodating this information – he is not adjusting his own worldview to take it into account. He is refusing to understand that although Amazon has physical access to the item, it does not have legal access to the item.]

Customer Service: We do not have an option of creating a replacement at all. If I had an option, I would have done it right away for you.

Customer: The only way I could now get the item would be to pay extreme prices compared to what I paid for it originally. And you have to admit that this situation was created by you, not me. I'm left in a position where there's nothing

I can do, I either hold on to a faulty item or I get a refund and I don't have the item I paid for.

You are in a position that you have items that you can send out and you're not prepared to do that. Is that what you're telling me, that you're not prepared to actually solve my problem?

[The customer is starting to hear more than is being said. There is a difference between being unable to solve a problem and unwilling to solve a problem. The customer is hearing that the customer service agent is unwilling to solve this problem.]

Customer Service: Right, sir. I told you earlier that I do not have an option of creating a replacement.

Customer: Yeah, well, I understand that. But, you know, my argument here is that I paid for an item.

Customer Service: I understand that, sir, I understand that you have paid for the item, and you can return the item for a full refund.

[At this point, the customer service agent is starting to find the conversation difficult. Her voice is becoming quieter and she sounds sad. There are occasional pauses in the conversation where it seems that she is lost for words. But she maintains most of the technical requirements of listening – she gives the customer space to talk and tells him that she understands.]

Customer: Yes. Should you not be bending over backwards to try and source me a replacement? This is what I'm asking you. Because as I say, I've said this before, this was a situation that was created by you. And, as I say, you actually have got the item in your warehouse. And it would seem to me that you have got a situation here that you can solve.

Customer Service: You are repeating the same thing again and again in spite of me providing you with the solution. What else do you want me to do? Because there is no option that I have where I can create a replacement for you.

[The customer has just presented an important piece of information that the service agent fails to assimilate. He says that Amazon should be 'bending over backwards' for him. Is this a correct or fair belief? The customer has explicitly voiced an opinion that is key to this conversation, and the service agent has not heard it, and so they lose the opportunity to discuss it. Instead she says he is repeating himself.]

Customer: OK. But do you understand where I'm coming from here? It's very easy for you to solve this. You have access to this item. You could get that item to me. There is no real reason other than . . .

[Now it is the customer's turn not to listen. He is accommodating the fact that while Amazon has physical access to the item, it does not have legal access to the item. But he cannot learn that it is in fact not 'very easy' for the agent to solve this problem.]

Customer Service: But if I don't have an option, how do you think that I can create a replacement for you?

Customer: So you understand that a discount isn't going to solve the issue. A refund isn't going to solve the issue.

Customer Service: Exactly. I understand that, sir. But apart from that, you think from my point of view as well, sir, if I would have an option, why would I not create a replacement for you?

[The agent is clearly saying that she is not solving the problem because she is unable to, not because she is unwilling to. The customer does not hear this. This is potentially useful information, because he could either have accepted her offer or asked if there was someone else who had the authority to be able to help him.]

Customer: I understand that. All I'm saying and I know I keep repeating myself here, but why is it not the situation that you could actually say to me, look, buy it from the third party seller and we'll replace the difference, given, you know, that this is a goodwill gesture, in effect? And I just don't understand why there's not more of an effort being made. It just seems odd that you almost have a kind of disdain for me as a customer. It just seems crazy that you guys don't seem to want to help me ... (silence) ... Hello?

[The customer is now hearing disdain and craziness. This is not what the customer service agent has communicated. The customer service agent falls silent as she tries to emotionally process this accusation.]

Customer Service: I'm listening, sir.

RULE 10: REACH OUT

One day, when I was a boy in Cape Town in the mid-1970s, we went to the travelling dolphin circus which had set up temporarily in Seapoint. That was worse, rather than not as bad as it sounds, as wild-caught dolphins were suspended in slings as they were transported in trucks from town to town, kept alive with water sprayed on their skins, and then required to perform tricks in small, shallow, portable pools of seawater. I was four years old and I was absolutely enchanted by the dolphins. When it came to that part of the show where they invited a young member of the audience to join the dolphin in the pool and be towed around without a life jacket in a small inflatable boat, I remember my conviction that the invitation was for me only. I could not swim, and I would be entering a watery enclosure with a wild animal without my mother's permission, let alone any minimum height check, or health and safety briefing. But earlier in the show one of the dolphin's tricks had been to rescue a plastic doll thrown into the pool and the audience probably assumed that, in the unlikely event of anything going wrong, the dolphin could have lifted me with its pectoral fins and tail-walked me to the side of the pool and into the trainer's arms. Nothing did go wrong; I sat in the boat, thrilled by my connection to the animal. I can still feel the strength of its surges through the water as it held the thin rope in its mouth and pulled me and the unstreamlined little boat through the choppy waves behind it.

Many years later, but when I was still young, I was working in my job as a scuba instructor. By now I had swum with whale sharks, turtles, eels and rays, but the dolphins that I still searched for normally avoided scuba divers and their noisy bubbles. One day after the students had finished diving, I was free to snorkel alone about a kilometre offshore in about eight metres of water. I heard the whistles and clicks of a pod of dolphins coming close, but underwater sound has no direction, so I did not know where they were coming from. Eventually they came up on me from behind and slipped underneath me. I kept pace with them for a while, but only one was interested in me – a baby dolphin swimming with his mother and aunt. He kept twisting onto his back to look at me and make eye contact from underneath them and I followed him hoping to get closer. He was curious about me and also wanted to be closer. We swam over the same patch of ocean floor for a while, gazing at each other, him at the bottom of the sea and me at the top, but his mother and his aunt shielded him from me with their bodies and eventually pushed him away from me into the murky water and I heard their clicks recede. I was left floating on the surface of the sea, enchanted, but slightly unsatisfied by the encounter.

But that was just the beginning. That whole summer, the dolphins wanted to play. I swam and surfed with them repeatedly. I was surfing one morning in a silver sea and paddled for a wave flanked by dolphins, close enough to touch on either side. We skimmed the water together, me just above the surface and them just beneath and, as the wave broke, instead of getting to my feet and riding the face, I sat up and pulled out of the wave so that we would not collide. One of them rode for a moment further, burst out of the back of the breaking wave and did a backwards somersault right in front of me, then splashed back into the water and disappeared. This is a memory from the intersection of childhood and adulthood. I may never repeat it, but I have felt privileged by it ever since. I do remember that longing, and that joy of connection.

When I was in my early twenties, I was hitting a ball by myself on the squash court when a man knocked on the door and asked if I wanted to play. We played and became regular partners, then friends (which we are still, 25 years later). Once a thought came to one of us just before I was about to serve and we stood on the court and debated some matter, rackets and ball in hand, for almost the entire period of the booking.

I enjoyed a much briefer encounter with a friend once. We lived in different countries and hadn't seen each other for years. My friend was flying somewhere and had a transfer through London. He scorched out of Heathrow and came to see me. We had time for two embraces and 15 minutes of joyful conversation, and it seemed that the effort we had made for that brief connection had really been worth it.

BIDS

When Claudia and I argue, sometimes when things are most heated, she will pause and sigh, and give me a look that is part frustration, part sadness. This is her way of saying that she wishes that we weren't having this argument. I don't know what my face is doing at this point because I am behind it, but this is my cue to reach out and touch her, and maybe kiss her on the cheek, after which we can resume arguing, although with reduced intensity. This is what John Gottman calls a bid, when one partner in a couple invites closeness, and the other partner accepts or declines.

There are different types of bids. Requests are simple appeals for help along the lines of 'Can you take the bins out tonight?' They are fairly innocuous in terms of the amount of time or effort that they are requesting. The response to the bid can be positive or negative, and the bid can be accepted or refused. So, on being asked to take the bins out, you could refuse angrily or acquiesce angrily. Or decline graciously or regretfully (hopefully with a good reason) or accept graciously. Each of these responses could have some degree of emotional impact on the relationship.

At work, we eat lunch in the canteen. After the meal, different people take turns to take the coffee order and serve it to everybody. I don't drink coffee, so I am excluded from this particular ritual, which makes me aware of how such a simple request as offering or accepting a coffee still creates a moment of shared pleasure and builds or maintains relationships over time.

Another form of bid is a request for attention. When I studied baboons on the Drakensberg mountains in the early 1990s, they would request attention from each other by plonking themselves down in front of another baboon, either sitting with their backs to them or flat on their backs, stomachs up. This was a bid for a flea hunt, but like the coffees in my canteen, the interaction played a deeper role than the surface activity. These requests take different forms. When humans talk, chat, listen and joke with someone, the attention we pay is a comment on our interest in the person, as much as what they are talking about. We have all had the experience of trying to start a conversation with a comment or a question and waiting for a second or two to see how our bid for attention or connection will be received.

When we are confident that our bids will be accepted, or that we will survive a refusal, we can make direct bids also. In the time I spent in the Drakensberg I saw many baboons make successful requests for a back scratch, and in 25 years of my own marriage, have found no way or reason to improve on their method of asking. But when we make more charged bids, where we would feel a refusal more keenly, they can become more subtle. This is why a request for a coffee, to take out the bins, or to listen to the story of the day can take on a deeper meaning.

One of these meanings is relationship building and confirming – countless daily actions that individually do not count for much, but collectively accumulate to significantly affect the long-term course of a relationship. Each one counts.

And sometimes we bid for something more immediate and non-routine. Sometimes when I come home from work, Claudia will detect from the tone of my voice that I just need to be listened to for a bit, and by giving me her full attention and acceptance, she helps share and relieve the emotion that has built up and is troubling me. Sometimes I just need to be listened to, and sometimes I need her advice or her participation in working something out. My mother tells me that when I was a little boy, I could never get lost, because as soon as she was out of sight I would start to wail so loudly that I would instantly be found. I do think I am mostly good at asking for help when I need it, although I know I have the advantage that it is easier to ask when you believe your request will be accepted.

Our adult sons are at a stage where we need to be more alert to bids from them. They are more independent now and contain much of their own emotion and solve most of their own problems. They often use friends for emotional support and are cautious of depending on us in the way that they did when they were boys. But as we reconfigure our relationship from parents of children to parents of adults, we still get subtle bids for support, when they want to get something off their chests or problem solve.

We can also bid for affection, and for company. In any bid, we are taking some degree of risk by indicating a vulnerability, desire or a need that we hope the person of whom we are making the request will support. One way of managing the risk is to disguise the bid or make it less obvious. Sometimes the more afraid we are of having a request refused, the more subtly we make the request. But a subtle bid is also more at risk of being missed or declined. In these cases, Rule 10 applies to both parties: reach out by making the request and reach out by being alert to and responding to it.

The First Minister of Scotland Nicola Sturgeon told a story about meeting the then British Prime Minister Theresa May. May was wearing fashionable shoes and Sturgeon complimented her on them, but May didn't respond to the invitation to discuss anything other than the political agenda. She had missed the bid.

In 1995, Nelson Mandela made a bid for reconciliation with white South Africans by making an appearance at the opening game of the Rugby World Cup. Rugby is historically a white sport in South Africa, and by walking out into the middle of the stadium in front of 50,000 mostly white fans, Mandela was risking rejection. Democracy was only one year old, and Mandela was a brand-new president reaching out to a part of the population that had kept him in jail for 27 years, but had now, for a variety of reasons, relinquished their non-democratic control of the country. How would they react to this bid? I remember feeling the tension as I watched it happen live on television. Slowly, and then raucously, the crowd began to chant Mandela's name. The bid had been made and accepted.

FRIENDLINESS

Another way to fulfil Rule 10 (reach out) is friendliness. We have just got a new puppy. When we went to fetch it, I was a little concerned about separating it from its mother, but as it turned out, it was her third litter and she had lost interest in the pups, so the goodbye was not traumatic for either of them. What was charged were the hellos. The puppy instantly worked out that we were his new family and set about making friends with us. Eye contact, physical contact, play, body language and agreeableness (doing what we asked him to do) were all deployed with full intensity. Dogs have lived with human beings for 60,000 years and have adapted to our code of bonding. The puppy was open to new connections, but he was alone and helpless in a big world. What was remarkable was the optimism with which he faced this situation.

When one of my sons was younger, he would similarly prioritise connecting with visitors when they came to the house for the first time. He would be sure to be in their proximity until he was satisfied that a bond had been established. Babies do this also, by making unabashed eye contact and smiling with their whole faces. Friendliness is communicating an openness to making a new connection. Comedian Jerry Seinfeld talks about this openness to new relationships at different stages of life.

He says that in your thirties, it's hard to make new friends. His idea is that you are committed to the friends that you have. His sitcom *Seinfeld* was about this 'for better or for worse' commitment to a group. He likens vacancies for friends to vacancies for jobs, and says, 'If I meet a guy in a club or a gym or something, I'm thinking, "Look I'm sure you're very nice person, you seem to have a lot of potential, we're just not hiring right now."' Seinfeld contrasts this no-vacancies adult state to the state of childhood, where we are more open to new friendships. He says that for a child, if someone is not a grown-up, and is standing in front of the child's house, they must be friends ... 'Come on in, let's jump on my bed.' And if two children discover anything in common, for example both liking cherry soda, it means they must be best friends.

For the puppy, and my young son, inviting contact through friendliness made sense. Both of them were in the stage of life where they, to use Seinfeld's terminology, had vacancies. This does not always seem to be the case. Once I was riding my bicycle home from work when I was surprised to see a famous athlete that I worked with walking alone down the street. I called out to him but was surprised by his response. He didn't recognise me in my cycling helmet and glasses and instantly shrank from my call. It seemed that he had been enjoying a moment of solitude and anonymity and I had threatened it. Once he realised it was me, he was back to his normal friendly self, but that moment did give me an insight into his world, that he was occasionally overwhelmed with requests for relationships and, at those times, valued solitude over friendliness.

You don't have to be famous to understand this caution; millions of people use it daily as they travel on London's public transport systems and don't greet or make eye contact with people that they may have been travelling with for years. Mobile phones and headphones increase the ability to disengage. Some people criticise this as unfriendliness, but most commuters are exposed to a crowded space for prolonged periods twice a day and may just be protecting themselves from being overwhelmed. If they were to raise their emotional barriers just slightly, it would mean admitting a lot of extra people.

Schoolchildren are cautious about friendship, as their relationships are high stakes. They will be spending years in close proximity with a broad group of people that they did not select and so need to measure their alliances and interactions within that group carefully. Rejected overtures for friendship would lead to a loss of status and receptiveness to the friendship of low status or outgroup members would also be socially costly. Judgements about who to be friendly with need to be carefully made.

After driving a car in South Africa, I find London traffic very friendly. People from other parts of the United Kingdom may have a different reference point, but I am struck by Londoners' willingness to give way in tight spaces and at intersections, usually with a smile and a wave, to ease the passage of somebody that they will likely never interact with again. The logic seems to be that individual friendliness feeds a systemic cooperation, which will in turn benefit each individual. In South Africa, sadly, there is no such agreement. Spaces of road are defended resolutely. Every time you want to change lanes or join a new road at an intersection, the interaction is like a staring match or a game of chicken. It's quite tiring to have to fight your way to work and home again every day, and even if you are not inclined to be aggressive, there is less incentive to be friendly because your good deeds are unlikely to find their way back to you.

The execution of friendliness is not complicated – an 11-week-old puppy can pull it off with total success. The difficulty is more in the judgement of when to be friendly, as our decisions about whether to initiate or accept friendliness are informed by the potential risks and rewards of opening a connection to somebody else. We are correct to discourage overtures that would be overwhelming in their number or intensity and also correct to reject friendliness that proposes a relationship that does not appear to be in our best interests. But sometimes we miss moments where, for the price of a smile, we could become part of a lightly connected group, or when contributing to a benevolent system could benefit us in turn. It is these judgements that Rule 10 reminds us not to miss. It is often a joy when we do initiate or accept friendliness to realise that it is not necessarily skill that limits us in the creation of new relationships.

CHARM VERSUS CHARISMA

Friendliness can be charming, but not all charm is friendly. Friendliness is an offering without insistence. It is a suggestion of openness for the consideration of the other person. Friendliness is tempered by a consideration for the person who is receiving it. When I greet somebody every morning on the forest path on my ride to work, part of the friendliness is the understanding between us of the limits to our relationship. Barring an unusual circumstance, like a lost dog or a punctured tyre, neither of us is looking to escalate the relationship. Other circumstances and other relationships may require deeper degrees of connection than a daily hello but, in all situations, too much friendliness would not be friendly. The charm of a baby who I do not know smiling at me is the transparency of the interaction – all the baby wants is a smile in return.

Sometimes charm can go beyond this limited, transparent offering. Some dictionary definitions of charm refer to it as the power or ability to attract. I was at a work dinner once and watched with a mixture of interest and concern as the married male colleague sitting next to me set about charming the young female waiter who was serving us. Ideally people will be friendly to waiters, but this colleague was paying the young woman a lot of attention. He placed her on a pedestal and openly admired her. There is nothing wrong with interest and admiration, these are the first two of John Gottman's seven principles of successful relationships. What was uncomfortable for those of us observing the situation is that we knew this interest was only temporary; it was a promise of future behaviour that this man had no intention of keeping. What made the man charming is that he was prepared to present a temporary version of himself. He was like a jogger speeding up to a run only when he passed other joggers coming in the opposite direction. And having presented the young woman with this high interest, high energy version of himself, he then behaved as if he was entitled to something in return. Friendliness does not imply obligation, but what is beguiling about charm is the assumption that we have been entered into a contract. Your interest in me warrants my return interest. The young woman had not invited the interest and may not have wanted any or every level of it, but the man was trying to make her feel obliged to return it. The colleague progressively escalated his interest into personal territory and became gradually more demanding until eventually he was rebuffed.

Charm has a direction and a peak of intensity and is best understood as an action. It is something that you do. Charisma is a quality; it is something that you have. When my colleague tried flattering the young woman, he wasn't presenting himself as someone particularly special, he was presenting himself as someone especially interested in her. Charisma attracts by suggesting a special quality rather than a special effort. Charisma appears effortless, whereas charm is better described as easy, or practised. Charismatic individuals portray special insight, composure or determination. Charming individuals reach out to us, but charisma does not need a direction – we are all drawn to it. Roger Federer is charismatic because we see the degree of his special understanding of the game of tennis, his willingness to endure tension, and his determination to prevail in long and difficult matches. Nelson Mandela was charismatic because we responded to the strength of his determination to endure 27 years in prison, the grace he showed to forgive his jailers and his integrity to include everybody in his vision of a fairer society.

Everyone has abilities, and all people have abilities that are needed by others. Even my helpless puppy, with his gratitude, enthusiasm and openness, has something that my family and I need. Charisma is not dependent on being remarkable. A schoolchild can be charismatic as she presents a homework project. While she is at a stage of life when her abilities are still developing, her acceptance and use of her current abilities can make her charismatic. Charismatic people make accurate judgements, neither overestimating nor underestimating their own skills and qualities, which allows them to be both confident and humble. They are sensitive to other people and to circumstance, which allows them to present their qualities proportionately and when required or requested. Teenage climate campaigner Greta Thunberg is not a soaring orator or an intimidatingly intelligent scientist. She balances confidence in her knowledge and her direct delivery style with the humble understanding of her own personal limitations, and that she is relaying rather than generating expert opinion. She is determined to deliver a message that she is sure matters. Her knowledge of who she is and what she is doing gives her charisma.

MANNERS

Apartheid succeeded in its design of separating people, but not completely. As a young white South African I still received some education in Zulu manners. Zulu is the dominant culture in the part of South Africa where I grew up. The Zulu greeting is *Sawubona*, which means, 'I see you', a form of acknowledgement and respect. Traditionally, the senior or older person will initiate the greeting and the junior person will reciprocate. Greetings are universal, it is good manners to greet strangers and ask after their health before initiating any other topic of conversation. When I was growing up, it would have been strange to walk past a black person in the street and not exchange greetings and enquire after each other's health. When white people walked past each other, we would mostly ignore each other. When I met a black person, although I was aware of many reasons for our separation, it was always some relief to be able to respond to a greeting in the correct way.

Sawubona (I see you)

Sawubona (I see you)

Uyaphila empilweni? (Are you well?)

Yebo ngiyaphila. Wena? (Yes I am well. And you?)

Ngiyaphila (I am well)

Manners vary from culture to culture. In Zulu culture, it would be considered rude for a junior party to initiate a greeting, make eye contact or to shake hands with someone while they are eating, whereas in England it is considered rude to not do these things. In her book *Watching the English,* anthropologist Kate Fox observes that while all cultures value inclusion, and all cultures value privacy, different cultures prioritise these contradictory values differently. It would be rude to intrude on a commuter's privacy while on the London Underground, but it would also be rude not to include a stranger on a rural Italian bus in even intimate conversation. Manners are a way of tempering oneself, with the purpose of demonstrating willingness to respect convention and confirm in-group status.

Manners are at their worst when they are arcane and exclude. Elaborate rituals and exaggerated accents can be used to indicate membership of an exclusive group. The manners of posh people in England and rich white people in the American south can play this role. By contrast, genuine courtesy is a respect for and appreciation of the other person – *I see you.* Manners are at their best when they temper our raw desires and indicate a willingness to fit in. When I have worked internationally, I have found that Zulu manners travel well, and I am glad to have been taught them.

Some time ago, I got into a battle of wills over not drinking Turkish tea in Istanbul. It started one evening in a restaurant when I refused my host's convivial offer of alcohol after the meal. I refused his offer of tea as well but, unlike alcohol, tea is a significant social ceremony in Turkey, and he could see no good reason why I would not participate. I don't drink tea because I normally avoid caffeine. But over the next few days, to the amusement and frustration of the third member of our party, a mutual friend, this issue escalated. Eventually my host was ordering tea for me at every meal, which would grow cold, untouched in front of me as the other people at the table participated in the ceremony. By the end of the five-day visit, our positions were so entrenched that I wanted nothing other than bottled water, and I would have had to have drunk pots of tea to have placated him.

A part of Rule 10 (reach out) is de-escalating. Some of this is linked to Rule 5 (keep the conversation safe). It helps to make the disagreement less significant. By the time I had finished not drinking tea in Turkey, our disagreement had grown to encompass issues of cultural respect and individual freedom and contained significant amounts of unexpressed emotion. A trivial disagreement had built to the point that it had become difficult to resolve.

THE WISE AGREEMENT

In addition to de-escalating the significance and emotion of the disagreement, another part of Rule 10 is de-escalating agreement – seeking to close the distance between the positions that you each hold. In Roger Fisher and William Ury's book *Getting to Yes*, they argue that we should be seeking a 'wise' agreement.

We should avoid bargaining, compromising and playing hard. When I was young and my siblings and I argued around the table about who had received the largest serving of food, my father used to tell a story about two children who were each served a share of a sausage for dinner. When the one child complained that the other's share was larger, the father cut off a small slice of the larger piece and ate it. The first child was satisfied, but the second child complained that the other portion was now larger. So the father cut a small slice off that piece and ate it also. The second child was satisfied, but the first child complained again. This carried on until there was no sausage left and both children were satisfied that they had been evenly treated, but hungry.

Bargaining and compromising can amount to one party accepting a suboptimal solution if the other person does also. Simple equality is not always the same as fairness. Pursuing equality simplistically through bargaining and compromise can decrease the overall utility of the agreement. Fisher and Ury's idea is – rather than just attempting to balance the initial opposing positions by transferring benefits between them or removing benefits from both in what is at best a zero-sum exercise – to cooperate to design a solution that, in sum, offers a greater benefit to both parties. This is especially wise when there will be future agreements between these or related parties.

The opposite of reaching out is the BATNA (best alternative to negotiated agreement). It means the best outcome you could enforce or achieve independently were a cooperative relationship to break down. If you are negotiating the price of a car, your BATNA might be that you could go to the dealer across the road. The dealer's BATNA may be that they could sell the car to somebody else. But if there is no dealer across the road, your BATNA may be to pay the full price, or keep your old car, and if there are no other customers, the dealer's BATNA may be to accept your first offer, or not sell it at all. Fisher and Ury say that you have to know your BATNA and the BATNA of the person that you are talking to, but these have to be used carefully. Sometimes they may be presented as a transparent threat, and other times, need to be used subtly to avoid damaging trust in the negotiation. In *Crucial Conversations*, the VitalSmarts team say that one of the ways of keeping a conversation safe (Rule 5) is commitment – saying something like, 'It's hard to see a solution to this conflict right now, but I'm committed to keeping working at it until we solve it.'

Sometimes negotiations are conducted in bad faith. In these circumstances, threatening or deploying BATNA is a guard against tactics like deception, dishonesty, threats, emotional pressure and moving the goalposts. But sincere negotiations often work better with commitment than threat. Premature deployment of BATNA happens when one or both parties fail to see that there is the potential for a negotiated agreement to be better than the BATNA. The spouse who threatens to 'pack my bags' may limit the potential of the marriage by invoking its alternative.

Disagreements have chronic and acute components. The chronic components are the abiding interests of each party. The acute components are the discord and emotion that arise as a consequence of the conflict. Fisher and Ury's idea of the wise agreement is one that meets the legitimate interests of each party to the greatest extent possible and that endures because it offers a solution to both parties that is palpably beneficial and fair in the long term. By contrast, when playing hard, parties hope to raise the acute discomfort of the disagreement to the point that a solution that is not satisfactory in the long term will appear appealing because of the relief it offers from short-term conflict. Salesmen who use the hard-sell technique are aiming to create a pressurised situation that the customer can only escape from by spending money on something that they don't really want. My colleague in the restaurant was hoping to force the waiter's interest in him by making her uncomfortable about not reciprocating his intense attention, rather than being sensitive to what she wanted or needed.

When we (Rule 1) know what we are talking for, reaching out becomes more possible. It is natural to feel close to those that we collaborate with, and if an impasse can be framed as a problem that disadvantages both sides, rather than as a zero-sum conflict which only the harder player can win, it is possible to be drawn closer to the other party by the shared quest of finding a solution that improves the situation for both of you.

DE-ESCALATING AGREEMENT

Nelson Mandela was arrested by the apartheid South African government in 1962 and spent 27 years in prison. Towards the end of his imprisonment, the apartheid government reached out to him and offered to release him if he compromised on some of his political principles. Mandela refused to compromise and eventually secured an unconditional release. Because of the success of censorship of the press, in 1990, I knew who he was, but had never seen his face, heard his voice or been exposed to his point of view. For 27 years, white South Africans had been told that Mandela was a terrorist.

At about the same time, in an academic department of the university where I was a student, in a thankfully less consequential leadership contest, one of my lecturers was appointed to head of department. Chairing an inaugural meeting with his erstwhile peers, he took the opposite approach to Mandela and outlined a plan of changes, authoritarian controls and score settling that so horrified his colleagues they immediately decided to remove him from the post – his leadership position had lasted for less than 30 minutes.

Part of the success of the negotiations to dismantle apartheid came from systematic de-escalation of the conflict. Black and white negotiators formed strong emotional bonds with each other. This is a story that is hard to understand unless you grew up in the era that I did, but National Party politician Roelf Meyer addressed black negotiators at the end of one day of talks and said to them, 'I was brought up to believe that you were animals,' and then burst into tears.

Mandela was released in February 1990 and the first democratic elections were held in April 1994. The elections produced a Government of National Unity, which governed for almost three years, and in which, as president, Mandela invited members of minority parties to join the cabinet and had two leaders of opposition parties as deputy presidents. It was only in 2004 that the ANC assumed all of the seats in government. In negotiating for a unity government, the negotiators closed the distance between their starting positions and had de-escalated agreement. This was not a compromise, as most parties considered it to be a better all-round solution. The constitutional requirement for a unity government lapsed in 1999, but it continued until 2004, 14 years after Mandela's release and 5 years after he left the presidency.

In 2017, I made a work trip to South Africa from London, which is where I now live. I had an English colleague with me, and my son had come also. On a day off, all of us and two of my South African nephews visited Hout Bay in Cape Town. To my delight, I discovered that a new unregulated marine mammal entertainment industry had sprung up there. Self-appointed seal trainers would use pieces of fish to entice completely wild seals out of the water and charge locals and tourists a fee to cuddle them and have their photographs taken with them. Fur seals grow up to almost two metres long and can weigh over 200 kilograms. They are predators. People were petting them unconcerned by the unlikely event of anything going wrong. The highlight of the show would be when the trainer would hang over the edge of the harbour with a piece of raw fish in his mouth and a seal would leap clean out of the water and snatch it from his mouth. The crowd would marvel that it had not bitten him in the face and pulled him into the water.

I was delighted because the seal show was everything that the dolphin show was not. The seals were voluntary participants – as soon as they had enough of the attention or the easy meals they would slip back into the sea and their daily lives. But the human desire to connect was the same. Strong enough that, a generation after I had risked drowning by entering a swimming pool with a wild animal, people were still risking bites and a dunking by posing with a large predator.

I see this same human desire to connect in my day job. When I visit India, the cricketers receive love and adulation from fans. I was walking into a hotel with one cricketer when a fan ran up to him and hugged him around his waist, with his head on his chest, as if he were a child hugging a parent. When I leave the sports training ground in London where I work daily, there are often fans gathered outside waiting for a glimpse of the athletes. And if I need to go somewhere in public in my training kit before I have had the chance to change, the team badge serves as an invitation for people to come and talk to me, either to tell me that they support the same team or to announce a friendly rivalry.

Anthropologist Kate Fox says that while some European countries have a reputation for friendliness, and the English have a reputation for reserve, the English are in fact as outgoing, tactile and expressive as any nation – just with dogs, not people. My son said that in one week of walking our new puppy he had spoken to more people than in four years of living in the neighbourhood previously. It seems that people really do want to connect, they just need an excuse or for someone else to take the initiative. It is gladdening to consider that people do want to reach out to each other.

But this desire to connect has a dark side also. When we create in-groups, we create out-groups. One evening, after watching a football match, I was walking amongst the crush of fans to the train station. One fan was particularly inspired by the match and was chanting and trying to get the crowd to sing along. He was chanting, 'We love [name of club]! We love [name of club]!' But the response was half-hearted. He then started singing about a rival club. 'We hate [name of club]! We hate [name of club]!' This time the other fans joined in much more enthusiastically.

When I write admiringly about the spirit of reconciliation that allowed the negotiated dismantling of apartheid, I am also aware that South Africa remains the most unequal country on earth. And despite the universal human desire to reach out – which often seems to need only a hint of permission or opportunity to express itself – this desire does not always manifest in actual connections.

White apartheid South Africa was rightly stigmatised internationally. Nobody in South Africa pretended that the polarisation of society was a good thing. At best it was considered to be a necessary evil, due to a unique and regrettable set of circumstances. But really, people knew it was wrong. I never expected that, 30 years later, the politics of separation would become popular again. If I am to follow Rule 8, I must accept that this is not a matter that can be addressed in a short paragraph. I will just observe that we have both a desire to reach out and a desire to separate, and the history that I have lived gives me caution about how I fuel and express them, and concern about how I see them being publicly expressed.

In this book, I tell some stories that cast me and my attitudes towards other people in a less than flattering light. During a discussion, a friend recently said to me, 'You are not a racist.' I said, 'I am not claiming not to be a racist.' I am not saying that I am. But because of my upbringing, and the unequal society in which I currently live, I am continually infected with ideas of prejudice and difference which I must actively work to undermine. These ideas form a barrier that I need to continually reach out through. But I am not the only person who needs to do this.

The South African comedian Trevor Noah tells a joke about the incendiary and inordinately wealthy black South African politician Julius Malema. He says while on a trip to South Africa, he was having dinner with Malema and told him that white people feared him. There were two German tourists sitting next to them in the restaurant and Malema turned to them and asked them, 'Are you afraid of me?'

The tourists said, 'No.'

'See,' said Malema, 'those white people are not afraid of me.'

Trevor Noah said, 'But those white people are not from here.'

Malema said, 'None of them are.'

As a white South African, I have experienced the advantages of the privileged and also the insecurity of being a non-native minority. As a privileged white person I had the responsibility to reach out, and as a member of a minority group I knew the relief when I was reached out to. From both sides, it felt better when it happened.

Key principles:

- Make and accept bids
- Be friendly
- Use charm and charisma appropriately
- Use manners
- Seek wise agreements
- De-escalate agreement

When Nelson Mandela gave his presidential inauguration speech in 1994, it was the culmination of a personal and political struggle which had occupied his entire life and had seen him endure 27 years in prison, suffer hard labour, lead an armed struggle and, at one stage, fear execution. It was a glorious victory. At this moment of vindication and triumph, in front of his nation and the world, he turned away from anger and chose reconciliation.

In his speech, Mandela refers to the nation as 'friends', 'comrades' and 'compatriots'. 'Comrades' was a term used amongst anti-apartheid activists, while the term 'compatriots' would have reassured white people who would not have considered themselves 'comrades' that they would not be excluded from the new South Africa. This speech is an overt use of friendliness;

Mandela is not risking that his bid will be overlooked. He refers to 'our people' and picks as an example the former white president (and at the time current vice-president), the 'honourable' F.W. de Klerk. Friendliness and bids for reconciliation run through the speech. Mandela says that 'each one of us is as intimately attached to the soil of this beautiful country as our famous Jacaranda trees of Pretoria, and the Mimosa trees of the bushveld'. What Western politician has spoken as deliberately and warmly, or been as friendly, to an immigrant population?

This is charismatic oratory, not just for its use of symbolism (Jacaranda trees are a non-native species and Mimosa trees are indigenous, but both have beautiful flowers), but also for its integrity. There was a lot of anger in the country at the time, and like other politicians do, Mandela could easily have played to this to secure his political support amongst a majority part of the country. He did not need the votes of white people. But he turned down this opportunity because he valued the country over his own political fortunes, and made the more difficult proposal, that 'out of an extraordinary human disaster that lasted too long must come a society of which all humanity can be proud.' This is the wise agreement. The wise agreement is not an easy one, the challenge of building a peaceful, prosperous, non-sexist, non-racist democracy is one that occupies South Africa still, but what makes it wise is that it is a principled long-term vision, one in which 'all South Africans, both black and white, will be able to walk tall without any fear in their hearts, assured of their inalienable right to human dignity.'

Mandela does not hide from the magnitude of the conflict from which South Africa suffered, but by referring to the shared 'pain we all carried in our hearts as we saw our country tear itself apart in terrible conflict', he de-escalates agreement – it is easier to agree that we want to be freed from this pain than it is to continue to argue.

Black African cultures in South Africa have a live oral tradition, and the manners of refined diplomacy are part of Mandela's skill, 'Distinguished guests, comrades, and friends today, by your presence here, you confer glory and hope to newborn liberty . . . We the people of South Africa, feel fulfilled that humanity has taken us back into its bosom . . . Never, never, and never again shall it be that this beautiful land will again experience the oppression of one by another.'

I am still grateful for the relief Nelson Mandela gave us from fear and shame when he reached out to white South Africans. Many years after this speech I visited South Africa from my new home in London. I took a taxi being driven by a black man about 15 years older than me. He was old enough to have lived through the full excesses of apartheid, and the fact that he was the taxi driver and I was the passenger in some ways reflected the enduring effects of the inequality that he had suffered. I would have understood if I had picked up some resentment or wariness from him, or an attitude that now I lived in a different country it was good riddance. We were chatting and he was asking me about my life in the United Kingdom. We spoke about many different things, but eventually he asked me the question many South Africans ask of emigrants: 'Will you ever come back?' The truth is that my children have a home in the UK now, and it is unlikely that I will ever return. But I did not want to say this, so deflected the question slightly, and said, 'When I am in South Africa I feel as if I am at home.' He turned to face me and said with feeling, 'This is your home!'

Earlier, I wrote that this book was an apology to the man with the red rucksack, and a wish that I can do better. It is also a thank-you to the taxi driver for reaching out, and a wish that I can do as well.

CONCLUSION

COMBINING THE RULES

Most of our conversations with each other are good ones. Even of those that are not, many only fail for a small, simple or arbitrary reason. These 'narrow-miss' conversations can usually be effectively redirected by applying a single rule, sometimes just once. But conversations exist on a broad spectrum from healthy and effective to unhealthy and ineffective, and while they are numerically clustered towards the healthy side, the ones nearer the darker end of the spectrum have particular salience, so we notice them more. These are the complex, recurring, seemingly intractable conversations that can persistently affect our lives and relationships. These conversations may need more than one rule, or for rules to be used more than once.

When we discuss values such as freedom, fairness, loyalty and authority, a complication is that they sometimes conflict. Loyalty to a family member may involve compromising fairness to a member of the broader society, and acceptance of authority may involve compromising freedom. Aspects of social justice can also conflict. Our right to get what we need may conflict with our right to get what we deserve, which may conflict with our right to equality. There is an idea that talking involves a compromise between effectiveness and safety, that 'deep breath' conversations, vigorous structured opposed debates such as in law courts and political chambers, and 'angry boss/coach' tirades and demands are necessary to get the right answer or outcome, despite the cost. A consequence of this belief is that bullying bosses and aggressive colleagues are sometimes excused on the grounds that they are high achievers or prioritising getting to the truth. This belief pitches Rule 3: Remember that most people are good, competent and worthy of respect and Rule 5: Keep the conversation safe, against Rule 6: Use resilience and Rule 7: Use rigor.

An alternative perspective is that safety and effectiveness complement rather than compromise each other. We are more persuasive and open to persuasion when we respect and feel respected, and we think more clearly when we are calm. But also, complying with Rule 7 and Rule 8: Use complexity will generally increase rather than decrease safety. A British Cabinet minister who in 2020 was reported as asking, 'Why is everyone so [expletive] useless?' may have been in contravention of rules about rigor and complexity as well as those about safety, this was likely a factually incorrect as well as unsafe comment.

Other rules combine well also – you can reach out by listening, talk slow to detect errors of rigor or complexity, and know what you are talking for and remember the worthiness of your interlocutor to keep the conversation safe. Rigor is made more rigorous by using complexity, and listening and safety are both improved by resilience.

Using the rules in combination allows us to have better and more complex conversations by applying three essential ideas.

Prime yourself

Priming is the process of deliberately training ourselves to automatically notice particular and relevant clues. Expertise requires being able to detect the useful signs from what can feel like a deluge of less important information. When we are talking, we need to be particularly alert for (1) the problems of being specific when we should be general and vice versa, (2) opposing other people's opinions with our own instead of collaborating to find answerable questions, and (3) forgetting that we and the people that we talk to are human, which means being fallible but also intelligent and good.

The specific/general level change is one of the most useful scenarios to be primed to detect. We get attached to our specific opinions, and often opposing one such opinion with another is fruitless. For example, it would be very difficult to convince someone of the specific case that Politician A is good and Politician B is not, if they have a prior opinion that the opposite is true. But a more general conversation about 'What qualities and values make for a good politician?' is less adversarial and more likely to succeed. If you can agree on these general values, you could progress to the more specific conversation about whether Politician A or B fits your agreed criteria.

Another useful and de-escalating example for moving from the specific to the general is when you have been given an instruction which you wish to contest. If you have been told to wash the dishes, instead of arguing about whether you should wash these specific dishes on this specific day, it could be more useful to discuss what the general rule is that determines who washes up. This could divert an argument to a more useful discussion about whether the rule is 'I cooked, so you wash up', or 'I washed up yesterday, so you wash up today'. A good question to insert into a debate is 'What is the general rule?'. If you do not have agreed general rules, the conversation needs to become even more general to address the question 'What is a fair rule for deciding who washes up?'

It is also useful to be able to detect when a conversation should become more specific. It is all very well to say that you generally do not like washing the dishes, but it is more useful to know that specifically it is washing the pots that really annoys you.

Rule 1: Agree what you are talking for, and Rule 7: Use rigor are both relevant to priming yourself to detect quickly whether the conversation is appropriately specific or general.

A second scenario that is worth priming yourself for is the opinion-versus-opinion arm wrestle. Some questions, particularly those about values and priorities are hard to answer definitively, but, when these have been agreed, many questions become answerable. We tend to divide questions into those that we do and do not know the answer to, but because we and the person with whom we are talking often overestimate our knowledge and underestimate our ignorance, the ensuing inadequately founded opinions are a common cause of disagreement. A more useful way to divide questions is into those that are answerable and those that are not. Judging a question to be answerable means seeing that it could be definitively or even probabilistically resolved by using facts. Being primed to interject, 'I don't know, but that's an answerable question' into a conversation can save you from much fruitless opposition. The focus of the conversation can then become collaborating to find the factual evidence that will lead you and your interlocutor to an objective answer. The third priming scenario involves applying Rule 3: Remember most people are good, competent and worthy of respect, Rule 4: Talk fast and slow, and Rule 8: Use complexity. Quickly spotting when we are incorrectly attributing disagreement to someone else's ignorance, incompetence, or malignity (Rule 3) can help us realign the conversation. Rule 4 helps us to detect the common human shortcuts and biases which increase the chance of disagreement.

Biases increase the chance that we will be unwittingly wrong, and therefore less likely to agree. Shortcuts increase the chance that even when we are right, we will be unaware of the method that we have used to form a correct opinion. This is a problem for agreement because we are less persuasive when we can't show our working.

Rule 8 reminds us to resist asking or answering either/or questions and remind ourselves to try to think on a spectrum. This means using probability and degree instead of categories. It is easier to manage difference when it is on a spectrum rather than when it is categorical. Rule 8 can prime us to look for these opportunities for agreement.

Types of conversations

We have different kinds of conversations. Many of our conversations are predictions. We may have shared interests, but we disagree about how those interests are best served. These conversations range across the spectrum from personal, through professional to political.

Because the answer to a prediction is not available at the point of disagreement, we do not have an objective outcome to discover and agree to. What we do have is an objectively deter-mined best method for making forecasts, which was described in Rule 7: Use rigor. Agreeing on methods is better than arguing about answers.

Another kind of conversation is about fairness, where there are competing interests, and the task is to work out the balance that will best satisfy those interests. Rule 3: Remember most peo-ple are good, competent and worthy of respect, is important for talking about fairness because it is easy to interpret unfairness as being completely deliberate, when more often it exists on a spec-trum somewhere between deliberate and unintended. Rule 6: Use resilience, is also important because the experience of being unfairly treated can provoke strong emotions. Conversations about fairness are more likely to be successful when they are practical rather than personal (Rule 3) and calm rather than overcharged (Rule 6).

But fairness conversations should not only be initiated by the aggrieved party. Following Rule 10: Reach out, gives us the oppor-tunity to redress inequity even when we are the beneficiaries of it. Making a specific sacrifice to preserve general fairness could be beneficial even to the party making the concession.

A third kind of conversation is about belonging. These can be some of our easiest and most pleasant conversations, when we joke with friends, chat with colleagues, or tell a family member that we love them, we are confirming that we belong to each other and to the same group. Rule 9: Listen, and Rule 10 are relevant to these conversations. But belonging conversations can also be amongst our most fraught: when we try to decide how in-laws fit into our families, or how people with different origins, skin colours and beliefs fit into our society. Rule 4 reminds us to be aware of our biases and the shortcuts that we take to reach conclusions. Our human tendency to create in-and out-groups, and to favour the former, needs to be mediated with Rule 3, so that we are reminded that people who are in different groups from us are still good people who are worthy of respect. Rule 7 reminds us to use a rigorous methodology to guard against lazy and harmful generalisations applied to some groups, and Rule 8 can warn us against categoric thinking that causes us to see defined groups and meaningful differences where they do not in fact exist.

Arenas for conversations

The third idea is that conversations happen in different arenas. Philosopher David Miller argues that we have three arenas of human relationship[14], broadly, personal, professional and political. This matters when we talk about fairness because the principles of fairness change depending on which arena we are in. At the personal or solidaristic community level, we are mainly concerned that people should get what they need. At the professional or instrumental association level, we are mainly concerned that people get what they deserve, and at the political or citizen level, we are mainly concerned with equality.

When we try to understand the needs of someone else, we need to listen and to use resilience so that we are not excessively threatened by the prospect of reallocating some of our resource to them. Rule 1 is useful for these conversations also. There is a difference between understanding and evaluating someone else's need and fulfilling it, and both of these are different from

---

[14] *Principles of Social Justice*

protecting our own interests. Knowing what we are talking for helps keep the conversation productively focused.

Talking about what we deserve takes rigor and complexity. We have to understand the relative value of contributions, and the role of individual intent, talent, and cost in making these contributions. Deserve conversations are usually about making, agreeing or applying some kind of contract. These conversations usually happen in the workplace or marketplace, but there are times when they happen in more narrow or more broad conversations. One of the reasons why divorce negotiations become so fraught is that the protagonists are moving from a relationship where the mode of fairness is mostly about need, to one where the mode of fairness is mostly about deserve (or what you have earned). Protagonists may feel that they are being treated unfairly because they feel (possibly correctly) that they are not getting what they need. This would have been unfair in the previous family relationship, but may not be unfair now because needs are less relevant to the contractual relationship.

Rule 1 is critical to justice conversations because it helps us understand which conversation we are having. Justice may or may not require us to treat people outside of our national borders equally, and this debate swings one way or another depending on what goods we are considering distributing. A key debate in social justice is defining the boundary within which we consider that people must be treated justly. What are the family limits within which you need to meet people's needs, what are the business and contractual limits within which you must give people what they deserve, and what are the social limits within which people must be treated equally?

My cousin likes to point out that it is hard to continue to hate somebody once you have actually met them, and this insight reflects a challenge we have in broader social or political conversations, that as human beings, we have difficulty in empathising and relating outside of a small or simply defined group. Seeing an emotion on somebody's face or hearing it in their voice makes us more inclined to respect and protect them, and seeing the look in their eyes motivates us to trust and be trusted. But if we are to have good conversations about social justice, we have to remember to talk slowly about who belongs to our group, and to think rigorously about the probable consequences of applying respect and justice narrowly or more broadly.

Corporate asset strippers make money by selling the assets of a company rather than its produce. Because the company needs the assets to make the produce, the short-term gain is achieved at a long-term cost. But the asset stripper has a short-term focus and keeps the profit while passing the loss on to others.

In political conversations, conventions of honesty, respect and expert rigor are assets necessary for the production of good and fair social policies. But social asset strippers compromise these conventions in order to achieve a short-term advantage in political arguments. It is easier to win a debate when you are not bound to be honest, respectful or rigorous, and the cost of the damage to the social utility of these conventions is passed on to others. But the loss of healthy conventions is not the only asset that can be stripped.

Because social justice is about fair distribution within defined groups, some operators have discovered that they can reallocate wealth and still maintain a veneer of fairness not by redefining distribution, but by redefining groups. By narrowing the definition of the group to which we feel beholden, ruthless operators are able to argue that justice demands that some or all of a group of social assets including healthcare, education and wealth should only be available to a narrow part of society, and thus could fairly be more plentifully available to members of that group. This is a win-win proposition for some voters, who are thus convinced that they can maintain their moral integrity while simultaneously securing a greater share of society's assets.

The counter to this argument is to demand rigor in the method by which these groups come to be defined as well as in the calculation of the general social cost to even the beneficiaries of an us-and-them split. Rule 3 says that most but not all people are good, and one application of all of the rules is to help us become conscious of how to detect the exceptions and hold them to account.

USING THE RULES

In the following conversation, I talk with a friend and fellow psychologist about how this book of rules could be used.

Tim: So, I wrote this book.

Clinton: Yes.

Tim: It started because I moved out of my private practice where I felt like I'd acquired a reasonable degree of competence and suddenly found myself in another job, which was an organisation, and I had to have much less structured, more spontaneous conversations with people who weren't necessarily wanting to have conversations with me. So, there was a little bit of a rude awakening, to realise that I'd been doing quite well with some conversations, but only a very particular kind of conversation. I realised strategy could be applied to a broader range of conversations than just the therapeutic encounter.

Clinton: So you discovered unconscious incompetence in your own ability to talk?

Tim: I realised in some specific areas of talking I was unconsciously incompetent. But the instant I realised, I became consciously incompetent, and that's a progression.

Clinton: And that was part of your motivation for writing the book?

Tim: Yes. Something I have tried to communicate is that some parts of talking are so difficult that we shouldn't be ashamed or afraid, or even surprised, at not being good at those parts. And when we can get over that fear, hopefully we can progress quite quickly from unconscious incompetence to conscious competence. Often, unsuccessful conversations end up getting repeated, which in some ways can feel like a bad thing, but actually this repetition gives us the opportunity to practise and improve. And hopefully that is something that this book can encourage people with too, that using the rules deliberately can get you into conscious competence. And that's also worthwhile progress.

Clinton: My experiences are very similar to yours. I think I'm also quite good at having therapeutic conversations, but when you've been doing them for years, they become quite easy. But the band that I play in, it's such a collaborative thing, I just realised when I was talking I was failing often to get my ideas across. I think I have some valuable ideas to add in certain situations, but I'm not always getting them across in the way that I'd like to, or they're not being received in the way that I think they might be worthy of.

Tim: Have you had any arguments?

Clinton: Plenty. Sometimes very heated.

Tim: How do those go?

Clinton: In the band we've gotten to a point, years down the line, where we, kind of, know each other very well and we . . .

Tim: But what does that mean?

Clinton: Well, we roll our eyes and choose which arguments to pick up and which to just leave, and actually we work very well together.

Tim: And that's a kind of acceptance?

Clinton: Yes.

Tim: Because you're not rolling your eyes at the person, you're sort of rolling your eyes at the circumstance.

I remember getting quite frustrated with a couple of work situations. I think, for me, I found that emotion would come into it. These were new relationships that I was trying to build, and the emotion was quite threatening to those relationships. Or maybe to the clarity of thought that I needed to talk things through.

Clinton: Yes, and somehow, that emotion, people pick up on that, and then I guess that takes away from the safety within the conversation. People instinctively respond to it sympathetically, or they back away.

Tim: Yes.

Clinton: I think when you create something, it's important for the people collaborating with you to really listen to the initial version and really just grasp that first. And when you're a bit more introverted and tend to be the quieter one in the room, it's very difficult to get the initial idea across.

Tim: One of the things I tried to explore is the idea of conversational levels. Take communicating a concept in a song, for example, that's a conversational level. But if that level isn't working you could try to move the conversation up a level. Instead of being a conversation about the essential idea, it becomes a conversation about the process of explaining the idea.

Clinton: I could see that would work if I was talking with you, but I'm not sure that works as well with people who just want to get on with it. They're not interested in stopping for a theoretical discussion, you know?

Tim: And then, again, keep retreating up the levels. If one level's not working, you've got to just bail out of that one and step up, and keep doing it. Part of the skill of using Rule 1 is learning to justify why we should talk about talking. Finding the right level and getting buy-in from the person that you are talking to – that's using Rule 1, and it's so important, that's why it is the first rule.

Clinton: And sometimes I think just stopping and changing tack is incredibly valuable in itself. I see that in relationships. All relationships. The better you get to know each other, the more unconscious patterns are formed. If you want to break out of them you have to consciously decide what to talk about, and why.

Tim: Yes.

Clinton: So, I'll do this and my wife would do that, and then I'll say this and she'll say that, and it builds up to this argument, and the more that's happened over the years, the less we worry about all the preceding steps – we just automatically cut straight to the argument. I think the way to break that pattern is for one of the two parties to have the guts, or the courage, or the awareness, to take it to a different level. And immediately the pattern's broken, because if she does it, I have to follow her there, otherwise I'll look stupid.

Tim: Yes. One of my worries was, 'Can people get better at this?' And I do think, as you say, what is encouraging is that sometimes it takes something relatively small to create a change.

Especially because I don't think a lot of people like arguing or like conflict, but they find themselves defending their corner and they don't see another option. But if they can find an option somehow, and sometimes those things can be quite little, and one of those options is becoming a little more aware of a pattern.

Clinton: And I think often when we argue, we are arguing about the same things again and again.

Tim: I think many couples that have been together for a long time can go, 'Well, we argue about this, and this, and this, and we do it with very similar outcomes every time.' And it would be great to just be able to break that pattern in some way, or at least become aware of it.

I was in an argument, and the person said to me, 'You're the one with the skills. You should be able to sort this out.' And I thought, 'What I'm not going to do is take sole responsibility for this argument.'

Clinton: Yes.

Tim: Now, that's not to say that I'm flawless, and I think it is important for me to be able to recognise where I am making mistakes. But I think it's also important to recognise where it's not me, or not only me, who's causing the argument. What I don't want to say to people reading the book is, 'Now you've read this book, you must take full responsibility for resolving everything.' I have noticed that when I've run seminars on communication, sometimes people come back and they go, 'Well, now I've just assumed all responsibility for sorting things out,' and that's not a healthy place to be.

Clinton: But the rules will be very useful to me, to help me clarify my thoughts and experiences in a discussion.

Tim: Yes, because, like we said, some of the changes don't have to be that big to just break the pattern. It may be that, in conversations, there are things that you can execute better or problems that you can avoid if you understand them more fundamentally, which hopefully is what the book is about – understanding the principles that make conversations work, or fail.

Clinton: Yes, and when you see the positive result of it, that's reinforcing in itself, and it increases the likelihood of . . .

Tim: Yes. It's just, 'Oh, that worked.' You know, 'I'll do that one again.'

Clinton: We think it's difficult to change, but actually, humans are good at change. People will try something new, but then they lose motivation because they don't get immediate results, or it's hard. And then they stop, and three months later they do it again for a week and then they get sick of it so they stop, and then six months later it's 1st January and they make a New Year's resolution and do it for another week, and so it goes. They'll tell you, 'I can't change. I've tried all these times.' But they're not recognising that they have been practising change. It's just been change in the wrong direction. They have spent 11 months changing from, for example, exercising to not exercising. And they have only spent one month changing from not exercising to exercising. No wonder they're better at the wrong change. That's what we have to take charge of, the direction of our change.

I think to make real change in your life, you need to be *gatvol* of the current scenario and be prepared to put up with the discomfort of consciously practising those rules for however long it takes to gradually get better at them. So, it absolutely is possible to change but unlike what people will try and tell you and sell you, there are no shortcuts. You need to be prepared to make yourself uncomfortable.

Tim: Yes, and that starts with becoming more aware of how uncomfortable changing in the wrong direction is.

Clinton: And sometimes I would say maybe it's comfort, because it's what I'm doing all the time. So it's comfortable in that it might be a negative state of affairs, but it's one that I'm used to, so it's a kind of comfort zone.

Tim: I think that part of the complexity of getting better at talking, is that in some ways bad talking is comfortable. But there is discomfort also, a kind of background hum of dissatisfaction or a dread or anxiety, that you know this thing's not going in the direction that you want it to go.

Clinton: It is really complex, because I think we have motives on different levels. I want to have great relationships, and good conversations, but on another level, I'm also motivated to stay comfortable. So, I think harnessing or being aware of the goals on different levels is important, and I don't know if we'll ever get them all pointing in the same direction, but . . .

Tim: . . . I think that's the thing, is to recognise that they don't . . .

Clinton: . . . and then make an overall decision. And that's why change does require discomfort.

Tim: Yes, absolutely.

Clinton: But I'm making an overall choice. Each option has pros and cons.

Tim: And accepting that is a commitment. I think that commitment comes from an understanding that it's not just a single, universal improvement, and you will have to struggle, you know. Sometimes getting your point of view across is difficult, and listening is also uncomfortable sometimes. It's hard work. Biting your tongue is hard work as well. There is great joy in a retort sometimes, and just allowing some of your emotional frustration to leak is a tremendous relief, and sometimes a tremendous pleasure.

Clinton: But it doesn't work in the bigger picture.

Tim: No, not long term. Learning new skills, there's an element of hard work to that. You and I went for a run a couple of days ago, and even while we were running, I was just thinking, 'This is so enjoyable. Just placing one foot in front of another is so pleasant.' And I think that people think of change as having a distant reward, but even in exercise or conversations, there's a tremendous joy just to feel like, 'This is working.'

Clinton: Yes, it would be nice to solve all the world's problems, but even incremental change . . .

Tim: . . . being able to have one more conversation with your spouse, or discuss one more topic that you normally can't, or hang in for one extra layer of understanding and recognise that as progress rather than reflecting on the fact that it did eventually blow up . . .

Clinton: It's about the little bits. But they can have big effects.

Tim: At the end of one of the first therapy sessions I ever did, I summarised the session. I wrapped it all up quite neatly, and I thought that's what you did. I told my supervisor about it, and he said, 'What did you do that for?' If I'd been your client, I think I would have asked you not to have summarised.' I'd never thought of it with that perspective – maybe the summary does not respect the complexity of the conversation that one is in.

Clinton: That's how any conversation is as well. So, conversation at one level comes to an end, but you know, it's not really the end of it.

Tim: That feels like something we could end on.

Clinton: Yes.

ACKNOWLEDGEMENTS

I wrote this book for myself and people like me, who have good and bad days and experiences as we fluctuate somewhere about the middle of the range of mental health and interpersonal skill, but who are still interested in getting better at or contributing more positively to personal and also professional and public conversations.

Thank you for reading it, I enjoyed writing it, and hope that it was some degree of interesting or useful, and that if it was, there is something in it that you can share.

Beyond you, the reader, more thanks are due.

First, thank you to the people who came to see me for therapy, who over the years have entrusted me with your stories, thoughts and feelings. I was a young man when I began to practise as a psychologist, and I am grateful to each person and all the parents of children who nonetheless collaborated with me when I was much more fresh-faced than I am now. I hope that our conversations were also worthwhile for you, because I gained from them deeply.

To my sports and business clients, thank you for the tremendous amount I have learnt from you. There is a literature of high performance, but its aggregations do not contain the full reasons why those individuals who excel do, and I am grateful for the opportunity to hear accounts of high performance from the actors of those performances.

I will thank my friends and family directly rather than in this page, but I must use this final space to thank my agent, David Luxton, without whose support and vision this book would just never have been written or published, Matthew Phillips from Bonnier Books, whose seemingly off-hand comment, 'Did you write the proposal? Yes? It's going to be ok then,' helped give a first-time author the confidence to take on this project, and lastly Beth Eynon, my editor, whose integrity, care, skill and collaboration made the process and hopefully the outcome of writing this book feel less like a monologue and more like a conversation.

BIBLIOGRAPHY

Christakis, Nicholas A. 2019, *Blueprint: The Evolutionary Origins of a Good Society*, Hachette Book Group

Coleman, Peter 2011, *The Five Percent: Finding Solutions to Seemingly Impossible Conflicts*, PublicAffairs

Banerjee, Abhijit & Duflo, Esther 2019, *Good Economics for Hard Times: Better Answers to Our Biggest Problems*, Allen Lane

Dweck, Carol 2017, *Mindset: Changing The Way You think To Fulfil Your Potential*, Robinson

Fox, Kate 2014, *Watching the English: The Hidden Rules of English Behaviour*, Hodder & Stoughton

Fredrickson, Barbara L. 2011, *Positivity: Groundbreaking Research To Release Your Inner Optimist And Thrive*, Oneworld

Gawande, Atul 2010, *The Checklist Manifesto: How To Get Things Right*, Profile

Gottman, John 2019, *The Seven Principles for Making Marriage Work*, Orion Spring

Haidt, Jonathan 2013, *The Righteous Mind: Why Good People are Divided by Politics and Religion*, Penguin

Kahneman, Daniel 2012, *Thinking Fast and Slow*, Penguin

Mandela, Nelson 1995 *The Long Walk to Freedom*, Little Brown

Miller, David 1999, *Principles of Social Justice*, Harvard University Press

Borgida, Eugene & Nisbett, Richard E. 1975, *Attribution and the Psychology of Prediction*, Journal of Personality and Social Psychology

Pantalon, Michael 2011, *Instant Influence*, Little Brown

Grenny, Joseph; Patterson, Kerry, et al. 2014, *Change Anything*, Piatkus

Grenny, Joseph; Patterson, Kerry, et al. 2011, *Crucial Conversations*, McGraw-Hill

Patton, Bruce; Stone, Douglas, et al. 1999, *Difficult Conversations*, Viking

Peters, Steve 2012, *The Chimp Paradox*, Vermilion

Seligman, Martin 2011, *Flourish*, Nicholas Brealey

Schultz, Kathryn 2010, *Being Wrong: Adventures in the Margins of Error*, Granta

Tetlock, Philip 2016, *Superforecasters: The Art and Science of Prediction*, Random House

Fisher, Roger; Ury, William et al. 2012, *Getting to Yes: Negotiating an agreement without giving in*, Random House

INDEX

(Page numbers in **bold** refer to main subject areas.)